ISLAMIC LAW AND FINANCE

ISLAMIC LAW AND FINANCE

Edited by

Chibli Mallat

with an introduction by

W M Ballantyne

Graham & Trotman
A member of the Kluwer Academic Publishers Group
LONDON/DORDRECHT/BOSTON

First published by
Graham & Trotman Limited
Sterling House
66 Wilton Road
London SW1V 1DE
UK

Graham & Trotman Inc
Wolters Kluwer Academic Publishers Group
101 Philip Drive
Assinippi Park
Norwell, MA 02061
USA

Proceedings of a conference convened by the Centre of Near and Middle Eastern Studies and the Law Department of the School of Oriental and African Studies, University of London, in April 1988.

The convenors of the conference and officials of the University of London, in which the sessions were held, do not necessarily share the views expressed in this publication.

British Library Cataloguing in Publication Data

Islamic law and finance.
1. Finance. Islamic law
I. Mallat, Chibli
340.5'9

ISBN 1-85333-121-X

Library of Congress data is available.

ISBN: 1 85333 121 X

Printed and bound in Great Britain by the Athenaeum Press

CONTENTS

NOTE ON THE CONTRIBUTORS

Mr David Baldwin is a Research Assistant with the Department of Economics at the University of Durham. He has been doing field work on Islamic banks in Turkey.

Mr William Ballantyne is a barrister and a Visiting Professor of Arab laws at SOAS. His publications include *Legal Developments in Arabia*, London 1980; *Commercial Law in the Arab Middle East: the Gulf States*, London 1986; *Register of Laws of the Arabian Gulf*, London 1986, and he is the general editor of the *Arab Law Quarterly*.

Ms Jane Connors is Lecturer in Law at the School of Oriental and African Studies. Her recent publications include *Confronting Violence*, 1987, and *Domestic Violence: A U.N. Study* , forthcoming 1988.

Mr Ian D. Edge is Lecturer in Law, SOAS, where he teaches Islamic Law, Law of the Modern Middle East, Commercial Law, and Private and Public International Law. He is a Barrister and a Legal Consultant.

Mr Chibli Mallat is a lawyer specializing in Islamic and International law. He has published articles on law and on the Middle East in the *American Journal of Comparative Law*, the *Financial Times*, *Maghreb-Machrek*, and the *Cahiers de l'Orient*.

Dr Abbas Mirakhor is with the Research Department of the International Monetary Fund, Washington, D.C,. He has published several studies on Islamic Finance and is the co-author of *Islamic Banking*, International Monetary Fund, 1987.

Dr Munir Morad is a writer on Middle Eastern affairs and especially on regional politics and security. He also writes on economic issues. The chapter in this volume is part of this aspect of his work.

Dr Volker Nienhaus is Professor of Economics at the University of Bochum, Federal Republic of Germany. His recent books include: *Islam and the Modern Economy* , 1982, *Arab and Islamic Banks* , 1984, co-authored by T. Wolhers-Scharf, *Economic Cooperation and Integration among Islamic Countries* ,1986.

Mr Nabil Saleh is a Law Consultant (London). His books include *The General Principles of Saudi Arabian and Omani Company laws*, London, 1981, and *Unlawful Gain and Legitimate Profit in Islamic Law*, Cambridge, 1986.

Dr Rodney Wilson teaches Economics at the University of Durham. His books include *Banking Without Interest*, Leicester, 1983, *Banking and Finance in the Arab Middle East*, London, 1983, and *Islamic Business: Theory and Practice*, London, 1986

PREFACE & ACKNOWLEDGEMENTS

One of the most interesting intellectual expressions in the Middle East of the 1980s has appeared in the arcane field of law and finance. Alongside the political turmoil that has accompanied the re-emergence of Islamic militancy, there has developed a discreet but consistent effort at legitimizing legal and financial practices with a different, Islamic, perspective.

A decade after the first systematic attempts to introduce Islamic banks in the world system, it is time to assess some related developments in law and finance. To claim that a society or an enterprise is acting in an 'Islamic' financial way is not sufficient. It is also necessary to look into the details of its operations, to see first whether the claim to novelty in that experience is founded, but more importantly, to examine whether the alternative model is successful. On the level of the state, as in the new Islamic banking laws in countries as different as Iran, Pakistan, and Malaysia, success means the contribution of the banking system as a whole to the growth of the economy. On a micro-economic level, success for an enterprise can only mean competitiveness, and profit.

It is particularly difficult for the analyst to see clearly into the thicket of a financial system, and in the case of the new Islamic modes, the difficulty is augmented by the unavailability of a model to follow, and of blueprints against which a particular performance can be measured. But there is a further complication, which originates in the composite systems which, on various levels, accompany the inquiry.

I. A multi-layered system

The relatively short story of Islamic law and finance is composite in many ways. The combination of law and finance, to start with, offers a first layer of analysis, for it differs epistemologically from any other example in world history. Islamic finance is not bound primarily by the market place; its first constraint is the *Shari'a*, the Law. As will appear in all the following essays, *Fiqh*, jurisprudence, and the Shari'a in general, form the background against which all the attempts in contemporary financial business find guidance and legitimacy. Taxation, insurance, banking, and even simple sales and loans contracts are bound in the theory of Islamic finance by the Shari'a.

Because there is no tradition of an independent field of Islamic economics, the reliance of modern financial and economic transactions on the vast legacy of Islamic law acquires a further dimension, which is cultural. Islam does not claim a fully-fledged economist as its father, and the absence of an Adam Smith or a Karl Marx who might have written at least the outlines of a system of economics has forced the financial world to improvise, or to rely heavily on the wealth of material constituted by the corpus of the Shari'a. In a sense, the combination of law and finance in Islam is inevitable. Finance has nowhere else to turn for guidance but the law.

Composite is also the set of milieux taken as references in these essays. Financial practitioners in the present Islamic world must keep an eye on several areas, simultaneously. Thus, Islamic banks must compare their profits not only amongst themselves, but also with the 'normal' banks. On a macro-economic level, Islamic state banking must also remain aware of the development of other state banking systems, Islamic and non-Islamic.

A third layer in the analysis, as well as in the practice of Islamic financial institutions, is historical. Islamic banks look for precedents in the early history of the Muslim community, because in the uncharted path which is taken at present, the example of the Prophet Muhammad and his Companions offers the solace of a workable model of the past , as well as an ideal to match. The ideal Islamic city looms over the whole financial world which is being constructed at present.

To some extent, this reconstruction is impossible, because the historical totality cannot be fully grasped. But also, the financial setting has obviously considerably changed. Nonetheless, and however difficult the reconstruction may be, it remains an important starting point, and does not only operate in a remote, theoretical, fashion. Through the system expounded by the Islamic law, the life of the Prophet, the *Sira*, as well as his teachings as have come down to us through his Companions' traditions, the *hadith*, form a significant part of the law. And it is through these signposts filtered historically and legally that financiers try to accommodate to the archetypal city of Islam.

What ultimately is at stake is adaptation to the modern world in a different, Islamic, fashion. The enterprise is vast, as it involves hundreds of millions of people. But it is also taken seriously. It is said that more than 25 billion dollars are handled by the Islamic Banking system, and this does not include the state systems of Iran, Pakistan and Malaysia. What these essays try to do is to bring some order of analysis in the various efforts to establish a system of Islamic law and finance on solid ground.

II. New essays in a new field

The essays collected in this book are new. To an extent, they could not escape being new, for the field is young. Though the literature has been growing systematically in the past decade, it has paled in comparison with the buoyant practice in the real world. When compared with the volume of transactions and the money involved, or the interest generated by the espousal of Islamic principles by vast Asian states, the literature in the field of Islamic law and finance looks negligible. This, in Goethe's words, is quite understandable, for 'Grey is the theory, and Green the Tree of life'. But there is a specific dimension of the debate that renders this reality even more acute in Islamic law and finance: the practitioners themselves are not at ease with their field. This is due not only because it is only a decade old, but because there is a real predicament inherent to the equation. This appears better in the light of the dichotomy Muslim/Islamic.

Many countries and individuals relate to Islam. But countries can be Muslim without being Islamic, though an individual can only be Muslim. One would speak of a Muslim person, not of an Islamic person. For countries, the most extreme example of a Muslim, but not Islamic, country would be Albania. Similarly, Iran is Muslim and Islamic interchangeably. The nuance resides perhaps in the *conscious adoption* of Islam as a system of reference.

That the same distinction cannot be deemed true for individuals may be explained by the fact that Islamicity is not pertinent for individuals. Whether a person consciously adopts Islam as a system of reference will not render him or her less or more Muslim. Whether on the other hand a country or an institution tries to be Islamic, then the whole set of references it has chosen, and the general course it takes, will be different.

The following essays share an interest in approaching institutions in the sense just delineated. What is investigated are the modes of operation of these institutions, as these modes of operation are consciously presented as *Islamic*. For despite the fact that practice has preceded theory, the theory remains an important part for an activity which is highly conscious of its aims and methods. The institutions and states under analysis in these essays want to recognize in their practices a fulfilment of their choices for Islam, as opposed to any other model.

The attempt to examine with some detail this 'Islamicity' in the field of law and finance will bring the discussion to a wide geographical area, with experiments of countries where millions of people are concerned, such as

Malaysia (Jane Connors), Iran and Pakistan (Abbas Mirakhor), Egypt (Ian Edge, Chibli Mallat); institutions, which by essence are international and cover a large and economically significant area of operations (Volker Nienhaus, David Baldwin and Rodney Wilson), laws (Ian Edge, Nabil Saleh) or taxation systems (Munir Morad). These countries, institutions and systems all share the vindication of Islamicity.

These essays have tried to remain close to practical details. In some instances, the subject-matter was more favourable than others, as is the case in Egypt, where the survey of commercial law by Ian Edge is documented by a rich legal tradition. It is too early to assess the performance of state banking in countries that have adopted it only two or three years ago, but a first description of the legal texts in Malaysia was carried out by Jane Connors. In the case of Iran and Pakistan, Abbas Mirakhor goes into more details of the progress of Islamic state banking, as the statutes are relatively older, and followed through more systematically. But practice is not always readily available for analysis, and as Munir Morad's article suggests, it is pointless to talk about Islamic taxation in practice, when there has been no true instance of a systematic attempt at introducing in a contemporary state a system of taxes consciously derived from the Shari'a. Still, one will find that Islamic banks have started to yield results, and some assessment, such as in the articles of Volker Nienhaus, David Baldwin and Rodney Wilson, can be made.

Theory in other articles appears predominant, but there has been a conscious effort on part of the contributors not to diverge too much from the incidence of the new Islamic modes on the real life of finance. Nabil Saleh's chapter develops the constraints on transactions delineated by the Shari'a, and Chibli Mallat's essay shows the incidence of the debate on riba on fundamental articles of the Egyptian Civil Code. In both cases, the importance of the dispositions of the Shari'a is evident.

Finally, it is hoped that these essays will contribute also to opening the debate in areas of the contemporary world that have gone so far intellectually unchallenged. Perhaps the greatest advantage in a field such as this one resides in the necessity to think anew basic issues that have so far been accepted without question. Fixed returns on loans, as exemplified by the concept of interest, are a good example of economic issues which are generally taken for granted. That there might be a financial alternative to related problems, such as the issue of world internal and external debt, is by itself a challenging, but immensely complicated question. As William Ballantyne shows in his introduction to the book, there are grave matters associated with the financial and legal choices of countries which face, as most do, a worrying debt problem. The question of the success or failure of

Islamic banking on a State, as well as on the enterprise level, will loom large over the availability of alternative, and realistic, solutions to the problem of world indebtedness.

III. About this book

The essays in this book were presented in an international symposium organized by the Centre of Near and Middle Eastern Studies and the Law Department at the School of Oriental and African Studies, University of London, held in April 1988. That the symposium was a success is owed both to the seriousness and depth of the contributions in a field where many questions with far-reaching consequences have been raised, and to the eagerness of specialists from the business and academic world to discuss the thorny theoretical and practical problems in the world of Islamic law and finance. For their keen interest and their support on the day of the conference, I would like to thank wholeheartedly Albert Hourani, who brought his encyclopedic scholarship to the discussions, Muazzam Ali, Chairman of the International Centre for Islamic Studies, and a pioneer of Islamic finance, Robert Annibale, Vice-President at Citibank, London, whose knowledge of finance and development in the countries of the Third World is hard to match, and David Suratgar, from Morgan Grenfell, who combines the best legal scholarship of East and West.

This publication was only possible because of the many dedicated people at the Centre of Near and Middle East Studies, who worked to prepare the material for the printer's deadline. The transliteration of Arabic and Persian words has been simplified, and foreign words are italicized the first time they appear in each chapter. This work is the joint editorial effort of several able people. I would like to mention in particular my fellow editors, David Jorjani, who assisted me in the most difficult tasks, Alan Nicol, Roula Majdalani and Ben Wedeman, who patiently reviewed the texts. We also received the timely assistance of many people, especially Mary O'Shea, Melanie Stimmler, Bridget Harney, and Diana Crosby. Particular thanks are due to Mark Datko, whose skills in computerese immensely shortened the task. Last and not least, I would like to acknowledge the friendly support of Professor William Ballantyne, who brought his scholarship and vast experience to the whole venture, chaired the conference, and made a great success of the symposium. Of course, I take responsibility for the mistakes that have remained.

Most importantly, I would like to thank Dr Tony Allan, the Chairman of the Centre of Near and Middle Eastern Studies at SOAS for his gentle and continued trust and his active support. Without him, neither the conference nor the book would have been.

Chibli Mallat

London, June 1988

INTRODUCTION: ISLAMIC LAW AND FINANCIAL TRANSACTIONS IN CONTEMPORARY PERSPECTIVE

William Ballantyne
Law Department, SOAS

In this introduction I want expressly to highlight some of the matters which I believe merit special consideration and continuing discussion. Nobody who has read or heard anything which I have uttered over the past few years will be in any doubt of my strong views as to the practical importance of an understanding of the *Shari'a* law at the present time in the context of the undoubted reassertion of Islam, and thus the Shari'a, which we are witnessing. I do not believe that anybody who knows the Muslim world will doubt this: I do not have space here to go into the justifications for this belief; I have dealt with the subject at some length in the Coulson Memorial Lecture, which I delivered at the School of Oriental and African Studies in March 1988.

The first paper in this book is on 'Financial Transactions and the Islamic Theory of Obligations and Contracts' by Nabil Saleh. Now, of course, the importance of the reassertion of Islam and the Shari'a goes a long way, far beyond the subject of this book, although it is in the context of banking that the difficulties inherent in the Shari'a have achieved most prominence in the world today. Commercial law overall is really basically a matter of contract, and an understanding of the legal background is of increasing and vital importance. Thus this paper of Nabil Saleh is itself of great importance. In particular, perhaps, Nabil will forgive me for quoting a phrase which appears in the course of his paper: 'inevitable clash or mutual tolerance'. He links this with a warning to those who may tend to view the possible collapse of Islamic banking with eagerness: as I say, I hope I may be forgiven for anticipating this, because it is a subject so close to my own heart. I would like directly to identify myself with the sentiments which he expresses. An earnest plea must be made for an attempt to co-ordinate the two systems of Islam and the West. Once again, time simply does not permit me to analyze how this might be done but it does seem to me that the least that is required is:-

1. An international Arab Code of the Shari'a -- a new *Majalla*? -- to remove the uncertainty surrounding the true, immutable precepts of the Shari'a in basic texts, *nusus*, so that at least we can all know where we are; and so that above all we can ascertain where there exists in the

Shari'a sufficient flexibility to make it adaptable to modern economic circumstances; and at the same time:

2. Flexibility on the part of the occidental systems of law and finance in considering how far the Islamic concepts really do constitute anathema, in so far as their interests are concerned. I shall return to this subject later.

It is not surprising that, given the title of this book, the main preoccupation should be with Islamic banking, although the title could take the matter further than that. Thus Munir Morad's paper on taxation, with its learned analyses, is very welcome.

It is, of course, easy for a lawyer who like myself has spent the whole of his professional life practising in and with the Arab world to become obsessed solely with the Arab jurisdictions, but in assessing the importance of our subject today, we must not forget that there are between 700 and 1,000 million Muslims, encompassing a vast area of the world. This is in part evidenced in the book by the fact that Jane Connors writes on the system in Malaysia, Abbas Mirakhor on Iran and Pakistan, and David Baldwin and Rodney Wilson make special reference to Turkey. Finally, Volker Nienhaus in dealing with the comparative performance of Islamic banks, makes specific reference to several jurisdictions, and -- I found this extremely interesting and significant -- emphasizes the importance of the agricultural sector and the tendency to neglect the rural areas.

That brings me to Chibli Mallat's paper on *riba* -- the great debate on riba. This points out, as always in studying this eternal subject, that the key element is *doubt*. There is still not even unanimity on what riba really means, or a proper definition, on the extent of its application. It is while such doubts remain that there can be no certainty in financial negotiations where there is any question of the Shari'a law being applicable. This doubt, of course, extends beyond riba to the concept of *gharar*, into the third difficulty highlighted by Al-Sanhuri, the ban on multiplicity of transactions, etc. It is for these considerations that in my opinion a unified codification of Shar'ia principles is of the utmost urgency, wherein those precepts of the Shari'a which are by common consent deemed to be immutable, that is to say as stemming from the Qur'an or the *Sunna,* from the Qur'an itself or from the traditions of the Prophet -- wherein such precepts can be defined by common consent between the Islamic jurisdictions -- an international convention to that effect. The Learned Academy of Islamic Jurisprudence is presumably engaged in some such exercise, but since its formation little has emerged. On the other side, as I have said, Western lawyers and economists should be urgently considering the extent to which flexibility exists in the Western system, whereby the two systems, Western and Islamic, may be brought closer together. May I briefly try to point out the importance and practical application of these difficulties by stating three propositions:-

1. That in a jurisdiction where the Shari'a applies, contracts not in accordance with its precepts are quite simply illegal: in our present context, banking transactions based upon the conventional Western system of interest;

2. That in Muslim eyes, not only is a system of economics which is not based on Shari'a principles anti-religious, illegal, and sinful, but that in the world today, the Islamic system is better;

3. That, as I have said, the alternative to some co-operation is a clash, a confrontation.

Let us consider these three in turn.

I

The Basic Illegality

Let me take a topical example -- I always consider practical examples better than theory -- a syndicated loan agreement. You are all familiar with these. Let us suppose several liability in a syndicate of banks for a period loan to an Arab State, probably with guarantees via ECGD, COFAS, EXIM, as the case may be. Interest is defined by a rate above an inter-bank rate, and in case of default there is interest upon interest. Let us suppose that in our example, it is a sterling loan, with payments to be made in London, and that there is a proper law clause which defines English law as the proper law of the agreement; and there is a jurisdiction clause giving non-exclusive jurisdiction to the English courts, but vesting jurisdiction also in the courts of the borrowing State and indeed any other courts which may properly have jurisdiction according to their own laws. There is usually also, in the case of the State, express waiver of sovereign immunity.

Now, as you all know, such agreements invariably contain a number of conditions precedent, not the least of them being the necessity for the opinion of a lawyer qualified in the law of the borrowing State to the effect that the agreement is legal according to the law of that State. Why is this necessary in view of the choice of law clause and the jurisdiction clause? There are, of course, a number or reasons, but not the least are that it may be necessary to sue upon the contract in the courts of the borrowing State, either directly or by way of enforcing a foreign judgment obtained on the contract: it is also not inconceivable that an English court or other appropriate foreign forum may, despite the choice of law clause in the contract, take cognizance of public policy provisions in the law of the borrowing State. Thus an expert or 'clearing' opinion is sought. The lawyer giving such opinion must of course be fully cognizant of the laws of the borrowing State, and where it is an Islamic State, the first question he must ask himself is, does the Shari'a have any application? In dealing with the Arab States, as I am accustomed to do, the answer to this depends upon the jurisdiction: to take examples at one end of the scale, in Kuwait and Bahrain (since its new Commercial Code of 1987), and as Mr Edge points out in his chapter, in Egypt, the answer would be 'no', but with a caveat that interest rates are pegged by the Central Banks. At the other end of the scale, Saudi Arabia, the answer would be 'yes', the Shari'a is most certainly relevant, and the whole contract is illegal. In various other jurisdictions, there are varying shades. Whether such contract would in any case be denied as being illegal in present circumstances is another matter; what the lawyer has to advise on is the position of that contract at law. Almost invariably, he has to add to his opinion a proviso to the effect that if the Shari'a were to be applied, the transaction would be void, or voidable. If, despite such caveats as may have to be entered, the bankers take, nonetheless, a commercial risk (and this has happened in many cases), that is entirely another matter; but this is hardly satisfactory! It is one thing where a State is obliged from a position of weakness to reschedule or renegotiate its loans; it is entirely another where that State has a valid legal or constitutional argument on which to base its renegotiation (vide infra).

In the simplest terms, the Shari'a forbids interest on monies lent. Western economies are structured upon it. With the onset of oil wealth, the Arab world has entered the Western system, and in the majority of cases the conflict has simply not been allowed to arise. However, for a lawyer this is hardly satisfactory when he has to advise his clients on the possible legal risks involved in such a transaction as we have been considering.

As to the generality of the prohibition of interest qua riba, we may refer to that great Hanbali jurist, Ibn Al-Qayyim, who, following Shafi'i's view, writes in *I'lam al-Muwaqqi'in*, *'Dirhams and dinars are the units of valuation of articles sold, and constitute the standard by which the evaluation of property is recognized. It must therefore be fixed and regulated so that it does not go up or down, since were the price (of currency) to go up or down like commodities we would not have a standard with which to value the articles sold. Indeed, everything is commodity, and the people's need for a price by which to value articles sold is a general and compelling one. Such valuing is not possible, save on the basis of a rate by which to know value. This requires a standard on the basis of which things are assessed, which continues upon one state of affairs, and which is not itself assessed by reference to anything else. If it becomes a commodity which goes up and down, then the transactions of people will be impaired....'*

II

Is the Islamic System Preferable ?

The second, and no doubt controversial, issue to which I direct your attention for discussion, is the extent not only to which the Muslims may now be largely committed to a system of Islamic financing, but the extent to which they may be justified in regarding this system as better than the conventional Western system. May I quote from what I said at the 1988 Coulson Memorial Lecture: *'Do the Arab States really wish, would they even be advised, to tamper with the existing concepts of riba at the present time? When they look at the world banking system, which is based essentially upon interest, and which may seem to them at times to be tottering on its base; when they see the most powerful nations in debt rather than in credit -- may this not provide, apart from basic beliefs which exist anyway, a powerful argument that what the Prophet uttered so long ago was entirely right, and that the principle of profit-sharing and partnership is better not only from the religious point of view but in practice? Is Islamic banking not true merchant banking? Why then, they may say, erode the principles of riba as they exist, when it may be contended that they provide the only solution to impending chaos? I am not saying that I subscribe to such an extreme view -- I am simply not sufficient of an economist -- but it is a solemn thought.'*

In order to give further background for a consideration of this subject, I would like to refer very briefly to the main incidents in the economic history of the Gulf States, since they provide, after all, the prime example of the sudden onset of vast wealth, and the necessity for its absorption into the world economic scene.

When I first went to the Gulf in 1948, it was common form for the oil concessions of the time to provide for a fixed royalty on the oil produced by the oil companies of 3 rupees 8 annas per ton! The rupee was then valued at 1s. 6d., and a ton of oil is seven barrels. Even these munificent terms were of largely academic interest over much of the area because virtually no oil was being produced: it did not suit the international oil cartel to fit it into the existing international marketing pattern. When I advised on the first 50/50 sharing agreement in Bahrain in 1952, the 50 per cent tax payable to the Ruler of Bahrain was calculated upon an inter-company price of $1.40 per barrel (the posted price at that time of comparable crude was, as far as I recall, $1.75). The average annual rent for a concession was 100,000 rupees, or £7,500. These undoubted exploitations of the early years were, of course, gradually redressed by the increasing power of OPEC and the demands of that organization, together with the increasing demands for energy, until in the latter 1970s the spot price for a barrel of oil in the Gulf reached \$41 - \$42, of which the OPEC countries were taking the major share. This led, of course, to astronomical increases in income. The current scene reveals an average price of \$15 per barrel, and it has been lower. As we know, in all the producing countries there have been drastic cut-backs, and recently Saudi Arabia went to the length of restoring personal income tax, not to control inflation or for any other like economic reason, but because the income was needed. This measure was almost immediately withdrawn, but it tells its own story.

Against this background, the Arabs, looking at the contemporary scene, and having subscribed to the Western economic system in large measure, may perhaps be forgiven for wondering where on earth they have got to!

The *Observer* Business Section on 3rd April 1988, said, under a heading 'The U.S. Bank Bust': '*Some 184 American banks failed last year, the largest number in a single year since the Great Depression. In the first three months of this year, another 44 have gone under. In 1987, America's 200 largest banks suffered a combined deficit of \$21 billion, while the top 25 lost more than \$7.2 billion. The major cause related to the necessity to raise provisions against Third World debt*'.

If I may give another quote, this time from *The World Debt Crisis and Its Resolution*, a publication by the United States Department of Agriculture (1987): '*Debt rescheduling has become increasingly common since 1982. Such a move, however, only superficially improves the immediate payment structure. The long term effect of rescheduling will probably be to make the total cost of the debt even more expensive, and to make overcoming the debt problem even more difficult. Developed countries and their lending institutions may find that the benefits of forgiving some portion of the debts outweigh the costs that will result. Forgiving some of the indebtedness of the developing countries may stimulate the world marketplace, leading to mutually beneficial trade among nations*'.

The report to which I have just referred indicates the commencement of the debt crisis as beginning ostensibly with the international debt repayment problems of Poland in 1981, followed by those of Mexico, Brazil and Argentina in 1982. The report accentuates the circular effect of the various forces which go to make up the problem into which we do not have time to go here: briefly, for our present purposes, we might sum up the progression as follows:-

1. Rapid growth in development in the 1960s and early 70s, when credit was readily available and inexpensive.

2. Excessive demand for resources, notably petroleum, resulting in a virtual monopoly position for OPEC.

3. Fourfold increase in petroleum prices initiated by OPEC in 1973-74.

4. A resulting vast liquidity in the OPEC countries recycled by international bankers in the form of 'petrodollar' deposits by a massive lending program to developing countries. To quote again from the report, *'these bankers anticipated high returns on investments, and assumed that a country guarantee was adequate provision against repayment defaults. The bankers did not ask if the funds were being invested in such a way that a stream of foreign exchange earnings would be forthcoming to repay the loan'.*

Pausing there for a moment, might not an Arab Islamic banker say that the attitude of the international banks would have been far different if Islamic principles had been adhered to, and if the banks themselves had had equity interests in the projects in which these vast amounts of money were to be invested? Would such a contention be a valid one? Let us bear in mind that the IMF itself has recently recommended the replacement of much of the burden of debt by equity investment. Then, let us recall that this is really what the Shari'a dictates by way of *mudaraba* and *musharaka* !

Well, as we all know, the 1973-74 oil price rise set the stage for the large debt accumulation, and then there came the second oil shock of 1979-80. This was too much, and the major industrial countries restricted available credit.

It must be salutary surely to reflect that the guarantee of a sovereign State to pay a debt, regarded historically as sacrosanct, rapidly loses its value in circumstances where the State simply cannot repay. It would appear that of the 25 countries rescheduling between 1981 and 1985, only two, Morocco and Sudan, were Arab States, and of these only one, the Sudan, may be regarded as having essentially an Islamic regime. It is, however, sobering to consider that in many Islamic jurisdictions, should difficulties arise, there might be a legal, even constitutional, argument at the Shari'a with which to bolster up renegotiation or rescheduling - the basic illegality of the original transaction.

III

Mutual Adjustment, or Confrontation ?

My third proposition is in effect -- can anything be done by cooperation between the two ideologies to regularize all this ? Because I believe that with the undoubted reassertion of Islam and the Shari'a which is upon us, the alternative is a clash. I gave my views on this situation at the 1988 Coulson lecture, and as those views have not changed since then, perhaps I may restate them here.

'What, if anything, can be done by the Western lawyer, other than to sit back and wait for an inevitable crash application of the Shari'a ? First of all, realize the existence of the problem, and problem it is ! Secondly, Western lawyers must show a great sympathy and understanding for this powerful religious and cultural background, and we have to devise where necessary (not as yet in all jurisdictions) our bridges -if indeed these can be built. There are many ifs. The Shari'a is a sacred subject, and apart from understanding on the Western side, any dialogue must require the cooperation of the Muslim side in what in many quarters is regarded as a forbidden subject. Certainly, let us never underestimate the importance of this subject at this time -- a classical and rigid application of the Shari'a to modern economic agreements could be catastrophic, and it is sobering to reflect that this could occur in most of the Arab jurisdictions with no need for prior legislation. Let it not be thought either that such application is relevant only within a Muslim jurisdiction -- what of the situation in a Western court directed by its conflict rules to apply to a contract the Shari'a law, proved by expert evidence to be the law applicable as the proper law of contract? Also, what of the enforcement of foreign judgments in the Muslim jurisdictions? These are grave matters'.

Perhaps what is required in today's climate is not just a restructuring of the Shari'a to fit Western economic concepts, but some restructuring of those concepts in order to meet the Shari'a: a study of just how far Western and Shari'a concepts are incompatible in the light of a new *ijtihad*. In so far as dialogue is possible, let us pursue it. The need for it is the reason that I insisted upon 'The Shari'a in Transnational Transactions' as the leading subject of the first conference of the International Bar Association to be held in an Arab country --Cairo, February 1987. The Arab Regional Committee of the IBA formed as a result of the outstanding success of the conference (of which I have the honour to be the first chairman) will, I hope, provide an opportunity for such dialogue. There will be a second major conference of that Committee in Bahrain in March 1989. Another hopeful initiative with which I am concerned is that of the Euro-Arab Chambers of Commerce in the field of arbitration.

We must take the opportunity for discussion while wise and moderate men are available to participate in it. Really, this can only be done by lawyers, and, in the final analysis Muslim lawyers at that -- such is the difficulty where the law is identified with religion. The political implications are, of course, obvious; but for the issue to become an international political issue, or to be overtly treated as such, is, I hope, unthinkable -- to say that that would be counterproductive is to understate the obvious. We are too apt to write learned memoranda based upon the material pros and cons of a situation. Our Arab friends can be supreme materialists; but also supreme romantic idealists, and, of course, religionists. Despite the obvious difficulties, I am optimistic enough to believe that something may be achieved.

It should not be impossible. We read in Mr Edge's paper, for example, of the international effort which subsumed the draft Law of Commercial Companies in Egypt in 1980. It is my sincere hope that the material presented here will provide at least a small stepping stone towards the realization of further achievement. There must be many more international fora for the discussion and analysis of these issues.

*****

PART ONE

LEGAL PERSPECTIVES

FINANCIAL TRANSACTIONS AND THE ISLAMIC THEORY OF OBLIGATIONS AND CONTRACTS

Nabil A. Saleh
Law Consultant, London

Introduction

During the Umayyad period (660-750 AD), the Qur'an's injunction (Qur'an II, 282) on the merits of writing down deferred transactions, because written acts would give more value to testimony and relieve the contracting parties from doubt, seems to have remained largely ignored. As a result, few written instruments and nearly no legal studies pertaining to the first century of Islam were transmitted to us. At the beginning of the Abbasid era occurred what appeared to be a sudden phenomenon, for we are put in presence of an important number of legal documents and treatises which bear witness to the existence of a significant corpus of law.

For some non-Muslim contemporary scholars, who also saw the nineteenth century adulteration of the *Shari'a*, this sudden emergence added to their conviction that Islamic law came into being as an idealistic system which remained independent from current practice. While it cannot be denied that, especially after the early tenth century, Muslim scholars and jurisconsults tackled in their treatises numerous hypothetical cases mostly in order to clarify difficult points of their teaching, and that some notions of Islamic law were not universally applied (e.g. the prohibition of dealing with *riba* and *gharar*) while some others were violated (e.g. criminal and constitutional laws, taxation), Islamic law was not a purely idealistic program never put to the test.

Thus, the law for marriage, divorce, inheritance and *waqf* is still Islamic in nearly all Muslim countries. Until the second half of the 19th century, that was also the case with regard to the law of obligations and contracts. Islamic law must in this contest be understood to comprise the law that is revealed, the teaching of the different schools and sects, customary practice, as well as an inevitable measure of foreign influence and alterations impelled by performance and the passage of time. In practice, Islamic law is instanced by old decisions of Cairo Shari'a courts (Chehata 1969, 55-56), by official registers and private papers in places like Riyad, Jeddah, Oman, the Yemen, Damascus and Baghdad, and by the much heralded manuscripts of the Cairo Geniza (Goitein 1964 , 314-357 and Udovitch 1970, 289-303).

From the second half of the nineteenth century onward, the Islamic law of contracts was in the Ottoman Empire and India affected by Western law, with, as a result, the emergence of a composite legal system which was not always systematic, and is still in the process of adaptation. Until the nineteenth century, there is little doubt that Islamic ethics, directives and prohibitions pervaded the field of contracts and obligations. Reported traditions of the Prophet, such as his delineation of the ambit of the Qur'anic riba prohibition[1] and his teachings with regard to misrepresentation in contracts[2], are witness to the unequivocal effect of Islamic law on the daily life of the believers.

The extensive number of legal stratagems (*hiyal*) that people, and especially merchants, had recourse to in order to avoid the Shari'a inconvenient mandatory dictates is an indirect evidence, although not particularly laudable from a religious prospect, of the Shari'a as the governing law of contracts. Even though divergences from the theory of Islamic law occurred from the outset, another system had not taken over. Rather, life's exigencies and the contact with other cultures have rapidly created a more lenient legal system parallel to the theoretical legal structure. The Shari'a was never purely idealistic and speculative.[3] And no other coherent system of law disputed or could dispute its position in the Islamic countries.

---

[1] The Qur'anic prohibition of riba is limited to loan agreements. It was to be extended by several *hadith* (traditions) to the exchange of currencies and denominated articles, which became properties susceptible of riba.

[2] A deceived buyer was thus given the option to retain an animal that was the object of misrepresentation, or to return it with a measure of dates, intended to compensate for the use of the animal since its purchase.

[3] Not the least for the reason stated by one author (Cahen 1977, 223) that examples drawn from modern age cannot apply to medieval time. The reverse is equally true.

Since the nineteenth century however, the Shari'a lost its exclusivity to govern financial transactions in Islamic countries to a combination of sacred and secular laws. In countries such as Saudi Arabia, Oman or North Yemen, where Islamic law remains dominant, a substantial number of mundane statutes curtail the Shari'a's ascendency significantly. Conversely, where in other Islamic countries secular laws seem to take precedence, the Shari'a has not been completely supplanted. The legal currents which exist side by side, i.e. the Shari'a and secular statutes or their combination, have ill-defined and ever shifting spheres of application. Practice, which also includes the ruler's whimsical dictates, adds another uncertainty to the state of financial transactions by creating or superseding the law as a matter of fact. To identify the legal rule governing a given problem is therefore an arduous and puzzling task. And the difficulties are compounded by the actual interpretation and practical implementation of the rule.

This paper will not discuss the actual law or laws which govern a particular transaction in a particular country, but it will point out those Shari'a features which in principle should have, but not always had, a material impact on the technique of concluding financial transactions. There will be occasional references to the actual statutes of one or another country.

I. Absence of Formalism

In the past a written agreement and an agreement not committed to writing had exactly the same value with regard to their probatory force. For both forms of agreement it was only the testimony of those who witness them which established their existence (Tyan 1945, 11 and 72). Because writing was not convenient or possible during the first century of Islam, contracts were often concluded by a witnessed exchange of words and that was deemed sufficient to tie up the contracting parties together (*'aqada*, the verbal root of *'aqd* - contract or transaction - means to tie up, to make a knot).

For more complex contracts or more orderly contracting parties, when writing was resorted to, it had to be witnessed as well. Contracts of trivial importance could even be concluded by mere conduct (*mu'atat*) with scarce words exchanged and with no need for witnesses.[4] Other contracts could only be perfected by the subject-matter passing hands from one contracting party to the other such as the loan of a non-fungible article, pledge and gift. But as

[4] Mu'atat is when the offer and acceptance are expressed by an act with no need for any formula. For example, when a shopper tenders five dirhams to a trader and takes two melons from the stall, and the trader takes the money and remains silent.

a general rule, contracts under Islamic law grew with no formalism if we except the requisite for uttering explicit words, in the past or present tense,[5] which are indicative of the contracting parties' intentions.[6] In certain market places, the contracting parties may clap or shake hands in order to close the bargain, but these are local customs which, technically speaking, have no part in the conclusion of the transaction. This lack of formalism found in the Shari'a Contract Law is remarkable compared to the then existing formalistic laws of neighbouring Byzantian and Sassanian Empires. One likely reason for the Islamic informality in the technique of contracting is the Qur'an's concern to spare the Islamic community from any undue hardship (Qur'an XXII ,78), that concern being a distinctive feature of the teaching of Islam. A better guarantee for the respect of contracts and transactions was not deemed in ceremonial but in observing the divine injunction 'O ye who believe fulfil [your] contracts' (Qur'an V, 1).

Nowadays, written evidence is deemed essential with respect to a growing number of transactions and contracts, often as a requirement of the local authorities and not necessarily as the expressed wish of the contracting parties. In that way memoranda and articles of association, commercial agency contracts and rent contracts are necessarily in writing and must be properly registered; otherwise they have no value in the eyes of the local authorities. In that way, the advantage that the Shari'a offered to Muslims in their dealing has faded away. But it is equally true that the disadvantages that accompanied a strict interpretation and implementation of the Shari'a law of contract have also considerably diminished, as the constraining factors, discussed in the next section, have lost ground.

II. Constraining Factors

Nearly all systems of law have developed and created limits and barriers which curtail to a certain extent the liberty of contracting. In capitalist and moderately socialist societies, mandatory provisions of the laws and Public Policy prevail over the accord of the parties. In communist countries strong state orientation is another curbing factor. The Shari'a has its own set of

---

5 A promise to contract is not, as a matter of principle, valid by Shari'a standards. Thus the contracting parties are urged to make use of the past tense or, less satisfactorily, the present tense, which indicates that there is no separation in time between their intention to transact and the transaction they pass.

6 Expressing the intent by other means than words, such as nodding, is not valid except for the mute. Contracts by mere conduct were first tolerated with respect to trivial subject-matters only.

requisites, abhorrences and ethics, which cannot be easily defeated by the agreement of two contracting parties. Changing the set is the more difficult since the Shari'a is given by God, and man is not allowed to tamper with it.

The Qur'anic prohibition of 'riba' which is translated into English as 'usury' or 'interest', and the Shari'a prohibition of 'gharar' which is generally designated in English as 'uncertainty', 'risk', 'speculation', are two landmarks of the Islamic legal system. Both of them constitute such a constraining factor on the technique of contracting that the famous jurist 'Abd ar-Razzaq as-Sanhuri branded them, in one of his treatises, as being the major impediment to the evolution of Islamic jurisprudence in line with the requirements of modern life (Sanhuri n.d., Vol. 3,14). Other curbing factors are the requisites set up by the Shari'a on the contracting parties to a particular nominate contract not to depart from the strict pattern devised by the fiqh for such a contract, as well as investigating the legality of the cause (*sabab*) of contracts.

A. The Prohibition of Riba and its Impact on Financial Transactions

Because Muslims are prevented from taking and giving interest accrued on capitals, they cannot perform most banking operations, as commonly practised, without committing a mortal sin sanctioned by severe punishment. Thus the loan of fungible commodities (*qard*) is to be discharged without any premium or advantage provided to the lender, unless this advantage is willingly granted to him, after settlement and not before, and not as a condition of the loan. The lender cannot even accept a gift from the borrower, except if it was customary for the lender, prior to the qard, to receive such a gift, or if after the qard an event occurs giving a good reason for the gift, such as marriage. This prohibition is not restricted to a gift as such but applies to any advantage or benefit that the lender might secure out of the qard, such as riding the borrower's mule, eating at his table, drinking his coffee or even taking advantage of the shade of his walls (Saleh 1986, 41-44).

Suftaja (bill of exchange) was therefore regarded with suspicion by the various schools of law, but it was not forbidden.[7] A bill of exchange (suftaja)

[7] Hanafis accept the concept of suftaja with aversion (*karahiyya*), (al-Kasani 1910 Vol 7, 395-6). Hanbalis deem suftaja lawful, provided it is agreed on following the conclusion of the qard and not as a prerequisite of the qard (Ibn Qudama n d, Vol 4, 356), as do Shafi'is

is defined as a loan of money repayable by the borrower to a person other than the lender in a place which could be different from the place where the money was handed over to the borrower. Suftaja's main purpose is to avoid the risk of transporting the money. This is reached by creating, besides the borrower's obligation to repay the money, another obligation, which is to pay that money to a person other than the lender and often in a different place. Because the lender derives from the suftaja -which is basically a loan of money- such an extra advantage, it was not readily adopted.

A similar prohibition from dealing with interest is valid for the depositor of a sum of money with a bank. The depositor cannot take any interest or indeed advantage out of his idle money.

The riba prohibition relates not only to large financial operations, it affects any monetary transaction, small as it may be. Thus the charge that a bank retains for services rendered to its client should in no way be related to the financial value of that service, such as for example being made proportional to the sum involved. However a service charge could be in proportion to the magnitude of the service actually rendered.

This is not to say that accommodation was not found. Most, if not all countries where Islam is prevalent, have ignored the prohibition of taking and giving interest, which is nowadays the most important field of application of the riba prohibition. No stone was left unturned to find a justification for a restricted scope of application of the riba prohibition. It suffices here to say that accommodation ranges from turning a blind eye to the dealing with interest, as is the case in Saudi Arabia, to an open legitimization of interest connected with commercial, as opposed to civil, transactions as instanced by Art.102 of the Kuwaiti Commercial Code of 1980.

Until the late seventies, opposition to such accommodation was relatively muted. Opposition was mainly confined to a limited number of traditionalist scholars whose teaching was more intended to keep the Shari'a torch alight than to impel a real change. Everyone seemed content with the situation, until the challenge came from two non-Arab countries, Iran and Pakistan, which set the stage for dramatic changes and invited other Islamic countries to join them in their reassessment of fundamental values. Whether Arab Islamic countries will fully respond to such an invitation is difficult to predict, but it is clear that paying lip-service to the Shari'a is less and less acceptable. Lenient views on the application of the riba prohibition not only

(ash-Shirazi 1343H., Vol 1, 304) and, apparently the Ibadis (as-Salimi 1344H, 384-5).

stumble against the outright Qur'anic condemnation, which would be limited to loan agreements, but also against a revival of religious fervour unconcerned with practicalities.

B. The Prohibition of Gharar and its Impact on Financial Transactions

Arising from the same wish to protect the weak against exploitation by the strong, the Shari'a established a principle of general application commanding that any transaction should be devoid of uncertainty, speculation or risk (gharar). Scholars elaborated sets of rules for the avoidance of gharar, which may be summed up in one precept: the contracting parties should have perfect knowledge of the countervalues intended to be exchanged as a result of their transaction. If the subject-matter of a contract was not existent or even not present at the time of contracting, the transaction was regarded with great suspicion by traditional authors.

When the money value of a transaction was not determined at the meeting of the contracting parties (*majlis al-'aqd*), that was deemed unacceptable by Shari'a standards. Of course payment could be postponed: such is the case when credit is given, but at least the price should be determined at the time of contracting. Even when the price is to be determined either through a decision taken by a given person, by reference to market price, or by analogy with a sale performed by a third party, Islamic schools of law, with perhaps a slight exception advocated by the Hanbali school, resist such practices on the ground that they include an element of gharar.

Gharar is dispelled only by the determination of the money value during the meeting of the contracting parties, whether this money is disbursed forthwith or at a later stage. The aversion to transactions which involve an element of risk or speculation has led to the virtual unanimity of Islamic schools of law in forbidding the practice of paying earnest money. This money was understood as a sum of money given by the potential purchaser to the potential seller as a portion of the total price in the event that the transaction is concluded and as a lump sum compensation in the event that the potential purchaser changes his mind and decides not to finalize the contract. Only Hanbalis do not condemn the practice of earnest money (Ibn Qudama n. d., Vol 4 , 256).

A strict interpretation of the prohibition of gharar by conservative scholars engaged in speculative studies would normally lead to the ban of 'contracts on future things' and the invalidity of the 'promise to contract'. Let us see the situation with regard to these two forms of contracting.

1) Contracts on Future Things

In reality not all Muslim scholars were unappreciative of practical pressures and practical needs; thus the teaching of the Maliki author Ibn Rushd, who said that in case of necessity (*darura*) and when the future inception of the subject-matter is certain, such as when during one harvest fruits are produced in continuing and connected succession, a sale contract of the whole harvest would be valid (Ibn Rushd 1981, Vol 2, 156). Although many other authors shared Ibn Rushd's views, it is with the great Ibn Qayyim al-Jawziyya that we have the most remarkable perception of the problem. Ibn Qayyim denounced the confusion between a non-existent subject-matter and between uncertainty which casts doubt on the future existence of the subject-matter. What the Shari'a condemns, he concludes, is not non-existence but that uncertainty (Ibn Qayyim al-Jawziyya 1970, Vol 1, 357-361).

Contemporary Arab authors and legislators were only too happy to rely on the teaching of such a prestigious predecessor who refused to be put off by an apparent deadlock. They focused their attention on gharar and disregarded the question of the thing's non-existence. And it is most probably in the wake of Ibn Qayyim's illuminating precedent that the provisions of Article 129.1 are to be found in Iraq's Civil Code of 1951. These provisions read in translation: 'The subject-matter of an obligation may be non-existent at the time of contracting, provided its future existence is possible and provided it is determined in a way which dispels want of knowledge (*jahl*) and risk (gharar)'. Qatar followed suit (see Art. 33 of the 1971 Civil and Commercial Law).

Even the more traditionalist Jordan's Civil Code of 1976 contains provisions to the effect that 'the subject-matter of a contract may be a thing in future provided risk (gharar) is averted' (Art. 160.1). In the following Art. 161 risk (gharar) is equated to an exorbitant want of knowledge. The Explanatory Memorandum of the Jordanian Civil Code (p. 155) tells us that the Hanafi school of law deems as a requisite that the subject-matter of a contract be in existence at the time the contract is concluded. But it considers that it may not be necessary in contracts such as hire (*ijara*), *salam* (a sale with advance payment for future delivery) and manufacture (*istisna'*).

Kuwait's modern legislator shares that view. Not only does Art. 168 of the 1980 Civil Code stipulate that 'the subject-matter of a contract may be a thing in the future unless its existence is dependent upon pure chance', but also the accompanying Explanatory Memorandum (p.138) emphasizes that exceptions and qualifications to the Shari'a principle (i.e. no thing in the future can be the subject-matter of a contract), are so numerous that it can be said that the principle does not receive application except when material gharar cannot be averted.

Consequently, it can be said that in contemporary Arab codifications, averting material gharar has replaced Shari'a requisite for the existence of the subject-matter at the time the contract is concluded. Material gharar and not the absence of the subject-matter causes voidance of contracts in the eyes of the modern Arab legislator.

In practical terms, after Ibn Qayyim, Sanhuri and anonymous legislators in the Arab world, contracts on futures are deemed valid provided they do not include a material element of uncertainty, risk or speculation.

2) Promise to Contract

A contract under Islamic law is expected to exhaust all its purposes as soon as it is concluded. That is not a sign of primitiveness, but an inescapable aspect of the theoretical system. The religiously-rooted requisite that transactions should be devoid of riba (unlawful advantage) and gharar (uncertainty, speculation, risk), has deeply stamped the entire Islamic system of law and most particularly the Law of Contract. The dual abhorrence of riba and gharar means that whenever a transaction involves the exchange of two countervalues, (a) that exchange, if it has to take place under conditions which could result in *riba an-nasi'a* (riba by way of deferment), should be concluded immediately and (b) these countervalues must be in existence, in their essence at least, and known to the contracting parties.

This theory strongly appealed to scholars and jurists, and they consequently overlooked the concept of obligation arising out of contracting, focusing their attention, instead, on the subject-matter. For them the accord of the contracting parties is expected to have an immediate impact on the subject-matter; nothing else really mattered. The logical complement of that theory is that an agreement to agree is a nullity in Islamic law (Coulson 1984, 44 and Vesey-Fitzgerald 1979,183) and that an exchange of obligation for obligation (*bay' ad-dayn bid-dayn*) is prohibited (Schacht 1984,146). Therefore a promise has no binding effect, even when the promisee expresses acceptance of the promisor's undertaking (Chehata 1970, 133-135).

But it is a fact that contracts do not always exhaust their purpose at the time of their conclusion. It may happen that, owing to a variety of reasons, the subject-matter remains for a time unaffected by the contract.That was acknowledged by traditional scholars who made room for a certain number of transactions deemed as exceptions to the principle. In that way, the validity of a sale with advance payment (bay' salam), of a contract of manufacture (istisna'), and of a hire contract (ijara), is not seriously questioned. But the legal requisites for the conclusion of such contracts are detailed in such a way as to minimize the risks of riba and gharar.

Although in bay' salam one of the countervalues is not at hand at the time the contract is concluded, and although in a contract of manufacture and in a hire contract both countervalues are unavailable at the time of contracting, an exact description of the unavailable countervalues was deemed sufficient to remedy the situation and to legitimize those contracts.

That was a convenient precedent which enabled contemporary Arab legislation to validate a promise to contract, provided all essential elements of the future contract, as well as the time during which it should be concluded, are determined (Art. 105.1 Jordan's Civil Code and Art. 72 Kuwait's Civil Code).

C. Choice of Special Conditions (*shurut*) Restricted under the Shari'a but not under Contemporary Statutes

The late Professor Coulson outlined the question of 'special conditions' (shurut) in the following manner: '[In Islamic Law] each nominate contract is strictly, and usually simply, defined in terms of its purposes and effect, and the question is how far, if at all, may the parties vary this rigid scheme by introducing agreed special terms and appendages to the particular contract they are purporting to conclude' (Coulson 1984, 51).

The answer offered by the different schools of law is that a special condition can be added to the pre-fixed terms and conditions of a nominate contract only if some specific requirements are met. Those requirements vary from one school to the other. If we take the Hanafi teaching as an example we are told that a special condition is readily and validly accepted as an appendage to a contract if it is necessary to the contract (*min muqtadayat al-'aqd*), for example the vendor retaining possession of the object of a sale until the time he receives payment; or if it is appropriate to the contract (*mula'im lil-'aqd*), such as the vendor asking for a pledge to secure payment of a sale price; or if the condition is customary to the inhabitants of the place where the contract is concluded.

The remaining schools adopted different criteria. The Hanbali school is considered the most lenient of those schools with regard to that particular problem. Under its teaching the validation of a special condition is the rule unless it falls under one of the two following categories:

(a) If it conflicts with the objective or the essence of the transaction, such as when the vendor requires that the buyer shall not sell or otherwise dispose of what he has acquired.

(b) If the special condition is contrary to a specific prohibition in the Shari'a, such as when the Prophet disallowed the presence of two conditions in one contract. The two conditions which are proscribed, according to the Hanbali interpretation, are those which bring an advantage to one of the contracting parties without being necessitated by or appropriate to the contract itself. The classic example of the combination of two such conditions in one contract is when the buyer of grain requires that the vendor mills it and carries it to him. But when the conditions, whether two or more, are necessary or appropriate to the contract itself, such as a sale made contingent upon the presentation of a pledge together with another security, then the conditions are valid.

If we revert now to some of the contemporary Civil Codes of the Gulf, we notice that Kuwait's Civil Code for example has not adopted any of the fiqh teachings with regard to special conditions, which in the circumstances would have been Maliki's teaching; what was chosen is not too different from what is expected to be seen in any Western-inspired secular statute, namely that 'a contract may contain any condition agreed by the contracting parties provided it is not prohibited by law, Public Policy or good morals' (para. 1 of Art. 175).

By contrast, para. 1 of Art. 164 of Jordan's Civil Code (which is identical to Art. 34 of Qatar's Civil and Commercial Law) sums up Hanafi teaching with respect to special conditions; it states in translation: 'A contract may contain a condition which confirms its content or is appropriate to that content or is found in customs and habits'. On the other hand para. 2 of the same Article is contrary to Hanafi teaching and reads as follows: 'A contract may also contain a condition which is to the advantage of one of the contracting parties or to a third party provided it is not prohibited by the legislator or is not contrary to Public Policy or morals, otherwise the condition is cancelled but the contract remains valid unless the cancelled condition was its motivation, in which case the contract is also cancelled'.

It is worth noting that fiqh deems invalid a condition which is to the advantage of one of the contracting parties (or even a third party) without being necessary or appropriate to the contract and without being prescribed by custom, for the reason that it amounts to an unlawful advantage (riba) secured out of the contract.

D. Investigating the Legality of the Contractual Cause (*sabab*)

In relation to contracts, cause (sabab) means the motive (*ba'ith*) which actually induces the parties to enter into a given contract; but it also means the purpose of contracting (*gharad*). Both meanings relate to the intent of the contracting parties. As is the case with other legal systems, the Shari'a forbids any contract which has a manifestly illegal cause such as a transaction designed to perpetrate an unlawful killing or a robbery.

Broadly speaking, the various Islamic schools of law approached the matter of legality of the cause in two different ways; the first approach relies on the opinion that respect due to legal acts should lead to taking into account the ostensible intention and disregarding the inner or real intention, even if the latter contradicts the former. That means that motive is not given a great value, is identified with the purpose, and is even assimilated to the subject-matter. The second approach is based on the belief that motive should be scrutinized in the light of moral and religious principles. This means that a transaction is to be measured against the degree of purity of the contracting parties' intention. For the Hanafis and Shafi'is, the ostensible meaning conveyed by the apparent terms of a contract is taken into account when the real inner intention is not easy to detect; the real intention, however, prevails when recognizable. Malikis and Hanbalis take a different stand and give great significance to real motives behind the apparent legal act (and indeed all acts) provided they are known to both parties.

Consequently, motives for the Malikis and Hanbalis determine the validity or invalidity of a contract whether or not they are identified in such a contract. Two classical examples of void contracts under Hanbali fiqh because of this illegality are the sale of grapes intended to be transformed into wine and the sale of arms intended to stir up trouble.

Thus, the basic rule taught by the schools of law that put emphasis on real motives even when unapparent, is that a contract which in itself fulfils all the criteria of validity and in all appearance contains no element of illegality, may yet be a nullity on the ground that it is inspired by improper motives. On the other hand the Hanafi and, to a lesser extent, the Shafi'i schools of law consider that it is not the function of the courts to investigate what stands behind apparently genuine transactions or to unveil their real inspiration. It is therefore not surprising that a carefully contrived range of legal stratagems (hiyal) under which illegal transactions can take place developed in countries where the Hanafi and Shafi'i schools are prevalent.

Indeed these legal stratagems are not acceptable to other schools. This, until recently, had little practical significance, for the countries where hiyal are repudiated did not have enough economic leverage and hence no real bearing outside their boundaries. That is no longer the case since the discovery of oil in the very countries where hiyal are banned. On that account this ban has now a much wider practical implication than it used to have some fifteen years ago. In addition, the law of contract is being increasingly affected by the resurgence of legal moralism based on the dicta of the Qur'an and the Sunna. That is to say that the real cause of contracts will be increasingly investigated and taken into account especially in the Gulf area where fiqh spurns legal stratagems (hiyal) and requires disclosure of the real sabab.

Let us examine at this stage how the 1980 Kuwaiti Civil Code and the 1976 Jordanian Civil Code have dealt with the concept of cause (sabab). It is no accident that Art. 165 para. 1 of Jordan's Civil Code defines sabab as being the immediate purpose (gharad) intended out of the contract; whereas Art. 176 para. 2 of Kuwait's Civil Code defines sabab as being the motive (ba'ith) which induces a contracting party to conclude a contract provided that such a motive is known to the other contracting party.

The explanation for this difference is simple: the Hanafi school prevails in Jordan whereas the Maliki school holds authority in Kuwait. However, both legal systems stress that sabab should be in existence as well as lawful (Art. 176 para. 1, Kuwait; Art. 165, para. 2, Jordan) and both legal systems make room for establishing the real cause (sabab) when there is doubt on the veracity of the apparent one (Art. 178, Kuwait; Art. 166 para. 2, Jordan).

III. Inevitable Clash or Mutual Tolerance ?

Until the mid-1970s, financial transactions performed by merchants were governed in most Arab countries by statutory provisions basically secular and Western-inspired, which paid nominal tribute to Shari'a. These statutes had been introduced in the Arab World under the Ottoman Empire, were reinforced during the colonial era and eventually given validation by Muslim jurists, such as the great Sanhuri, the main architect of the Egyptian Civil Code of 1948 after which so many Arab civil codes are modelled.

Several factors contributed to holding the Shari'a aloof; not the least of these factors was the wide assumption that the Shari'a cannot provide for matters of commercial law without considerable distortion. Thus, most Arab countries were keen to adopt the distinction found in France and some European States, but not in common law countries, between Civil Law and Commercial Law as separate bodies of law, frequently set out in distinct codes. Commercial Law is applicable only to commercial men (merchants) and governs acts of trade. It is mainly distinguished from Civil Law by a less formalistic way in concluding contracts, more flexible rules of evidence, presumed solidarity among debtors, often shorter delays for the statutes of limitation, and exposure to bankruptcy rules.

At present, financial transactions remain governed by statutory provisions, secular by and large. However, the challenge presented by the Shari'a's champions is everywhere on the increase. In some areas such as in the banking sector, it has generated total disarray, at least for a time, and this has compelled Saudi and U.A.E. legislators to take prompt action, something they are habitually reluctant to do, with the aim at appeasing the Shari'a's champions and reassuring international financial and banking communities. It is not certain that they have entirely succeeded.

Moreover, another type of challenge has emerged during the last decade and that is the revival of operations traditional to fiqh such as the Islamic partnership (*musharaka*), the cost-plus-profit contract (*murabaha*), the commenda partnership (*mudaraba*) as well as various other operations of lesser importance. Altogether they represent a *modus operandi* promoted by banks which claim to function on the basis of Islamic ethics.

The challenge they represent is certainly directed against the financial and banking system as practised in nearly all Western and Eastern countries, but it has another, self-directed, dimension. In fact we are not any more presented with abstract principles and tenets which could well be uttered with no intent to see them implemented. Instead long forgotten concepts and operations are revived and put into practice.

That was the most daring move; for a financial system described as Islamic is made to compete with an already existing and confirmed system. But the stakes are high. If the newly introduced system fails or wanes, such setback will bring lack of credibility to the Islamic financial system as a whole.

I hasten to say that those who anticipate failure of the system with eagerness, should think twice before they start rejoicing, for its collapse, if it ever occurs, will develop resentment, frustration and a further mistrust of Western standards and values. Only religious radicalism will reap advantage from such a situation, and the divorce between East and West will be nearly complete in case the financial and economic systems collide and their legal systems segregate. Religions, cultures and languages being already distinct, no common ground or interest would remain to bring the two worlds near each other.

Until now the legal currents which exist side by side in all Islamic countries, i.e. Shari'a law and secular statutes or their combination, are being transformed gradually and not without difficulty and temporary setbacks into an original system which is expected to assert itself with time. The reintroduced financial and economic system based on Islamic ethics awaits some positive response from a West which until now has spurned the newly proposed system and failed to adopt a constructive attitude. With more understanding and joint efforts, modifications and limitations may well be injected into the new proposals in order to make the Islamic system more acceptable to Western techniques. In case appropriate adjustments take place, it is not unreasonable to assume that a blending operation will occur one day. What is unreasonable is to take for granted that total rejection will be devoid of consequences which will be adverse to both West and East.

References

Cahen C 1977, *Les peuples Musulmans dans l'histoire medievale*, Institut Français de Damas, Damascus

Chehata C 1969, *Théorie générale de l'obligation*, Editions Sirey, Paris

Chehata C 1970, *Droit Musulman- Applications au Proche-Orient*, Dalloz, Paris

Coulson N J 1984, *Commercial Law in the Gulf States*, Graham & Trotman, London

Goitein S D 1964, 'Commercial and Family Partnerships in the Countries of Medieval Islam', *Islamic Studies*, Vol 3, pp 314-357

Ibn Qayyim al-Jawziyya 1970, *I'lam al-muwaqqi'in*, 4 Vols, Dar al-Jeel, Beirut

Ibn Qudama M n d, *al-Mughni*, 9 Vols, Maktabat al-Riyad al-haditha, Riyad

Ibn Rushd 1981, *Bidayat al-mujtahid wa-nihayat al-muqtasid*, 2 Vols, Dar al-ma'rifa, Beirut

al-Kasani 1982, *Bada'i' al-Sana'i' fi tartib al-shara'i'*, 7 Vols, Dar al-kitab al-'arabi, Beirut

Schacht J 1984, *An Introduction to Islamic Law*, Clarendon press, Oxford

Saleh N A 1986, *Unlawful Gain and Legitimate Profit in Islamic Law*, Cambridge University Press, Cambridge

al-Salimi N 1344 H, *Jawhar al nizam fi 'ilmay al-adyan wa'l-ahkam*, al Matba'a al-'arabiyya, Cairo

Sanhuri A n.d., *Masadir al-haqq fil-fiqh al-islami*, 6 Vols, al-majma' al-'arabi al-islami, Beirut. Originally published between 1954 and 1959

al-Shirazi 1343 H, *al-Muhadhdhab*, 2 Vols, Cairo

Tyan E 1945, 'Le notariat et le régime de la preuve par écrit dans la pratique du droit Musulman', *Annales de l'école Française de droit de Beyrouth*, Beirut

Udovitch A 1970, 'Theory and Practice of Islamic Law: Some Evidence from the Geniza', *Studia Islamica*, Vol 32, pp 289-303

Vesey-Fitzgerald S 1979, *Muhammadan Law*, Scientia Verlag Aalen, Germany

*****

SHARI'A AND COMMERCE IN CONTEMPORARY EGYPT

Ian D. Edge
Law Department, SOAS

Introduction

Egypt is a land of intense paradoxes.

It lies at the centre of the Arab World with a unique geostrategic position that touches Africa, Asia and Europe, which has clearly coloured and influenced its history.

It is generally considered to be one of the main centres of Sunni Islam. Cairo is home to one of the oldest Islamic Universities (Al-Azhar) which is a fount of Islamic teaching for the Sunni schools of Islamic law (the *Shari'a)* and one of the main educators of Islamic religious scholars (*shuyukh*) in the Arab World. Yet, since antiquity, Egypt has been subject to varying degrees of foreign control which have clearly influenced and pervaded its attitudes to law, politics and the economy. Each foreign conqueror had his own attitude to the Shari'a which was generally one of restricting its jurisdiction. Non-Islamic foreign influence, beginning in the late eighteenth century, gradually increased until by the late nineteenth century it threatened to subsume all but a part of the Shari'a. Once finally released from the shackles of foreign domination, the country experienced secular (generally Socialist) revolutions which have produced possibly the most liberal political and social regime in the entire Middle East with a vast corpus of almost entirely secular laws at its heart.

At one and the same time, therefore, Egypt has coexisting elements of both the most traditional religious and the most secular customs and practices of any of the Arab states and it is this contemporary dynamic that I want to consider in this article.

Firstly, therefore I shall need to consider in outline Egypt's attitude to the Shari'a since the advent of the European political control of Egypt in the nineteenth century.

Secondly, I will look at and consider the present day influence of the Shari'a in three areas: (1) the law making process - the Constitution and legislation; (2) the law enunciating bodies - the courts and judicial decisions; and (3) future developments in the economy and new financial legal structures based on the Shari'a. From this I shall be able to attempt an assessment of the importance of the role of the Shari'a in modern Egypt.

The Shari'a in Nineteenth Century Egypt

In pre-nineteenth century Egypt the Shari'a was supreme. Shari'a courts existed extolling the principles of the main Hanafi school of law, although at various times other schools were allowed their own courts.[1] All manner of disputes were taken to these courts, which existed side by side with the courts of other religious communities (the *millet* courts) and some non-religious courts (e.g. that of the *muhtasib* - a kind of medieval Director General of Fair Trading)[2]. But from the time of Muhammad 'Ali the Shari'a and Shari'a courts were in retreat before European inspired laws and practices.

In the first half of the nineteenth century there was considerable interest amongst Egyptian scholars in European law and legal method. European law codes were translated into Arabic[3] as were the works of Roman law such as parts of Justinian's *Corpus Juris*.[4] As a result of this there was considerable debate on the possibility of codification of the Shari'a and Qadri Pasha (minister of justice) produced three famous codifications on the Shari'a law pertaining to personal status, *waqf* and civil transactions. These were intended to be adopted as official texts. In the event this never occurred, but the courts (both Shari'a and non Shari'a) used the codes as works of reference on Shari'a law well into the twentieth century.

During this time Shari'a courts applying Shari'a law lost jurisdiction over increasing areas of legal matters to more secular tribunals. This began with the

---

1 See Escovitz 1985.

2 The records of the Shari'a courts in Egypt are probably the largest, oldest and most comprehensive of any state in the Middle East and have been inadequately studied. One of the major problems is that they are written in an almost incomprehensible legal shorthand (the *Qirma* script) knowledge of which is available to only a few scholars. See the appendix on court records to Tucker 1985.

3 See the work of Tahtawi and his assistants referred to by Ziadeh 1968, chapter 1.

4 For example, the work of Abd al-'Aziz Fahmy Pasha and Sufi Abu-Talib.

implementation of commercial tribunals in Alexandria and Cairo in 1850 and ended with the creation of the Mixed Courts in 1876 and the National Courts in 1883.[5]

These new secular tribunals used an accumulation of codes and civil and commercial laws based almost entirely on European (generally French) models. In this way the commercial life of Egypt was transformed. The Shari'a courts operated in only a rump of cases involving mainly personal status.

At the same time as this limitation of judicial competence was taking place, certain Islamic scholars were also questioning the application of the traditional rules of the Shari'a *qua* traditional rules. Three scholars stand out: Al-Afghani (1838-1894); Muhammed 'Abduh (1849-1905) and Rashid Rida (d. 1935) who together instigated a debate whose reverberations have yet to be stilled, about the need of the Shari'a to reform itself to take account of modern conditions - yet keeping within the framework of the sources of the Shari'a. Of these perhaps Muhammed 'Abduh was the most influential as he held the important position of Mufti of Egypt from 1899 to his death in 1905. His published opinions (*fatawa*) run to many volumes and are an important source for Islamic modernists.[6] Needless to say these opinions were extremely controversial and treated by some as pure heterodoxy. They engendered debates as to what was the Shari'a and whether the Shari'a had any capacity to change and whether it could be codified at all. As a result it is extremely difficult (particularly for a non-Muslim) to pronounce with certainty on the validity of any modern legal concept according to Shari'a law.

In summary, the history of the Shari'a in Egypt in the nineteenth century is one of encroachment and limitation, mainly at the hands of European dominance, but with at least the connivance and support of a portion of the Egyptian elite.

---

5 See generally Ziadeh op.cit. and Brinton 1968. For a general history of Egyptian law from 1800 to 1876, see Zaghlul 1900, 158-291.

6 See Kerr 1966.

The Shari'a in Early Twentieth Century Egypt

Egypt gained independence (of a sort) in 1922 and its first constitution in 1923, yet the legal system remained European-dominated for another 25 years.

Independence for the legal system was not attained until October 1949, upon the demise of the Mixed Courts and the system of capitulations in accordance with the Montreux Convention of 1937, which had extended their life for a fixed period of 12 years.[7]

The system did not change overnight. Essentially all the cases extant in the Mixed Courts were transferred to the National Courts which continued to use the codes and laws drawn up in the nineteenth century. The Shari'a courts continued to exercise their authority in a limited number of cases but even that separate jurisdiction was taken away in 1955,[8] after which one merged set of national courts existed. It was (and is) a system in which the Shari'a has little relevance outside matters of personal status law - and even there, there were modest reforms by laws enacted in 1920, 1923, 1929 and 1931. The Islamic scholars of Al-Azhar were reduced to a teaching and advisory role - their judicial functions being taken over by judges of the National Courts who specialized in Shari'a matters.

Reaction, however, was not far away and during this period a number of fundamentalist Islamic organizations were established which posited a return to (so called) fundamental and traditional values, which almost always included a call for a reimposition or return to the Shari'a in Egypt ('the Qur'an is our constitution' was an early slogan).

The largest and most well known organization was (and is) the Ikhwan al Muslimun (the Muslim Brotherhood or Brethren) which was set up by a Shaykh of Al Azhar, Hasan al Banna, in 1929. It soon attracted a lot of attention and began a campaign of both vocal and active opposition to government and its operations were often temporarily proscribed. It overstepped the mark however in the early period of the Free Officers Revolution in 1954 when one of its members attempted to assassinate Nasser. Subsequent investigations purported to find an organized plot by the Ikhwan to overthrow the regime. Whether or not this was true, a revolutionary court (*Mahkamat al thawra*) was set up which *inter alia* tried and executed a number of

---

7 See generally Vatikiotis 1980, and Brinton, op.cit.

8 By laws 461 and 462 of 1955. The courts of the non-Muslim religious communities were also abolished by these laws.

the Muslim Brethren for treason. It was at this time that the organization as a whole was proscribed by presidential decree. Thereafter, its activities (and those of similar but less well known organizations) would be furtive and subject to state surveillance and harassment.[9]

The Shari'a in Modern Egypt

From the foregoing it can be clearly seen that by 1955 the role of the Shari'a had been circumscribed in practice and principle: practically, it was applied by partly secular trained judges in secular courts in cases of more and more limited scope and ideologically it was attacked as being inappropriate in some of its detail (though not in essence) to the modern world.

To all intents and purposes the Shari'a had little role to play in Egyptian law and politics from 1955 to the 1970s; but as the leftist revolutionary policies of the 1950s showed themselves to be ill fitted to the needs of modern Egypt, the search for new ideologies intensified. Sadat heralded a new era with the promulgation of legislation opening Egypt's markets to capitalist influences and promoting foreign investment - the much vaunted economic opening up or *infitah*- but this only made more apparent the great disparities of wealth and influence existing in Egyptian society, which led to increasing calls for a return to traditional values via the seamless web of the true spirit of Islam (an ideological infitah). Fundamentalist groups mushroomed, fuelling public opinion through papers and journals (e.g. the well known monthly *al-Da'wa* of the Ikhwan) and with them came the decrying of the social state of Egypt and the warcry 'Back to the Shari'a'. The apotheosis of this was the assassination of President Sadat, portrayed as the arch-secularist, but paradoxically privately a very religious man, in 1981. Repressive measures were then undertaken against the more militant fundamentalist groups and, hence, the remaining organizations have been careful to work within the limited legal framework to attain stated goals; they are steadily and carefully gaining political legitimacy.

In this section I want to consider the role of the Shari'a (and its exponents) in contemporary Egypt in areas of the law making processes (the Parliament, the Constitution and legislation) and the law enunciating bodies (the courts and judicial decisions) and finally to consider pending changes and the future of the Shari'a in Egypt.

---

9 See generally Mitchell, 1969.

(1) The Law Making Processes

(a) The Constitution

Egypt's first Constitution of 1923 was based on the Belgian Constitution of 1831 and the Ottoman Constitution of 1876. It lacked any provision on the hierarchy of sources of law or what those sources were and the Shari'a was not mentioned in it at all. This was to be repeated in the Constitutions of 1952, 1956 and 1964. Not until 1971 was any provision on the sources of law found in any Egyptian Constitution. In the Constitution of 1971, Article 2 provided that:

> 'the principles of the Islamic Shari'a are a principal source of law'.

This did not completely satisfy the fundamentalists and after considerable political turmoil in the late 1970s, with fighting between Muslims and Copts and pressure from independent members of the People's Assembly (Maglis ash-sha'b), Article 2 was amended (by referendum) to read instead:

> 'the principles of the Islamic Shari'a are *the* principal source of law'

This change, as we shall see, caused a number of problems for the courts as to its interpretation and the effect to be given to it.

(b) The People's Assembly (Maglis ash-sha'b)

Since the Ikhwan were proscribed as a political organization in 1954, no Islamic fundamentalist has been able to canvas openly as a member of a fundamentalist political party. However with the beginnings of liberalization of the political process in Egypt in the 1970s[10] certain people of known pro-Islamic reform views were either elected or appointed to the People's Assembly as independents. Within the main political parties certain deputies clearly showed

[10] By law 38 of 1972 on the People's Assembly and law 40 of 1977 (as amended) on the formation of political parties. Under the electoral law only certain approved political parties are allowed to present themselves as parties in elections to the People's Assembly and the Ikhwan has never been accorded this right nor has any other avowedly fundamentalist party.

their pro-Islamic stance; for example, the former speaker of the Assembly Sufi Abu-Talib and the former chairman of the Bar, the late Gamal el-Oteifi.

But with the growth of support for the fundamentalist groups and the general upswelling of feeling for Islam as an answer for modern problems, the government in the last two elections has turned a blind eye to the fact that members of the Ikhwan have been included with the ranks of some of the main opposition parties.

In the elections of 1984 a few Ikhwan entered the People's Assembly as members of the Wafd opposition party but they were clearly a subsidiary part of the party and soon came into conflict with the other Wafd members. In the elections of May 1987, an alliance of the liberal party (Hizb al-Ahrar), the Labour Party (Hizb al-'amal al-ishtiraki) and the Umma party, disguised a majority of Ikhwani candidates but at the hustings their stance was clear. In this way a large number of Ikhwanis entered the People's Assembly as deputies and the alliance gained more popular support than any other opposition group. It is as yet early days to assess their influence in the Assembly but it is clear that the reimposition of the Shari'a is one of their main aims, as is also their desire to be accepted as a political party in their own right. As yet however sloganeering does not seem to have been replaced by many concrete suggestions for change.[11]

(c) Legislation

(i) Generally

Most of the contemporary legislation in Egypt is European inspired. The Commercial Code remains that promulgated for use in the National Courts in 1883 although it has been amended many times since then though never entirely replaced. The Civil Code of 1949 is an extremely interesting legal compilation. It was twelve years in the making and involved many of the finest Egyptian legal scholars as well as some of the greatest European Civil lawyers (mainly French). Under the chairmanship of 'Abd al-Razzaq al-Sanhuri a massive comparative study of Shari'a and Western civil law was undertaken. The result is a comparative law gem. In the main the code is a development of the previous Egyptian civil codes of the Mixed Courts (1876) and the National Courts (1893), but a considerable number of Shari'a principles are to be found

11 The Ikhwan candidates of the coalition fought the election under the slogan 'Islam is the solution'.

in it: particularly in the formation and termination of contract and in rules of pre-emption (*shuf'a*). Civil law concepts were also introduced but often altered to suit Egyptian circumstances or improved to produce a more logical or ideal provision.

For example, French administrative law developed the doctrine of *imprévision*, whereby if external circumstances relevant to a contract alter so that the performance of one of the parties becomes crushingly difficult, then the court has the power to rewrite the terms of the contract accordingly. This power has not, however, been extended to contracts generally and exists only for the specific category of administrative contracts. The doctrine of imprévision is included in the Egyptian civil code but without such limitations so that it applies to *all* contracts. Thus, the Egyptian civil code is not in this (nor many other instances) a slavish imitation of a civil law model, but a code made as ideal and far reaching as possible, using Egyptian and European sources, and amended to suit Egyptian conditions. It can therefore truly be called an Egyptian code.

It is perhaps for this reason that so little of the civil code has been altered or reformed since its inception - a fate known to few Egyptian laws - and also why projected reforms to it produce results little different from the present code.

(ii) Recent calls for reform

In recent years, pro-Islamic sympathisers and Ikhwani Parliamentary deputies have made (or assisted in) calls for the reimposition of the Shari'a both generally and in particular areas of law. It has been a regular topic of debate before the People's Assembly in the last ten years. In most cases the Government has stalled debates on such matters by using a number of expedients such as parliamentary procedure or the setting up of long running committees to investigate the demands and only in a few cases has it actually considered Shari'a based legislation.

After the intense debate of 1971 as to the role the Shari'a should play in the law and the Constitution, which culminated in the establishment of Article 2 of the Constitution, a special legislative committee was set up in the People's Assembly (under the chairmanship of Gamal el-Oteifi) charged with its implementation. Although the regime projected an image of supporting the Shari'a and the aims of reforming the law to bring it into conformity with the Shari'a, few changes occurred though many were put forward. The parliamentary procedure whereby draft laws have to be submitted to the Speaker of the Assembly who decides whether or not to put them on to the Assembly's agenda was often used to delay consideration of Shari'a laws.

In the early 1970s the following laws were presented in draft, but by one of the above manoeuvres each was prevented from being considered: laws on *hadd* punishments for theft and unlawful sexual intercourse (*zina*); a law prohibiting alcohol; a law prohibiting interest between individuals (only); a law prohibiting all kinds of interest and others. Only a watered down law on consumption of alcohol (limiting it to tourist establishments) became law by presidential decree in 1986.[12]

(iii) The Draft Codes of 1982

In 1978 a special committee for the codification of the Shari'a was set up by the Assembly under the chairmanship of the new speaker, Sufi Abu Talib. The aim of this committee was to reconsider the major Egyptian codes and produce Islamic equivalents conforming to the Shari'a. This included the civil code which the draftsman al-Sanhuri had said had taken as much from the Shari'a as it was possible to take. The result was a collection of draft laws: civil, commercial, civil and commercial procedure, maritime commerce and criminal, all of which purported to conform to the Shari'a. They were not fully produced until 1982 and each had a large explanatory memorandum giving the Shari'a source from which each provision derived.

The draft codes were presented to the Assembly[13] and immediately disappeared into committee where they remained until 1985. In that year, in a debate on the implementation of the amended article 2 of the Constitution, it was suggested that the draft codes be considered by the Assembly for immediate adoption. The speaker side-stepped this by deciding that the draft codes had not been properly put onto the Assembly's agenda and could not be considered in that session; hence, once again the codes were consigned to the committee shelf.[14]

The content of the draft codes is much as one would expect.[15] The most clearly Islamic is the criminal draft code which provides for the application of the hadd penalties for theft, highway robbery, unlawful intercourse (zina), slanderous accusations of zina, drinking wine and apostasy. The latter particularly raised the ire of the Christian (Coptic) community in Egypt.

---

12 See Altman 1979, 199-219.

13 *Madbatat maglis ash-sha'b* 1982, 32-41; Hill 1987, 123-35. I am indebted to Professor Hill for the use of the proceedings of the People's Assembly.

14 *Madbatat maglis ash-sha'b* 1985, 14-35.

15 I am indebted to Sayf el-Din el-Oteifi for providing me with copies of some of these draft codes, through the good offices of Michael Davis.

The civil and commercial codes are surprisingly little changed and it is interesting to see that the explanatory memorandum of these laws provides support from the Shari'a texts for established provisions in the present codes, which are clearly of European origin. A good example of this is the provisions on decennial liability in Articles 651-654 of the present civil code. These provide that the architect or constructor of a building is absolutely liable for a period of ten years after construction for faults that appear in the construction. This liability was taken from the codes of the Mixed Courts and the National Courts (though extended and clarified) which in turn was taken from French law. Almost identical provisions are found in the draft Islamic code of civil transactions. Interestingly the liability is supported, as conforming to the Shari'a, by reference to the contract of *ijara* (hire) and equates decennial liability with the *daman* (civil liability) that an *ajir mushtarak* (independent contractor) under a contract of ijara is subject to in cases of defective work. Unfortunately, these slight references in the explanatory memorandum to Islamic legal concepts obscure more than they clarify. Daman is a form of tortious liability whereas decennial liability is considered an extended contractual liability and more worryingly, in classical Shari'a law before daman can operate one needs to show some illicit act (*ta'addi*) or negligence (*tafrit*) by the ajir mushtarak whereas decennial liability is a form of strict liability, thus, the references to Shari'a are clearly misplaced and would convince only the ignorant.

Even more interesting are the provisions concerning insurance.[16] There is an extensive commentary on insurance in the draft civil code which concludes by saying that the Islamic jurists (*fuqaha*) were divided in their views as to the validity of the contract of insurance. However, the commentary goes on to say that if insurance is organized as a system of cooperation (*nizam ta'awuni*) then it might be valid and it refers to opinions (fatawa) of Shaykh Muhamed 'Abduh that a contract of life insurance is permissible if it is in the form of a *mudaraba* contract. The insured person provides capital by way of premiums, the insurer provides the labour (he undertakes the administration and investment of the insurance funds) and the profit is divided between the two parties in agreed proportions. Thus, insurance is seen as a type of joint venture, a method of investing money, rather than as a way of merely providing compensation for the happening of uncertain events.[17] Needless to say the funds must be invested in accordance with Shari'a principles.

---

[16] Draft code of civil transactions 1982, articles 747-769.

[17] Such a contract would break the Shari'a cardinal principle of *gharar* (uncertainty).

The draft civil code also addressed the issue of the payment of interest on debt.[18] Interest on civil and commercial debts has been part of Egyptian law since the nineteenth century. The Mixed Civil Code of 1876 provided for the payment of up to a maximum of 12 per cent interest on civil and commercial debts. In 1882 this was amended by decree to 7 per cent in civil and 9 per cent in commercial matters, unless the parties agreed otherwise, subject to a ceiling of 12 per cent. These became the provisions of the National Courts Civil Code of 1883. One final change occurred in 1892 when the interest rates were altered to 5 per cent in civil matters, 7 per cent in commercial matters, unless otherwise agreed, subject to a ceiling of 9 per cent. The original provisions and each of these changes mirrored changes in French law.

When the 1949 civil code was promulgated it too provided for payment of interest on debts. The figures were again different and lower still (perhaps adverting to the legislators aversion to interest and the draftors desire to make the code as Shari'a orientated as possible): 4 per cent in civil matters, 5 per cent for commercial matters unless otherwise agreed, subject to a ceiling of 7 per cent.[19]

However the draft of the 1982 civil code is uncompromisingly clear. Any agreement for the payment of interest is void, and included within the term interest (*fa'idat*) is any commission for which no services have been rendered or any postponed benefit.[20] This has been one of the most controversial provisions and the commercial community have said many times that the approval and bringing into force of a law prohibiting interest would seriously affect the already precarious economy of Egypt.

Overall therefore the civil transactions code seeks to uphold the established principles of the present law, even to the extent of providing new, or blatantly modern, interpretations of Shari'a law (and even occasionally spurious ones). The code only rejects the most glaringly anti-Islamic provisions of the present

---

18 Like French law, Egyptian law distinguishes between interest for delay in payment and interest agreed by the parties. The former, although called interest, is a form of damages payable to the creditor for the prejudice suffered in being kept out of his money: e.g. Civil Code Articles 226-233. This interest ('moratoire') is calculated from the date the case is brought before the courts to demand repayment of the debt - which accords with French law pre-1900.

19 Articles 226 and 227 of Civil Code, 1949.

20 Draft code of civil transactions 1982, Articles 235-6. The provisions mirror articles in the Civil Code of Kuwait, 1980. The clause refers to interest generally and not just interest in delay in payment as referred to in Articles 226 and 227 of the present code.

laws. This is clearly an attempt to harmonize established Egyptian law with the Shari'a, to try and produce a code exhibiting the best of both systems and as such its underlying philosophy of reform mirrors that of al-Sanhuri in the 1930's and 40's.

(iv) Company Law (law 159 of 1981)

With the advent of the Foreign Investment laws of 1971 and 1974 and the desire to open Egypt to foreign investors (the so called economic infitah) it became obvious that the 1954 Company Law was outdated and outmoded for use in a modern capitalist-orientated economy, as many of its provisions related to a more state governed, monopolistic, and socialist economy. The government decided to produce a new company law and in an unprecedented move consulted and acted in collaboration with a host of foreign (generally non Arab) organizations and advisors. Intimately involved were USAID, the Ford Foundation and the French Centre of Legal Studies. A conference was held in Cairo in 1980 at which top level lawyers, professors and bureaucrats participated mainly from the USA, France and England. The result was the company law of 1981, a wholly secular law, based almost solely on French and US laws.

Overall, the Shari'a had no role to play at all in the company law which was wholly western in inspiration. A report by the Capital Market Authority for the conference does (rather tongue in cheek) say that one minor provision - that limited liability companies require a minimum of two members which may include a married couple, whereas in the old law the minimum was three if a married couple was included, counting them as a unity - was more in consonance with the Shari'a which treats the financial status of husband and wife as distinct!

(v) Islamic Banks

Islamic Banks do operate in Egypt but they are all are regulated by individual laws which set them up, accord them corporate status, and which lay down clearly their powers and (most importantly) their exemptions from the application of the general Banking Act provisions.[21]

[21] See Mayer 1985, 32-50 for the background; also *Business Monthly*, the journal of the American Chamber of Commerce in Egypt, February 1982. My thanks to Anahid Harrison for providing me with back copies of *Business Monthly*.

The largest Islamic Bank is the Faisal Islamic Bank (FIB) set up by law 47 of 1977. Under this statute the FIB enjoys a special status as a private Islamic Institution. It is exempt from many of the regulations governing labour and company law; it is guaranteed against nationalization and has tax and customs exemptions. It is Saudi controlled and in the first year of operation attracted over £LE 60 million in deposits.

Like most Islamic Banks it has two basic accounts for investors: a current account in which money earns no interest but is repayable on demand and an investment account in which the depositor/investor receives a return proportionate to the bank's profit (or loss) as a whole on its investments (the rudiments of the *mudaraba* joint venture contract which Islamic law accepts as valid and which is the basis for most Islamic banking operations).

It is an unusual phenomenon of the Middle East (Egypt particularly) and indicative of the wide social adherence of the population to Islamic precepts, that because the payment of interest is purportedly forbidden in the Qur'an,[22] current accounts on which the depositor receives no interest can be used and indeed elicit considerable funds.

Even though the Islamic Banks operate under special laws they are little controlled by the banking system as to where and what they actually invest their money. Considerable apprehension has recently arisen as to whether the actual investments of Islamic Banks conform to the Shari'a and are restricted to Islamic investments (i.e. those that the Shari'a would consider valid transactions). Many of the banks set aside money for soft or charitable loans to the poor. These are generally without interest, but may be with or without a charge for administration or insurance. Generally the banks are supposed to invest by means of joint ventures in projects in which they negotiate for a specified return of profits. It is widely believed, however, (as their accounts are not public no one can know for sure) that the banks also speculate in foreign exchange and commodities markets in the West, hold equity in Western companies and have deposits at interest in Western banks. Such investments are particularly attractive when a major form of deposit is the foreign currency of migrant workers outside Egypt. If such investment is rife then the banks must have suffered considerable losses in the October 1987 Stock market crash, though none have yet admitted to doing so. It would only be a matter of time before it affected the returns to investor depositors.

---

22 The precise meaning of riba, which is what the Qur'an actually prohibits (see sura 2, verse 275), is controversial, but the majority of modern jurists assume that the payment of interest is included.

Overall, there can only continue to be a question mark over how far in practice these Islamic Banks are truly Islamic.

(2) Law Enunciating Bodies (Courts and Judicial Decisions)

According to Article 1 of the Egyptian Civil Code 1949[23] a judge in any civil matter is to apply the provisions of any applicable law, and in their absence custom and in the absence of custom the principles of the Islamic Shari'a. Thus the Shari'a is relegated to a subsidiary role in the hierarchy of sources of civil law. It is an indication of the comprehensiveness of the civil code and the background of the judges that virtually no civil cases (other than personal status) are found before the 1970s in which the judges refer to the Shari'a.

With the new constitutional provision in 1971 that the Islamic law was a principal source of law, the position of the Shari'a was considerably bolstered and became more frequently referred to by lawyers pleading cases before the courts.

As early as 1948 the Maglis al-dawla (the Council of State), the highest administrative court, had accepted the argument that the Constitution was a superior law and that in the case of conflict with an ordinary law the Constitution must prevail.[24] Thence the administrative courts (and to a lesser extent the ordinary courts) developed the concept of lack of constitutionality (*'adam dusturiyya*) and assumed to themselves the ad hoc right to determine the constitutionality of laws. This power was eventually consolidated and given to a special court, the Mahkamat 'ulya (Supreme Court) in 1969. Very soon this court was inundated with pleas (based on Article 2 of the 1971 Constitution) to hold laws unconstitutional because they conflicted with the Shari'a.

In an important decision in 1976[25], the Mahkamat 'ulya ruled, in a case concerning imprisonment of a husband for failure to pay maintenance, that in accordance with Article 2 of the 1971 Constitution, the Shari'a was one of the criteria for testing the constitutionality of legislation, regardless of when it had been enacted, so that it applied to a consideration of the earlier personal status legislation of 1920 and 1929. The court went on, however, to uphold the relevant provision as conforming with the Shari'a.

---

23 For an English translation see Perrott et al. n d.

24 *Majmu'at maglis al-dawla: Ahkam al-qada' al-idari* 1950, 315-327.

25 *Majmu'at ahkam wa qararat al-Mahkamat al-'ulya* , 432-441.

The Mahkamat 'ulya was replaced in 1979 by the Mahkamat al-dusturiyya al-'ulya (the Supreme Consitutional Court)[26] which was a much more independent and non-political body than its predecessor. The 1980 amendment to the Constitution followed close on its formation and has produced a large number of cases before the court in which the constitutionality of legislation has been called into question. For example, cases on the punishments for theft and adultery in the criminal codes; the personal status laws; the law of murder; the law of succession - particularly the provisions on obligatory bequest and finally in another important decision, the payment of interest in accordance with the 1949 civil code.

The case on interest was *Rector of Al Azhar v. Fouad Goudah et al* [27] and was decided by the S.C.C. in May 1985. Fouad Goudah had claimed before an administrative court for the payment of £LE 292 (being the balance outstanding on a contract for the supply of certain medical instruments to the faculty of medicine of the university of al-Azhar) together with interest on the debt at 4 per cent from the date of the action, in accordance with Article 226 of the civil code of 1949.

The Rector of Al-Azhar raised the question of the constitutionality of Article 226 and the matter was transferred at the Rector's request from the administrative court to the S.C.C. The S.C.C. rejected the Rector's claim, without having to consider whether or not the payment of interest was prohibited by the Shari'a, on the procedural ground that Article 2 did not apply retrospectively but only prospectively. The court supported this view by referring to the Report of the People's Assembly on the amendment, to the non-specific nature of the consequences to attend the Article 2 amendment and also to the commercial confusion and instability that would result from any other decision.

Although the S.C.C. did not expressly refer to the earlier 1976 decision of the Mahkamat 'ulya, insofar as it contradicts the later decision it must presumably be considered as now over-ruled. The decision of the Mahkamat 'ulya (a partial

---

[26] Hereinafter referred to as the S.C.C.

[27] Al-Mahkamat al-dusturiyya al-'ulya 1984-1986, 209-224; also in *al-Garida al-rasmiyya* 1985, 999; for an English translation see Arab Law Quarterly 1985,100-107 and see the commentary by the eminent Egyptian lawyer Dr Saba Habachy K.B.E., at ALQ 1985, 239-241. I am indebted to counsellor Dr Awad al-Morr (judge of the S.C.C.) for his help and patience in aiding my understanding of the S.C.C. and to the president of the court, Dr Mamduh Mustafa Hasan, for his help and courteous interest and in providing me with copies of the decisions of the S.C.C. and its predecessor.

body whose members were presidential appointments having limited tenure of office) was not referred to by the S.C.C. at all - perhaps because the S.C.C. is considered a new court and not a mere continuation or rearrangement of the Mahkamat 'ulya. In any event, the S.C.C. is not bound by precedent and only occasionally refers to its own or any other judgments of other courts.

The S.C.C. said further that Article 2 placed the onus of harmonizing past and future legislation with the Shari'a squarely on the legislator - that it prescribed guidelines for the People's Assembly and not the judiciary.[28] In fact in no case since 1980 has the S.C.C. used Article 2 to declare any legislation unconstitutional as being contrary to the Shari'a.

The decision of the S.C.C. was greeted with relief by commercial lawyers and businessmen. It is not entirely clear, however, how far it extends. On the facts it only applies to judicial interest on civil debts (set by the civil code at 4 per cent). It does not refer to judicial interest on commercial debts (set by the civil code at 5 per cent) nor to bank interest or credit transactions which fall outside the civil code and are (and have been) governed by special legislation. Most lawyers consider that the judgment clearly covers judicial interest on commercial interest by simple analogy, but whether or not bank interest and credit facilities are included is controversial. The main legislation governing bank interest is law 20 of 1975 (as amended) which predates the 1980 amendment but postdates the original provision in the 1971 Constitution.

A case is, however, pending before the S.C.C. on the constitutionality of a provision of law 120 of 1975 concerning interest.[29] It concerns a bank loan in Egyptian pounds at variable interest secured on land (i.e. a mortgage). Section 7(d) of law 120 of 1975 allows a bank to vary the amount of interest charged on a loan in certain circumstances. As a result of an early repayment of part of the loan by the debtors the bank increased the interest on the outstanding loan. The debtors challenged the validity of this increase *inter alia* on the ground that the provisions of law 120 of 1975 giving the bank power to charge (and increase)

---

28 I was informed in 1981 by the then Attorney General that the then President of the Mahkamat al-naqd (civil supreme court) had issued a circular to all the judges to the same effect soon after the promulgation of the amendment to the Constitution in 1980 and in an attempt to stop lower judges exercising their own discretion to apply the Shari'a using the amendment. The newspapers at the time reported a number of cases of first instance judges attempting to apply Shari'a punishments for theft and apostasy in reliance on the 1980 amendment to Article 2. All such attempts were quashed on appeal.

29 I am indebted to Dr al-Morr for details of this case and for a copy of the claimants submissions to the court.

interest rates on loans were unconstitutional as being contrary to Article 2 of the Constitution.

In the 1985 S.C.C. case the court seemed to indicate in an obiter dictum that, while it was not relevant to the determination of the case at hand, they accepted the argument that the payment of any interest is contrary to the Shari'a. In the pending case the report of the *mufawidin* (the government delegates or functionaries attached to the court who prepare a report for the court and attempt to present the government's view of the case) was in favour of holding the provision of law 120 of 1975 unconstitutional for this reason.[30] The court is not bound by the report of the mufawidin, but it is of course the starting point for discussion. At present the court is deliberating and debating as to what it can and should do and a decision is not expected for many months. The procedural evasion used in the 1985 case cannot be used on the facts of this case, so subject to any other procedural sidestepping of the issue the court will have to rule on the substantive application of Article 2 to a subsequently promulgated law. It remains to be seen whether the SCC will grasp the nettle of trying to reconcile bank interest on loans with the Shari'a prohibition of riba, as some would argue is possible.

The final decision is eagerly awaited and is certain to be very controversial whatever it decides.

(3) Development in the Economy and New Financial Legal Structures

In this section I want to look at some commercial trends in Egypt including the development of the Stock Exchange and some problems of investment and credit.

30 The report was compiled by a member of the mufawidin who has since been appointed to the court and who is thus prevented from sitting on the court to ensure there is no conflict of interest.

(a) The Stock Exchange[31]

After the nationalizations of 1958-1961 the stock market in Egypt became almost defunct. Investor confidence sank and is still affected even though in the last five years the volume of listings has increased enormously as a result of company law 159 of 1981 which requires that all new joint stock companies list their shares within one year of their public offering or, if there is no public offering, within three months of publishing the accounts for the third year.

As of February 1988, 430 companies were listed in the Cairo Exchange. Last year the volume of trade was £LE 270 million (= £70 million) a drop in the ocean compared with the volume in trade in London or New York, but not insubstantial in Egypt.

Trading activity on the two exchanges (Cairo and Alexandria) is limited to government bonds or shares in public sector controlled or mixed joint stock companies. The government bonds are few, mainly housing or development bonds. There are no other debt securities, such as company debentures or company loan stock: debt financing is arranged through the banking system. The reason for this is clear. Under the civil code the maximum interest on any debt security is 7 per cent and hence there is little enthusiasm amongst lenders for such debt financing when bank deposits provide interest of 15 per cent or more according to the type of bank and currency. There is at present a bill before the People's Assembly to amend this provision of the civil code as regards corporate debt.[32]

Another possible extension of the Exchange activities would be the development of a futures market, but although the civil code accepts the validity of a contract involving future obligations,[33] it is uncertain whether this would include futures contracts where there is no intention to make a final delivery, as this is clearly against Shari'a principles of certainty in contracts (gharar) and gambling (*maysir*). The government delegate to the Stock Exchange, when asked about this, said that it was against the mentality of Egyptians to develop such a market.

---

31 I am indebted to Dr Mahmud Fahmy, former Chairman of the Capital Market Authority for arranging access for me to the Stock Exchange and also to Mr Gasser Fahmy (the government delegate to the Exchange) and the stockbrokers (particularly Mr Nasir Nasmy) for their help and interest.

32 I am indebted to Mr Gasser Fahmy for this information.

33 See article 131 of the civil code, 1949.

The Stock Exchange is however considering the introduction of a share index. At the moment they are studying movements of shares to decide what shares to include in the index, which will probably be quoted in Egyptian pounds (for shares quoted in pounds) and in dollars (for shares quoted in dollars).

(b) Islamic Investment Companies[34]

It is clear that ordinary Egyptians do not invest in the Stock Exchange because of the ease with which they can get better (and more comprehensible) returns on investments from other sources. At the moment the commercial banks offer around 14 per cent to 15 per cent interest on long term certificates of deposit and the Islamic banks offer up to 20 per cent. However, the biggest returns in Egypt at the moment are those given by the so called Islamic Investment Companies which in some cases tops 30 per cent.

These organizations are legally set up as individual partnerships or sole traders. They advertise and make much of the fact that they act according to Islamic principles. Investors deposit money with them, which they supposedly invest in ways that conform to the Shari'a. Any resulting profits (or losses) are shared between the 'company' and the investors. So far they have been able to distribute profits that represent well over the commercial banks interest rates and hence have had an enormous, even spectacular, growth over the last five years. The biggest of them, al-Rayyan, is thought to have over 150,000 depositors and funds of over £LE 2 billion. The second largest, al-Sharif, is thought to have over 125,000 depositors and funds of at least £LE 1 billion. Altogether it is speculated that there are about 2-3,000 of these 'companies' with 2-3 million depositors and deposits of almost £LE 5 billion.

Like the Holy Roman Empire, however, they are neither Islamic nor investing nor companies. They are set up as partnerships (not companies) and hence escape the provision of the companies law 1981. As a result they do not need to publish accounts or indicate what funds are held and in what investments they are channelled. Hence, it is impossible to know whether the deposits are invested according to the Shari'a or to decide how the 'profits' are distributed or interest is calculated. They act as deposit takers, but are not governed by the banking laws. In essence, they are accountable to no one and the main worry about their spectacular growth and returns is that they are practically unregulated by law. There is intense speculation as to how such returns are funded and many critics are of the opinion that their activities must include investment in

---

[34] *Sharikat Tawzif al-Amwal*, literally 'companies for the investment of funds'. See article by Dr Mahmud Fahmy in *al-Ahram al-Iqtisadi* 1987, 16-18 and the *Financial Times*, 6/1/1988.

Western shares, commodities and futures (hardly Islamic), while some go so far as to allege that they are also involved in such illegal activities as drug trafficking, illegal foreign exchange dealing or payment out of principal.[35]

When al-Rayyan suffered a run on its deposits in 1986 due to alleged losses on the gold market, it was widely assumed that it was helped by the other Investment Companies, anxious about the effect on public opinion of the weakening or collapse of one of their number.

The size and spectacular growth of these 'companies' is another clear indication of the pull of commerce and financing that purports to be Islamic and it has given the heads of these 'companies' immense power, including the power to make or break currency reform. A previous Minister of the Economy resigned after one Investment Company threatened to withdraw millions of dollars deposited with the National Bank of Egypt, which the Bank could not meet, in response to suggested currency reform.

Recently, however, the government has taken the offensive and called for regulation of these investment companies and they themselves have attempted to improve their official image, by being seen to act responsibly. They have set up many subsidiaries as companies, subject to the 1981 legislation, to organize their various commercial investments. Al-Rayyan has, for example, set up a food company, a jewellery company, a restaurant company, a finance company, and many other such ventures, including a property company offering cheap flats and mortgages. Al-Sharif's plastics company operates profit-sharing schemes with its workers and is generally considered a model employer. In this way the investment companies are attempting to improve their public image, while still being loathe to disclose the financial basis and stability of the central holding partnership.

Nevertheless, the government has decided that the companies act legislation should apply to them and a bill to that effect is at present before the People's Assembly. Depositors will have their deposits converted to equity and the investment companies themselves will have to issue shares to the public. The

35 There is no evidence to support any of these allegations. Egypt has admittedly had its fair share of corruption trials recently where allegations such as these have been made (and sometimes upheld) against reputable companies and banks. A special court, the Mahkamat al-Qiyam (Court of Values) was set up to hear such cases in 1980. It has heard a number of important corruption cases since its formation, especially those of Othman Ahmed Othman (reputedly Egypt's richest individual and one time Minister of Construction) and Sadat's brother, Esmat Sadat.

new companies will then be obliged to reveal their financial state by publishing their accounts; they will also be required to deposit money with the Central Bank and pay taxes. Money and investments held abroad will have to be declared and may have to be liquidated and repatriated.

Islamic Investment Houses are not and never were truly 'Islamic'. It is tragic that when (for their demise is inevitable) they fall they will besmirch the idea of 'Islamic' Investment in the minds of many upon which they have deceitfully and wrongfully puffed. The present government would do well to consider whether or not to restrict the use of the words 'Islam' or 'Islamic' in the names of companies and in advertisements: possibly to register the use of such words and subject their use to the scrutiny of a council of 'ulama who would test the veracity of the subjects claim to follow the tenets of Islam.

It remains to be seen whether the phenomenon of the Islamic Investment Company will survive the public scrutiny to which it is about to be subjected, particularly if the result is a substantial reduction on its returns on deposits.[36]

36 The beginning of the end may have come sooner than expected, because in May 1988 the major Islamic Investment Companies declared a moratorium on transactions and new business : See *Financial Times* 23/5/88, 4/6/88, 6/6/88, and 8/6/88.

Conclusion

In this article I have tried to investigate and assess the role that Islamic law plays in contemporary Egypt. I have shown that Islamic law as such has been reduced to a very minor role in the Egyptian legal system, but that Egypt remains a society in which Islam continues to exercise an important hold on the minds and actions of the population. Thus it is forward looking and yet traditional and conservative.

Egyptian legislation is predominantly Western in inspiration, although the civil code is a truly Egyptian code which attempts a synthesis of Western and Islamic principles into a law suitable to the needs of Egypt. Al-Sanhuri, in drafting the civil code and also in establishing the maglis al-dawla (the Council of State), was producing modern laws and modern legal institutions for a modern state. Yet, Islamic law had its role to play and was not forgotten. The judiciary however that applied the laws was in the main brought up and imbued with the European civil law tradition and inevitably their interpretative approach has been more secular than Islamic.

The contemporary reaction against foreign and secular influence is seen in the increased calls for the implementation of 'pure' Islam and Islamic law. Very little time however is given over to expounding exactly what this involves, particularly in the field of commerce. Islamic commercial law proceeded generally from wide prohibitions against certain types of speculative activity. Necessity and customary usage, therefore, were used to validate many contracts and instruments of commerce, that strictly should have been held invalid. Now more than at any time is there a need for a set of Islamic Commercial or Investment principles which would produce order out of this chaos and which would lay down rules concerning all manner of modern contracts and instruments of commerce that the medieval jurists knew nothing of. Only by such detailed research will commercial men be won over to an Islamic approach, which has very valid ideas to offer to the modern business community.

Vague and open-ended calls for implementation of the Shari'a are not conducive of anything. Article 2 of the Constitution may have been seen as a battering ram against an edifice of secular legislation, but the existing system has blunted its force and effectively neutralized its impact.

So what of the future?

The trends are obvious and disturbing. The Egyptian population is growing at a rate of 1 million people every 10 months. The Egyptian economy, based almost entirely on tourism, oil and foreign workers remittances, is in the doldrums.

Egypt is not self sufficient in food and imports vast amounts of wheat. The government is going to find it increasingly difficult to support its burgeoning population which will turn to whoever offers help. Already some of the fundamentalist groups operate some of the best clinics and health care centres in parts of Cairo.

Within the legal system there are already signs of breakdown and of a new order. Law student numbers have vastly increased (Cairo University accepts 2-3000 a year!) with a consequent decline in standards. Little or no work is now done on comparative law nor on European civil law. Judges of the Council of State used regularly to spend a year or more in France in their French counterpart. This no longer operates, beyond a cursory visit funded by the French authorities. Cases have multiplied and delays are legion. Good lawyers are few as the profession of lawyer is not highly regarded (though paradoxically a judge has a high status). The result is that the new generation of lawyers (soon to be judges) is less concerned to adhere to the principles of the civil law and Egypt's civil law past. The next generation of judges may be radically different and they will be in position just as the system seems most likely to receive the most potent calls for change. Thus the future is uncertain but looks like being exciting and challenging.

At present the Shari'a remains little more than a slogan in modern Egypt. It remains to be seen whether the Ikhwan's election slogan 'Islam is the solution' can be converted into legal and commercial concepts adequate and acceptable in a modern state.

* * * * *

References

Arab Law Quarterly 1985, vol.1, part 1, pp 100-107.

Altman 1979, 'Islamic legislation in Egypt in the 1970s', *Asian and African Studies*, vol.13, pp 199-219.

Brinton J.Y. 1968, *Mixed Courts of Egypt,* Yale University Press.

Business Monthly , Cairo.

Escovitz 1984, *The Office of the Qadi al Qudat under the Bahri Mamluks,* FVG, Stuttgart.

Fahmy Mahmud 1987, in *al-Ahram al-Iqtisadi,* no. 941, 25/1/1987, pp 16-18.

Financial Times, London.

al-Garida al-rasmiyya (Official Gazette) 1985, 16/5/1985.

Habachy Saba 1985, 'Commentary', *Arab Law Quarterly,* vol.1, part 2, pp 239-241.

Hill Enid 1987, *Al-Sanhuri and Islamic Law,* Cairo Papers in Social Science vol.10, Monograph 1.

Kerr Malcolm 1966, *Islamic Reform: the political and legal theories of Muhammad 'Abduh and Rashid Rida,* Berkeley.

Madbatat maglis ash-sha'b (Proceedings of the People's Assembly) 1982, 70th Session, 1 July 1982, pp 32-41.

Madbatat maglis ash-sha'b (Proceedings of the People's' Assembly) 1985, 74th session 4 May 1985, pp 14-35.

al-Mahkamat al-dusturiyya al-'ulya (the Supreme Constitutional Court [decisions]) 1984-1986, vol.3 , Session 4/5/1985, pp 209-224.

Majmu'at ahkam wa qararat al-Mahkamat al-'ulya (Collection of the decisions and opinions of the Supreme Court) 1978, vol.1, part 1, pp 432-441.

Majmu'at maglis al-dawla: Ahkam al qada' al idari (Collection of the Council of State decisions of the administrative courts) 1950, Session of 10/2/1948, Year 2, pp 315-327.

Mayer Ann 1985 'Islamic Banking and Credit Policies in the Sadat Era: the social origins of Islamic Banking in Egypt', *Arab Law Quarterly* vol.1, part 1, pp 32-50.

Mitchell Richard 1969, *The Society of the Muslim Brothers,* Oxford University Press.

Perrott et al. tr. n d (circa 1949), *The Egyptian Civil Code,* Cairo.

Tucker J. 1985, *Women in Nineteenth Century Egypt* , American University of Cairo.

Vatikiotis P.J. 1980, *The History of Egypt from Muhamed Ali to Sadat,* 2nd edition, London.

Zaghlul Ahmad Fathi 1900, *al-Muhamat* , Cairo.

Ziadeh Farhat 1968, *Lawyers, the Rule of Law and Liberalism in Modern Egypt*, Hoover Institute, Stanford.

* * * * *

TOWARDS A SYSTEM OF ISLAMIC FINANCE IN MALAYSIA

Jane Connors
Law Department, SOAS

Introduction

Malaysia, which achieved independence from Britain in 1957, is a multi-racial, religiously plural society. It is comprised of three main racial groups - the Malays, the Chinese and the sub-continental Indians - while the balance of the population of approximately sixteen million is made up of various aboriginal groups, such as the Kelabit, Iban and Kadazan of East Malaysia and others, including Europeans.

To some extent, the principles of Islamic law entered Malaysia in the fifteenth century, when codes such as the *Undang Undang Melaka* reduced some aspects of Islamic law, such as the law relating to marriage, sale and legal procedure to writing.[1] Certainly, when the British colonised the territory, all treaties and agreements entered into between them and the Malay rulers required the colonisers to refrain from intervening in matters of Malay custom and Islamic law (Tun Haji 1986, 6-7). In practice, however, the colonisers did interfere with the administration of Islamic law in the territory. This resulted in the curtailment of the jurisdiction of the *Shari'a* court, which became subordinated to the jurisdiction of the civil courts.

After independence and the passage of the Federal Constitution in 1957, the Shari'a court became entrenched in the Malaysian system. Article 3 of the Constitution states that Islam is the religion of the Federation although 'other religions may be practised in peace and harmony in any part of the Federation.' Malaysia is not, however, an Islamic state, but a secular society, where the jurisdiction of the Shari'a courts and the area generally covered by Islamic law are confined to that relating to personal and family law. The jurisdiction of the Shari'a courts is limited by Article 121 of the Federal Constitution which provides that the judicial power of the Federation shall be vested in the High Courts of the State of Malaysia and Borneo and in such

[1]These texts were hybrid, varied in origin and often diffuse in purpose. See Sandu and Wheatley 1983, 191.

inferior courts as may be provided by Federal law (Ismail 1985). Power is given to the States to make laws relating to the constitution, organisation and procedure of the Shari'a courts which have jurisdiction only over Muslims and the limited legislative subjects allotted to the State in the Constitution.[2]

Notwithstanding the fact that Malaysia is thus a secular state and the power to make law which is particularly Islamic in character appears to be circumscribed, an increasing deference to Islam has become manifest in the country. At the outset, these manifestations were confined to the State level where the Islamic law governed the personal lives of Muslims. At the Federal level, such manifestations have been slower and more delicate both because of the nature of the Federal legislative powers and because the Federal legislature has found itself compelled to a greater extent than the States to pay regard to non-Muslim interests. Recently, however, two pieces of legistation have indicated that this deference to Islam is now being paid even at the Federal level. Both pieces of legislation, the *Islamic Banking Act,* 1983, and the *Takaful Act,* 1984, attempt to introduce principles of Islamic finance into the Federation. This attempt may be problematic given that there is only a bare majority - if that - of Muslims in Malaysia[3] and given that the corporate sector is largely in the hands of non-Muslims. Further, neither Act seeks to replace the current banking and insurance systems, thus the success of the ventures will depend on how successfully the Islamic institutions can compete with traditional structures. Both pieces of legislation have been in operation for a short time only, there have been no disputes concerning their operation and certainly no litigation with respect of either.

I. Islamic Banking Act, 1983

The passage of the *Islamic Banking Act* was preceded by eleven months of research by a government-sponsored committee -headed by the Prime Minister's special economic adviser, Raja Mohar Badiozaman-, which studied the operation of the Faisal Islamic Bank in Egypt and the Sudan.[4] Its report,

---

[2] The Federal Constitution, Para. 1, State List, 9th Schedule allots family law, *waqfs* and other religious trusts, *zakat* and Islamic religious revenue, the organisation and conduct of mosques and the Shari'a court and offences by Muslims against the tenets of their religion as within State power.
[3] All Malays are Muslim, Article 160 of the Federal Constitution defining a Malay as 'a person who professes the religion of Islam, habitually speaks the Malay language and conforms to Malay custom.'
[4] Much of the information for this part comes from Segal 1982.

which was presented to the Prime Minister, Datuk Sri Mahathir Mohamed, outlined the Islamic law relating to banking and economics, concluding that *riba* was forbidden, but that the principle of sharing of profits and losses was acceptable. It saw this as promotable in four ways. First, by *mudaraba*, where one party provides 100 per cent of the capital for a particular project, takes no management role, but splits the profits with the entrepreneur according to a pre-arranged ratio. Second, by *murabaha*, where goods are sold at a price which covers the cost of purchase and an agreed profit margin. Third, *musharaka*, which involves full profit sharing and a decision-making partnership between a financier and an entrepreneur and finally, *wadi'a*, which allows the owner of an asset to deposit it with another, who is then able to make use of it with the other's agreement.

On a practical level, the report suggested that customers' current and deposit accounts should bear neither interest nor a share of the profits. The bank could, however, provide 'gifts' to savers as a token of appreciation for keeping money in the bank, but there would be no contractual obligation on the bank to provide such a gift. Money making deposits would take two forms, both based on *mudaraba*. General investment deposits of over 500 ringgit would earn a share or profits from a general pool of investments for a fixed period of three months or more, while special investment accounts would earn income from specific projects or sectors stipulated by the customer.

With respect to investments by the bank itself, short-term investments would create a specific problem for it, as the prohibition against riba would prevent it from buying treasury bills and short-term government securities, which are both interest-bearing. Hence, a new *Investment Act* [5] allowing the Government to issue short-dated investment certificates which would pay dividends, rather than interest, was advocated. The medium- and long-term investments of the bank were to fall into four main categories. First, finance fixed capital requirements, such as land, buildings, plant and machinery, where the bank could usually be the sole provider of funds or a business partner. Second, cash for equipment on the principles of murabaha, in other words, as a loan transformed into a sale and purchase or on leasing - *bai' mu'ajjal* - deferred sales. Third, finance of a company's inventory, where the bank would carry the risk unto the point of sale, where the profits would be split and, finally, bridging and end-finance for property, where the bank would buy premises and resell them to purchasers on instalments with a negotiated profit margin. This latter could be achieved also by the substitution of an assumed rental value for profits.

[5] This became the *Investment Act*, 1983.

Following the Report, the Act providing for the establishment of Islamic banks was passed, coming into effect on March 11, 1983. The Act itself is modelled on the conventional Malaysian *Banking Act,* 1973, but contains suitable modifications so that Islamic banks can conform to Islamic banking principles. Thus, section 2 defines 'Islamic banking business' as 'banking whose aims and operations do not involve any element which is not approved by the Religion of Islam'.

A licence will be issued to a company to transact such business by the Minister after the company applies for such a licence through the Central Bank, which will consider the application and make appropriate recommendations to the Minister.[6] The Central Bank is not empowered to make a positive recommendation unless it or the Minister is satisfied that the aims and operations of the banking business which the company desire to carry on will not involve any element which is not approved by the Religion of Islam.[7] Moreover, section 3(5)(b) provides, unusually, that a licence will not be granted unless the articles of association of the proposed bank provide for the establishment of a Shari'a advisory body to advise the bank on the operations of its banking business contrary to the precepts of Islam. The Minister has power to vary or revoke any condition of a licence or impose conditions or additional conditions, this power being exercisable on the recommendation of the Central Bank and after giving an opportunity to the Islamic bank to submit reasons against the proposed action.[8] The Islamic bank must pay the Central Bank an annual licence fee such as prescribed [9] and the Minister is given power to revoke the banking licence of the Islamic bank on the recommendation of the Central Bank. The circumstances where such revocation may take place are laid down in section 11(1) and include 'pursuing aims, or carrying on operations, involving any element which is not approved by the Religion of Islam.'[10] Before such action is taken, the Islamic bank must be given an opportunity to submit reasons against the revocation of the licence.[11] An appeal lies against such a revocation to the High Court[12] and the Central bank is entitled to be heard on such appeal.[13]

All other provisions within the Act are similar to those which may be found in conventional banking legislation. Thus, Part III sets out the requirements for

---

[6] Section 3.
[7] Section 3(5).
[8] Section 4(2).
[9] Section 9.
[10] Section 11(1)(a).
[11] Section 11(2).
[12] Section 11(5).
[13] Section 11(4).

the maintenance of capital reserves, the annual appointment of an auditor, the preparation of audited balance sheets and statements of assets and liabilities. Part IV and V set out guidelines for the ownership, control, management and restriction on the business of Islamic banks, while Part VI places Islamic banks under the supervision and control of the Central Bank. Thus any Islamic bank, like any other Malaysian bank[14] is under the control of the Central Bank and has a duty, if it considers that it is likely to become unable to meet its obligations or is about to suspend payment, to inform the Central Bank, which upon investigation, may, among other things, assume control of, and carry on, the business of the bank or appoint some other person to assume control of, and carry on, the business of the bank.[15] The Act, like the *Banking Act*, 1973, also includes a provision to ensure banking secrecy.[16]

There has been only one bank licenced under the Act. This bank has a structure similar to any commercial bank, with a board of directors heading departments which deal with investments, funding and administration. Unlike conventional banks, this board is paralleled by a religious supervisory council which consists of between three and seven Islamic scholars, whose role is to ensure that the banks activities comply with Islamic law. The equity structure of the bank is unusual, 30 per cent of its paid up capital of one million ringgit being taken by the Federal Government, 10 per cent by the Pilgrims' Fund Management Board (LUTH), 5 per cent by Perkim, the Muslim Welfare Association, 25 per cent by religious departments of the States, while the remaining 30 per cent is split equally between government agencies such as the Federal Land Development Authority and other qualified bodies such as Permodalan Nasional - the national equity corporation - and other state level religious organisation.

II. Takaful Act, 1984

The *Takaful Act*, which aims to provide an acceptable scheme of insurance for Muslims was, like the *Islamic Banking Act*, preceded by close study of schemes which exist in other parts of the world, such as the Sudan, Saudi-Arabia, Pakistan and Switzerland (Penubuhan Syarikat Takaful 1984). The report of this study indicated that present day conventional insurance schemes were barred to Muslims because of three factors which characterised them.[17] The

14 *Banking Act*, 1973.

15 *Islamic Banking Act*, 1983, Sections 36 and 37.

16 Section 34.

17 Much of what follows is derived from Fadzli Yusuf 1986. Mr. Fadzli is one of the employees of the Takaful company.

first, *gharar*, which exists because of uncertain or unknown factors which characterise both life and general insurance. In both, the insured or policy holder agrees to pay a certain premium, while the insurance company guarantees to pay compensation on the occurrence of a certain event. The insured or policy holder is not informed how the amount of compensation that the company will pay him is to be derived. Second, *maisir* or gambling, which arises as a consequence of the presence of gharar. This is particularly so with life insurance, because when a life policy holder dies before the end of the period of his insurance policy after paying only part of the premium, his dependents will receive a certain sum of money, the derivation of which is not clear to the policy holder at the beginning of the contract. The final aspect of an insurance contract which is repugnant to Islam is riba, the practice of interest and other related practices, which are part of the investment activities of conventional insurance companies.

The report suggested that *takaful* - or joint guarantee - should be the basis of Islamic insurance. In practice, this means that members of a group would agree jointly that if any of them were to suffer loss he would receive a certain sum of money to cover such loss. In other words, a takaful scheme amounts to a mutual agreement to provide help of and when it is needed.[18] The scheme is based on mudaraba - the sharing of profit and loss in business. In practical terms, the entrepreneur, the takaful operator, accepts payment of the takaful contributions from the investors or providers of capital - the takaful participants. To avoid any element of gharar or uncertainty, the contract stipulates how the profit or surplus from the operations of the takaful as managed by the operator is to be shared, which is, of course, in accordance with mudaraba. Moreover, the contract states how the takaful instalments paid by the participants are to be employed by the operator. In sum, therefore, the takaful contract states clearly the rights and obligations of both participants and the takaful operator.

The takaful contract also involves the concept of *tabarru'* - to donate, to contribute. Hence, participants agree to relinquish as donations made in accordance with the concept of tabarru' certain proportions of their takaful instalments or contributions in order to fulfil their obligations of mutual help embodied in the concept of takaful. As stipulated in the contract, the purpose of tabarru' is to enable participants to assist and help fellow participants who might suffer loss or damage. Any sharing or profit or surplus mudaraba is made only after the obligations of assisting fellow participants have been fulfilled.

---

[18] The scheme as presented bears a similarity to Ship Owners' Mutual Protection and Indemnity Associations.

Essentially, therefore, the report advocated the establishment of a takaful scheme, or a form of business which aims to embody the virtues of co-operation, mutual help and shared responsibility among the participants. It suggested a financial plan which accumulated profits and whose participants would agree to donate or relinquish their capital or part thereof and the investment profits gained therefrom as tabarru' for the purpose of sharing any loss or damage suffered by any of them.

Accordingly, the *Takaful Act* which seeks to provide for the licensing and regulation of takaful business was passed and gazetted in 1984. The Act, which is modelled on the *Malaysian Insurance Act*, 1983 is divided into four parts. Part I provides for preliminary matters and interpretation, the classification of takaful business and the construction of references to matters pertaining to takaful. It defined takaful as a scheme based on brotherhood, solidarity and mutual assistance which provides for mutual financial aid and assistance to its participants in the case of need, whereby the participants mutually agree to contribute for that purpose. It goes on to provide that a takaful business is the business of takaful whose aims and operations do not involve any element which is not approved by the Shari'a. Finally, it divides takaful business into family solidarity business and general business, a division which corresponds to life and general insurance in conventional schemes.

Part II provides for the conduct of takaful business, setting out the requirements for carrying out such business, the conditions for registration, the imposition of an annual registration fee and restriction on takaful operators.

The Part includes section 8, which is the central provision in terms of Islamic law. This provides that the Director-General of Takaful shall be responsible for the registraion of takaful operators. Application for registration must be made by a company and before such registration will be allowed, the Director-General must be satisfied, among other things, that the aims and operations of the takaful business which the company desired to carry out in no way involve an element which is not approved by the Shari'a. Further, the Articles of Association of the operator must provide for the establishment of a Shari'a supervisory council, the purpose of which is to advise the operator on the operations of its takaful business in order to ensure that is does not involve itself in any element which is not approved by the Shari'a. If a registered operator does pursue any aim or carries on operations involving any element which is not approved by the Shari'a, the Director-General may cancel the registration of such an operator.[19]

---

[19] Section 11 (1)(a).

The Part goes on to deal with the establishment and allocation of funds and the allocation of any surplus. It outlines the requirements of the assets of takaful funds, the payment of dividends, the grants of advances, loan credit facility and financial facility. There is a provision for the establishment and maintenance of a takaful guarantee fund and the payment of money out of the fund.

The Act makes clear that a takaful operator is required to maintain a deposit, the amount of which will be prescribed by the Minister, with the Accountant General of Malaysia. This deposit may be invested with the approval of the Director-General of Takaful in any manner which is not contrary to the Shari'a.[20] This requirement will be held to be fulfilled if any bank licensed under the *Islamic Banking Act*, 1983 covenants with the Government to deposit with the Accountant General a specified sum in cash on account of the operator's deposit.[21]

Part II goes on to provide for *retakaful*, the conduct of takaful business and assumption of risks by takaful operators.

Part III of the Act provides for investigations to be carried out by the Director-General of Takaful, returns and the winding up and transfer of business. It sets up a requirement of annual accounting and reports and the right of the Director-General to issue directions and investigate the affairs of a takaful operator. It outlines the powers of the Director-General of Takaful, the duties and responsibilities of takaful operators and the malpractices, such as misleading statements, that may be associated with the running of such a business. Further, it sets out the capacity of an infant to enter into a contract of takaful and the effect of other contractual disabilities.

Finally, Part IV of the Act deals with administration and enforcement matters in general. Provisions exist with regard to indemnity, annual reports, offences under the Act and the prosecution of such offences.

Following the passage of this legislation, the *Sharikat Takaful Malaysia Sindirian Berhad*, which operates as a composite company managing both the family takaful business and the general takaful business was incorporated on November 29, 1984 as a private limited company under the *Companies Act*. The memorandum of association of the company is prefaced with a statement that 'all businesses of the company will be transacted in accordance with Islamic principles, rules and practices'. Furthermore, in accordance with section 8 of the Act, the memorandum provides for a Shari'a supervisory council with has a minimum of three and a maximum of seven members. The

---

[20] Section 13.
[21] Section 14.

authorised capital of the company is 100 million ringgit, divided into 100 million ordinary shares of one ringgit each, the present paid up capital of ten million ringgit being held equally between the Islamic Bank and State religious councils and agencies.

Conclusion

At present, steps towards Islamic finance in Malaysia have not progressed beyond the passage of the above legislation and the introduction of the Islamic Bank and Takaful company. It has been suggested however, that Islamic pawnshops which would function without the imposition of interest will be introduced shortly. Both pieces of legislation described and the institutions that have been set up under them are very new. Further, the legislation is regulatory and does not provide any statement of the substantive law to be applied in cases of dispute. This may prove to be problematic as any litigation concerning both Acts will be before the civil, rather that the Shari'a, courts, which are staffed by Western educated judges.

Both institutions pose a number of practical problems. The major problem presented by the Bank - a problem which had been foreseen by its Director Dr. Abdul Halim Ismail (who is also the Director-General of Takaful) - is that its clientele is uncertain (Segal 1982).

The Muslim owned corporate sector in Malaysia is weak, a factor which makes it difficult for the Bank to achieve the standard deposit breakdown of most commercial banks, while individual Muslim investors have the option of placing their money with the Pilgrims' Fund or the national unit trust scheme. However, only one Islamic bank has been licensed for the country and it appears, following recommendations to the Prime Minister, it will be the only bank so licensed until at least 1993. At present the Bank has over 116,000 accounts, mainly derived from lower and middle income groups although it is understood that the Bank has promises of joint ventures from foreign investors (Ibid.). The other problem which faces the Bank is that close vetting of any investment initiatives suggested to it is crucial, because within the terms of mudaraba the Bank must bear any investment losses alone.

Insofar as the Takaful company is concerned, perhaps the most obvious flaw in the legislation is that it sets up a Shari'a supervisory council to advise the company on its operations, but there is no such council to advise the Director-General of Takaful himself.

The moves to introduce Islamic financial institutions in Malaysia will prove interesting to observe, particularly in view of the large numbers of non-Muslims who are natives of Malaysia and because of the fact that the financial power in the country is largely in the hands of non-Muslims. Further, tension between secular elements and Islamic principles is evident in the legislative framework of the country, as such statutes as the *Social and Welfare Services Lottery Board*, the *Racing (Totalisator) Board*, 1961 and the *Racing Club (Public Sweep-states Act)*, 1965 made clear, and this tension will, no doubt, continue. Finally, doubts have been expressed as to the sincerity of the Government's aim in the introduction of such measures, some commentators suggesting that the initiatives are political opportunism, rather than proper commercial ventures. Indeed, one critic concludes: '*The Islamic Bank is but another bank. It may abolish interest but, given the capitalist structure of the economy, the Bank, like other commercial banks, will continue to mobilize the savings of the ordinary people for investments that will earn profits, which will almost always benefit those in the middle and upper echelons of society....the abolition of interest in a capitalist economy without other fundamental changes can only lead to greater injustices and inequities..*'(Muzaffar 1987, 82).

* * * * *

References

Fadzli Yusof M. 1986, 'Takaful- Islamic Alternative to Insurance', Law Seminar, Kulliyyah of Laws International Islamic University, Petaling Jaya, July 26-27, 1986.

Ismail A.R. 1985, 'Administration of Islamic Law in Malaysia and the Shariah Court', Paper presented at the 8th Malaysian Law Conference, Kuala Lumpur, 14-16 November 1985.

Muzaffar C. 1987, *Islamic Resurgence in Malaysia*, Penerbit Fajar Bakti Sdn. Bhd., Petaling Jaya.

Sandhu K.S. and Wheatly P. eds. 1983, *Melaka: The Transformation of a Malay Capital 1400-1980*, Vol.1, Oxford University Press.

Tun Haji M.S. 1986, 'Traditional Elements of the Malaysian Constitution', in Trindade F. and Lee H., *The Constitution of Malaysia: Further Perspectives and Developments,* Oxford University Press.

* * * * *

THE DEBATE ON RIBA AND INTEREST IN TWENTIETH CENTURY JURISPRUDENCE

Chibli Mallat
Law Department, SOAS

Introduction

The definition of the word *Riba* has been the subject of a protracted jurisprudential debate in the Arab and Muslim world in the twentieth century. It is not surprising that the question of Riba would come under strong scrutiny: a significant legal problem appears whenever the concept of interest falls in the purview of its definition.

The illustration of this axiom is simple. If Riba is understood to mean simply usury, then, as long as interest rates have not hit unusual ceilings, all transactions conducted in society are valid. But if Riba is in essence defined as interest, then the whole civil and commercial structure of society becomes tainted with illegality.

The word Riba and its derivatives appears in various instances in the Qur'an, and in some *hadiths*.[1] In a concise form, the rule can be stated thus: 'God has forbidden Riba' (Qur'an: II,275). Depending on the domain subsumed under the word, a number of financial, commercial, and civil transactions can be included or excluded from the ambit of the prohibition.

The development of modern banking in the 70s has triggered in the Middle East a renewed and active debate over Riba. As things stand at present, the Arab-speaking countries of the Muslim world have all adopted banking systems that follow a Western model, and they fundamentally accept the

[1] The most famous hadith of the Prophet relating to Riba appears in all the main compilations of the traditions, except Bukhari's: 'Gold for gold, silver for silver, wheat for wheat, barley for barley, dates for dates, salt for salt, each kind for each kind, in hand; he who increases or asks for increase commits Riba (*Arba*), alike whether he gives or takes'.

charging of interest in most forms of commercial transacting. But the model has recently been challenged by a number of States and institutions, as it was accused of being in clear breach of the Shari'a.

But long before the oil boom and the concomitant emergence of a banking system, the debate over Riba had taken root. In its most sophisticated form, it has been developing in the recurring polemic among Egyptian jurists, laypersons, and 'ulama throughout the century.

Obviously, the cyclical resurgence has preceded modern times, and crises originating around practices considered Riba-ridden have been documented in the Ottoman empire over fixed interest related to waqfs (Mandaville 1979). But the age-old debate was probably enhanced in Egypt by the early growth of modern finance, and the accompanying debt problems (Landes 1958), and by the legal renewal that developed eagerly in Egypt since the turn of the twentieth century (on Riba, see generally Saleh 1986).

This fertile ground found its most enriching dimension when basic transactions had to be reconsidered. A comprehensive redesigning of the basic civil laws of Egypt was started in the 30s under the supervision of 'Abd ar-Razzaq as-Sanhuri, and was coronated by the adoption some twenty years later of a comprehensive Civil Code that was meant to combine the best legal traditions of East and West (Hill 1987). But the intensity of the polemic in the 30s and 40s echoed and continued an earlier important debate, which, at the turn of the century, had involved the highest circles of the Azhar, in the person of the great reformist Muhammad 'Abduh, and in the laity, in the person of the Khedive. The two waves were strangely complementary, as the arguments became more and more refined.

The polemic in Egypt has revived again in recent years, and acquired a constitutional and jurisprudential dimension which places it in the limelight (See Ian Edge's article in this volume.) But the arguments have remained essentially grounded in the civil law, particularly in the dispositions on the legal ceiling on interest of Art. 227 of the Egyptian Civil Code.

This chapter will try to describe the legal arguments over Riba developed in the jurisprudence of the twentieth century. Section I addresses the first polemic, known as the Sunduq at-Tawfir affair. Section II introduces the relevant dispositions of the Egyptian Civil Code. Section III will present some of the arguments of Muhammad Abu Zahra, an important religious figure of contemporary Egypt. Section IV will present the polemic in its most sophisticated form, as it developed over some thirty years between 'Abd ar-Razzaq as-Sanhuri and Ibrahim Zaki al-Badawi. The last section will briefly show how the debate rebounded in the 80s.

I. The *Sunduq at-Tawfir* Affair

The polemic over Riba developed in Egypt out of circumstances that in part bore the imprint of a local conflict. But in fin-de-siècle Cairo, they also seemed inevitable. As capitalist penetration had developed in the country, a number of small-scale financial institutions had been created alongside the major foreign banks, following an imported model that had little concern for the religious sensitivities of the population. In the early twentieth century, like similar institutions in the West, the Egyptian Administration of Posts established a 'Savings Fund' (*Sunduq at-Tawfir,* also known under its French name, *Caisse d'épargne*) which yielded to the depositors/savers a return in the form of a fixed interest. 'Over 3000 from among the depositors refused, out of religious conviction (*Tadayyunan*), to take their interest fixed by the decree of the Khedive'. Consequently, 'some men in government, including the director of the Administration of the Posts, asked the Mufti informally... if there was a legal way that would authorize Muslims to take the profit earned by their monies in the Savings Fund' (*Manar* 1917, 529).

But the story of the Sunduq at-Tawfir is still not totally elucidated either in its outcome, or in the theories that accompanied the debate between Muhammad 'Abduh and the Khedive. A recent account indicates how the problems were obscured: '...The government sought a plan from Rida and Mufti Misr to avoid its being construed as Riba, the former agreeing, arguing that Riba involved exploitation and this was to the contrary an obvious benefit for the employees, which the latter refused angrily, arguing that it most clearly was Riba. So the Khedive assembled a group of 'Ulama in Qasr al-Qubba [the Khedive's residence] and charged them to draft a Shar'i [in accordance with the Shari'a] interpretation for Sanduq at-Tawfir, so that it would be religiously acceptable to the people. Rida found the result of their deliberation to be the same as the plan that he had suggested' (Eccel 1984, 416).

The debate over the legality of the Fund's operations was complicated by two extraneous factors:

A notorious enmity had developed between the Khedive Abbas and Muhammad 'Abduh, as they were both vying for intellectual leadership in Egypt. The Khedive, who, as the head of the administration, had fixed the interest rate of the Fund's deposits, was manifestly shaken by 'Abduh's negative opinion. But he recouped by appointing a board of 'Ulama from the Azhar to revise the Posts' case, thereby bringing competition to the decision-making power of the Mufti. But as the affair developed, according to the

Manar, the board of 'ulama appointed by the Khedive presented a plan which was similar to the one originally suggested by 'Abduh. In the meantime, the Khedive had secured the needed religious support; and though 'Abduh and the Board Abbas had appointed reached the same conclusions, the Khedive accused 'Abduh of wanting to force Riba on pious Muslims.

More significantly however, an external element that renders the controversy particularly intricate in hindsight, stems from the intellectual relationship between 'Abduh and Rida (for more details on the relation, see Kerr 1966). The Posts' affair is a conspicuous example of the difficulty in deciding, in what has reached us from 'Abduh through Rida, which opinion is truly the teacher's, and which the disciple's. When they match, the problem is obliterated, but in the case of Riba, the slightest nuance in the formulation carries far-reaching consequences when the opinions of the two great reformers do not coincide completely.

From the outset of the affair, the debate appears complex, as it took place within the delicate alleys of religious-legal circles. But if a definitive conclusion cannot be reached on the exact position of 'Abduh, partly because the texts that have reached us are themselves inconclusive, and partly because of the deforming intermediation of 'Abduh's disciple, Muhammad Rashid Rida, it is possible to see, already in the texts of the early century, most of the shape of arguments to come.

In Rida's account, who was relating events that took place in 1903, the Mufti, Muhammed 'Abduh, was dissatisfied with the system introduced by the Savings Fund: 'He (Muhammed 'Abduh) said: in no way can the mentioned (*Mansus*) Riba be accepted, and since the Posts' administration exploits the monies which it takes from the people (the depositors) and does not borrow from them out of necessity, it is possible for these monies to be put to use (*Istighlal*) on the basis of the commenda partnership (*Sharikat al-Mudaraba*)' (*Manar* 1917, 528).

According to a later account however, 'Abduh was the first thinker of Islam to have justified the exclusion of the 'loan for interest, *al-Qard bil-Fa'ida* (or at least some of its forms), from the ambit of the prohibited Riba'. That, however, happened 'only in his private conversations' and he 'apparently did not reach final satisfaction with this conclusion' as he refused to take the step of carrying it into the open and to bear responsibility for this conclusion to the people who followed him. Furthermore, his opinion on Riba was not written in his own hand, and it was only conveyed by Muhammad Rashid Rida, 'who is known to have often mixed his own ideas with his master's'. (Badawi 1964, 223)

The texts, however, are not so clear, and they tend to point at a different conclusion: 'Abduh was, contrary to what Badawi suggests, opposed to the first scheme laid out by the Posts' Administration. The 1917 remembrances of Rida in the *Manar* suggest that 'Abduh saw in the alternative of the commenda a way that would avoid the Riba transaction, and he did not, at least in the recorded text, admit the operations carried out by the Fund. It is true, however, that already, a qualification voiced by 'Abduh - which he did not deem applicable in the case at hand - would later pave the way for more leeway in the interpretation of modern banking operations. This was the concept of need, *Haja*, which absolved the banks from the Ribawi interdiction, but this example was qualified as exceptional in the discourse of 'Abduh-Rida, and the principle of the prohibition of interest-bearing loan operations was bolstered by rationales which remain to date among the most eloquent and persuasive.

In a text published in 1906 (*Manar* 1906, 332ff.), the connection with the modern world of banks is clearly made. Money, says 'Abduh in his comments on the verses on Riba in the second Sura of the Qur'an, is merely an indicator of the value (*Qima*) of commodities. If this is altered to making money the object (*Maqsud*) of the production of wealth, '*then this will lead to the stripping of wealth from the hands of most people and to concentrating it in the hands of those who limit their works to the exploitation* (istighlal) *of money by money. Thus, money expands (*yarbu) *with them* ('Indahum), *and is hoarded in the safes* (Sanadiq, *plural of* Sunduq) *and in financial houses* (Buyut Maliyya) *known as banks* (Bunuk), *and the labourers* ('amilun) *are stripped from the value of their labour, because most of the profit would then derive from the money itself (he [i.e. 'Abduh; the narrator is Rida] means that most of the profit goes to the capitalist* (Rabb al-Mal), *not to the worker), and thus die the poor*' (*Manar* 1906, 348).

The framework in which early in the century the debate is perceived by 'Abduh and Rida will constantly be repeated in the renewed efforts towards an alternative financial system. The terminology used by 'Abduh comes remarkably early in the populist literature of the colonial Middle East, and is noteworthy for the early use of expressions which will permeate much later the economic discourse of revolutionaries of Socialist and Islamic varieties. That 'Abduh, as early as the first decade of the century, used standard signifiers of later dissidents, is all the more remarkable since propounders of Islamic banking of much more sedate and conservative leaning kept using a similar phraseology.

Typical formulations run nowadays thus: 'The principles and underlying ideas in the [Islamic economic and financial] system are clear cut and any Muslim can easily understand them. It [the banking system] is based on the idea of social justice.' (Saud 1985, 103). Another Islamic banker uses the same theme for the advocacy of a smooth social development: 'Islamic banking as I see it is not only a matter of satisfying the religious wealthy Muslims who are willing to derive a legitimate (*halal*) income. Islamic banking should be viewed as a way that still can give hope for providing a remedial solution to the long standing problems between those who won the wealth and those who can work to make it increase' (Homoud 1985, 74).

But from the documents that have reached us on the Sunduq at-Tawfir affair, some conclusions can be reached:

- Neither the Khedive, nor Muhammad 'Abduh or Rashid Rida were comfortable about the interest yielded to the depositors on their monies, but they seem to have tolerated it if a scheme of *mudaraba* could be devised to legitimize the interest on the employees' deposits.

- What was called mudaraba however was not elaborated on significantly. The texts do not mention any return akin to a varying dividend, and the Sunduq at-Tawfir's activities seem to have gone on unperturbed.

- Nonetheless, the arguments presented on the pages of the *Manar* have remained the yardstick by which the logic of the rejection/acceptance of Riba-interest has worked: on the side of allowing interest, the idea was that of the need to move forward and facilitate transactions over money. Against Riba was presented the danger of letting money yield profit without the intermediation of work, and, as a consequence, permitting the concentration of capital in few hands and the 'exploitation of the poor by the rich' (*Manar* 1904, 28).

II. The Dispositions on Interest in the Egyptian Civil Code

The episode of the Sunduq at-Tawfir was insignificant in terms of the sums of money involved. But it triggered the twentieth century debate at the highest intellectual and institutional level.

When in the late 30s the debate resurfaced, the context of its production was even more significant. It engulfed many prominent thinkers, among whom jurists from the Azhar and from secular circles. But the issues discussed had a much more ominous ring than at the time of the Sunduq at-Tawfir affair.

The central issue was related to a legal development of great importance, the establishment of a new Civil Code. Until then, the civil laws of Egypt had been constituted in the main by a mixed system partly inherited from the French, and partly fashioned by Qadri Basha's *Murshid al-Hayran*. In the mid-30s, a committee was established for the drafting of the new laws, and 'Abd ar-Razzaq as-Sanhuri was entrusted with bringing the project into a full Code. The work took more than a decade, and in 1949, the new Egyptian Civil Code was passed into law.

Among the rules that had been thoroughly studied were the dispositions relating to interest. In the former compendium of Qadri Basha, the article on loans and interests permitted, in the fashion of the European Civil Codes of the time, interest with a maximum ceiling of 8 per cent. Article 125/185 read: '*It is absolutely forbidden for the contracting parties to agree on interests that exceed 8 per cent per annum... Any agreement stipulating an interest rate that exceeds this limit will be reduced to the maximum interest rate allowed [by this law] in the contract*'.

When the door was opened to redraft the old rules, the place of the Shari'a in the new Code was obviously a matter for long discussions, and the introductory articles placed it as one of the major sources for the Egyptian civil law. On a substantial level, the debate of 'Abduh and the Khedive rebounded. The question was whether a fixed interest over a contractual loan would remain possible.

On the whole, the old principles remained valid, but some measures were retained to keep the former dispositions under tighter check:

1) Article 232 stipulates that 'interests on interests (*Fawa'id 'ala Mutajammid al-Fawa'id*) are prohibited'. Under the previous Code, such interest was permitted under two conditions: (a) That accrued interests be running for no less than a year; and (b) that an express stipulation in the contract between lender and borrower allow such interest accrual. In the absence of such a stipulation, the creditor-lender would have to bring the matter before the court for a decision.

2) If borrower and lender do not agree on an interest on the loan, Art. 542 considers that 'the loan will be deemed interest-free'.

3) In case of delay after the payment is due, an interest of 4 per cent in civil, and 5 per cent in commercial, transactions will eventually be owed by the defaulting borrower (Art. 226). In this case however, procedural rules are favourable to the debtor. A summons by the creditor, even if official, would not be sufficient for the legal interest to start running. The lender-creditor must file his complaint with the court, and specify in the writ brought to the tribunal that his right is

not limited to the principal (*Ra's al-Mal*), but that it extends to the interest arising from the delay.

4) The totality of interests due will not be superior to the principal. But this disposition, adopted probably in line with the Qur'anic injunction prohibiting 'the eating of money times over' (*La Ta'kulu Amwalakum Ad'afan Muda'afa*, Qur'an: III, 130), is not taken into account for long-term productive investments (Art. 232).

5) If the creditor proves bad faith in claiming the debt, the judge is allowed to reduce the legal interest and even completely dispense with it (Art. 229).

6) If the borrower decides to repay the loan before it is due, Art.544 allows him to proceed without requiring the lender's agreement. Accelerated repayment cannot be precluded in the contract. But the borrower can exercise his right only six months after the contract, and he has six months to execute this intention. The debtor however, incurs the interest on the debt for the full six months .

But despite all these stipulations in favour of the debtor, the most important principle adopted by the Egyptian Civil Code is posited in Art. 227 (1): *'The contracting parties can agree on a different rate of interest, whether in return for a delay in payment [this is related to Art. 226] or in any other situation [which includes the loan for interest], on condition that this rate does not exceed 7 per cent. If they agree on an interest that exceeds this rate, this interest will be reduced to 7 per cent, and any surplus already paid must be returned [to the borrower].'*

How did the architects of the Code reach these conclusions, which, except for some constraints put on the creditor's presumed strong position, do not question the legitimacy of lending for a fixed interest?

Before discussing the background to the adoption of Art. 227, it is worth examining the reaction to Riba of a prominent conservative jurist from the Azhar, Shaykh Muhammad Abu Zahra.

III. Muhammad Abu Zahra: the Conservative Approach

Like 'Abduh and Rida before him, the position of Abu Zahra (1898-1974) was not clear cut, particularly when the criticism entailed the rejection of a Civil Code widely respected in Egypt and the Arab world for its quality. In his most developed contribution to the subject (Abu Zahra n.d.), Muhammad

Abu Zahra addressed the Egyptian civil law tangentially, and did not openly disagree with their stipulations. But modern banks, he added, should not work as they do at present. They should rather '*turn their activities from the loan with interest to other productive activities. In reality, the work of banks is not only limited to lending with interest. They have other activities, like taking shares in industrial and other companies, so that instead of loans being loans with interest, loans would all be on the basis of participation in commercial and industrial companies, a participation in the profits and losses of these companies.*' (Abu Zahra , 57)

This, in his view, would be in accordance with the civil laws of Egypt and with the injunction of the Qur'an that 'your capitals will be given back to you, then you will have committed no injustice, nor would an injustice have been done to you' (Qur'an II, 279). Alluding to Art. 232 of the Code, Abu Zahra continues: 'The modern Civil Code of Egypt has established this Qur'anic principle, and decided that [the aggregate of] interests cannot exceed the principal.' (Ibid., 56.)

But despite this assertion on the correspondence between Egyptian laws and the Shari'a, the gist of Abu Zahra's essay is opposed to this conclusion. The question of the aggregate interests is only marginal to the principle of the loan with interest, and when it comes to this central issue, his arguments contradict Art. 227 of the Civil Code. There is no doubt that Abu Zahra, like Rida and 'Abduh before him, were wary of too rigid a condemnation of positive laws and widespread practice, especially when they have no way to implement their opinions. But their convictions were clearly in contradiction with the practices they were witnessing.

In Abu Zahra's *Tahrim ar-Riba*, several arguments are adduced against considerations which in his opinion have been invoked for the defence of Riba in modern transactions:

One argument develops the theory of need/necessity (*haja/darura).* For the advocates of Riba, writes Abu Zahra, 'necessity (*darura*) requires the taking of interest, and if there is no necessity, then general welfare, *Maslaha*, will be taken into account; for wherein welfare is the law of God' (Abu Zahra, 36). This argument, he continues, is likened to the prohibition of eating pork and drinking wine, which could be lifted in critical situations. But the necessity in the case of interest, notes Abu Zahra, is certainly not akin to these extreme situations. 'It is not of the same kind, and if it were, it would work only on an individual, and not on a social, level. Even in the case [of necessity favouring Riba on an personal basis], which is an exception, this cannot be accepted. On the institutional level, necessity would apply to the borrower, never to the lender.' (Id., 43) Here Abu Zahra introduces two further distinctions. He acknowledges a difference between Haja and Darura, and between borrowing and lending.

A hypothesis is used to clarify these distinctions. In one debate on Riba, Muhammad Abu Zahra writes, he was put the rhetorical question of a Muslim country at war, in dire need for weapons to defend itself. Can this country underwrite a transaction in which Riba is involved, under the theory of necessity, darura ? This hypothesis, Abu Zahra argues, is unrealistic. Even if one were to accept the possibility of such an extreme situation, a Muslim country should do everything in its power to avoid resorting to a loan against fixed interest. But even in this extreme situation, only borrowing for interest, and not lending, would be permitted.

Abu Zahra takes the distinction a step further. All those involved in the practice of Riba, according to the hadith, whether close or remote, fall under the heaviest opprobrium. But there is a legal difference between borrowing for Riba and lending for Riba. 'Borrowing for Riba is forbidden, *haram*, as proxy (*li-ghayrihi*); it is a haram of ends '*saddan lidh-Dhari'a*', whereas lending for Riba is haram per se. Consequently, borrowing can be allowed out of need and not out of necessity, *yubah lil-haja, la lid-Darura*'. In that instance, he continues, a) both lending and borrowing for interest are haram, and b) the lender in that case is in double infringement, and his responsibility for the crime is of first-degree nature, whereas the borrower's is accessory, *bit-Taba'* "(Id., 43).

Secondly, Abu Zahra criticizes those who try to allow interest on the basis of a loose reading of a report of the Caliph 'Umar Ibn al-Khattab, in which 'Umar is said to have lamented that the Prophet died without clarifying the meaning of Riba. Such a loose interpretation cannot be upheld, Abu Zahra retorts. What 'Umar insisted on was the necessity to be extremely careful in matters related to Riba since, precisely, they were unclear. It was better to avoid falling into Riba by avoiding any doubtful practice which might, even minimally, lead to commit it. This is what the saying related to 'Umar means. It certainly does not entail that Riba should be allowed because we are left in the dark as to its exact meaning. Furthermore, writes Abu Zahra, 'Umar knew exactly what the *Jahili* Riba meant. And the Jahili Riba is the exact form of the present loan for interest (Id., 36-37).

Finally, the holders of a permissive attitude have advocated, according to Abu Zahra, the differentiation between a loan contracted for consumption (*istihlak*), and a loan for labour use (*istighlal*). Only loans for consumption in this new theory should be banned. But loans for labour use are in modern times of great necessity and of immense benefit to the economics of production. Abu Zahra agrees that capital is helpful to build up the economy.

But he quickly adds that there are ways to raise such capital without having to resort to a fixed interest: the commenda partnership is the perfect way to raise capital fruitfully, without versing into Riba.

These arguments by Abu Zahra clearly contradict Art. 227 of the Egyptian Code. That he never came to admit it openly is beside the point. But Abu Zahra offers a perspective, which was shared, and continues to be shared, by many jurists and 'ulama who feel uneasy about the framework set out by the Egyptian Civil Code.

IV. The Legal Debate between Badawi and Sanhuri

And yet the arguments for and against the equating of Riba and simple interest had not, with all the 'ulama and jurists who had participated in the debate since the Sunduq at-Tawfir controversy, taken their most sophisticated form. All the arguments presented had consisted of legal briefs, in the form of *fatwas* and short studies, some occasionally as booklets, as in the case of Abu Zahra. With Ibrahim Zaki al-Badawi and Abd ar-Razzaq as-Sanhuri arguments became systematic, and acquired book-length treatment.

The debate took place, like its predecessor at the turn of the century, in circumstances that rendered it particularly complicated, especially since one of its poles, Badawi, diametrically reversed his position more than twenty years after his initial opinion. But the stakes were also particularly high, because the whole accordance of the new Egyptian Civil Code with the Shari'a was at stake.

In 1939, as the preparatory work on the project of a new Civil Code was under way, Badawi was working in 'the section on Islamic Law', and Sanhuri, who was the head of the Preparatory Commission for the Code, asked him to prepare a study that would bring the idea of interest in accordance with the projected articles of the Code. A long report resulted, which impressed and pleased Sanhuri so much that he sent it for immediate publication to the law journal of the Fu'ad I (later Cairo) Law School, *Majallat al-Qanun wal-Iqtisad*, to date the most prominent law periodical in the Arab world. Badawi's study, '*Nazariyyat ar-Riba al-Muharram*', ('The theory of the Forbidden Riba') was published in two parts, in the April and May 1939 issues, and instantly became a major work of reference in Egypt on Riba (Badawi 1939).

Many jurists adopted the conclusions of this work. Among them was 'Abd ar-Razzaq as-Sanhuri himself. But as time passed, Badawi became less and less comfortable with the conclusions of his 1939 article. After his main conclusions were quoted approvingly in Sanhuri's *Masadir al-Haqq* (Sanhuri 1954), he felt compelled to present the 'maturer' views that he had reached, and in 1964, he published in Cairo a book that bore the exact same title of his 1939 article (Badawi 1964).

In contrast with Rida and 'Abduh, Badawi offers a systematic attempt at coherence in both his 1939 and 1964 works. Also, his familiarity with the texts of the classical legal tradition is more genuine than the other scholars, including the Azharites. Furthermore, the background of the debate being a precise legal text rather than undefined transactions carried out by a small money-house, the terms of reference of the debate helped to achieve a better marshalling of the arguments.

In this chapter, it is not possible to develop the whole view on Riba that Badawi constructed in his two studies. But some of the most interesting elements he developed will be presented.

A- Badawi 1939: The Limiting Theory

The main thrust of Badawi's 1939 interpretation of Riba is subsumed under what he calls, in the wake of Ibn 'Abbas, 'the limiting theory'. In this interpretation of one of the most prominent companions of the Prophet, 'Riba was limited to the Nasi'a, i.e. the Riba of the Jahiliyya [the Jahiliyya is the period that preceded the Prophet's call], which means the increase in the debt principal *at the time of the accrual* [underlined in original] in order to receive a new loan' (Badawi 1939, 563).

There follow five main observations:

1 - Like Ibn al-Qayyim and other adherents of the limiting theory of Ibn 'Abbas, *Riba al-Fadl*, though forbidden, should not be covered by as strict a prohibition as the case is with *Riba an-Nasi'a*, 'for what was forbidden for itself, *Tahrim al-Wasa'el* , should not be construed as strictly as what has been forbidden for its ends, *Tahrim al-Maqased*. Riba al-Fadl is consequently allowed in case of need (haja)' (Id., 564). Thus, selling dates that have ripened is permitted despite the hadith enjoining only the sale of 'dates against dates', as are allowed instances of credit sale. The analogy for Ibn al-Qayyim and Badawi can be extended to jewellery made out of gold and silver, or, following Malik, the sale of a smaller quantity of coins of better

quality against a larger quantity of low-mint coins. Furthermore, following the Zahiris, Badawi strictly limits Riba al-Fadl to the six categories of the hadith (Id).

2 - Loans predicated on benefits (*Qard bi-Naf' Mashrut*) should not be forbidden on the basis of Riba. The difference between the two categories lies in that 'the increase in Riba an-Nasi'a occurs at the time of accrual, whereas it occurs in the loan with interest at the moment of contracting..., and is therefore not based on compulsion... Even if we were to accept the analogy, its measurement changes over time, and the theory of the loan has evolved as the debt has for the borrower stopped from being barren and non-productive, to become the source of profuse profits which it is fair to allow the lender to take his share from' (Id., 565-566).

3 - Most new financial operations are free from Riba, such as the purchase of commercial papers (i.e., bonds, debts, etc.), which is allowed as a type of assignment (*hawala*) (Id., 555-557).

4 - Profits on loans made as deposits, as in the episode of Sunduq at-Tawfir, are permitted, following 'Abduh who likened them to Mudaraba contracts. But Badawi adds that this is not properly Mudaraba, which cannot be fixed (Id., 551,555); stock exchange activities are also legal (Id., 555-562); as well as insurance contracts. (Id., 562.)

5 - On a more general level, the concept of necessity is used extensively to legitimize current financial transactions, 'The principle ruling transactions (*mu'amalat*) is that they are permitted because they are related to the financial interest of the people, and what they agreed on as a necessity for them. There is nothing forbidden except what the legislator expressly forbids. Mere doubt (*ishtibah*) is not sufficient (Id.).

B- Badawi 1964: The Expanded Theory

Twenty five years after the publication of his article in *Majallat al-Qanun wal-Iqtisad*, Badawi took a diametrically opposed stance to his original views and published a full-length book on the theory of Riba. In this book, the basis of Badawi's self-criticism is articulated on Art. 227 of the Egyptian Civil Code, which, by allowing a ceiling of 7 per cent on loans, had implicitly accepted the principle of a fixed reward on money. Ironically, Badawi's theses of 1939 had paved the way for the codifiers of the Civil Code to rest the acceptance of the limiting theory of Riba on the conviction, which was partly based on Badawi's commissioned study, that it conformed to the received Shari'a.

Badawi was obviously not comfortable with his own change of mind. He did acknowledge that Sanhuri took into account the views he expressed in the 1939 article, which was '*a mixture of the alleged view (ra'i maz'um) of Ibn 'Abbas and his friends, and the alleged view of Ibn al-Qayyim. (Sanhuri) took from the first his opinion that the forbidden Riba of the Qur'an is nothing else than the multiplied (Muda'af) Riba over Capital, and that outside this definition, any other Riba would not fall under the Qur'anic prohibition (like Riba an-Nasai'a and Riba al-Fadl expressed in the hadith of the six categories). And Sanhuri took from the second [i.e. the theory of Ibn al-Qayyim] the view that Riba is forbidden for it being an ends and not for being a means. The prohibition of Riba as means is acceptable in case of need (haja); so Sanhuri took his last view from Ibn al-Qayyim and introduced in it - as an instance of a prohibition of Riba for it being a prohibition of means - the Riba an-Nasi'a mentioned in the hadith, and considered it to belong to that category*'. (Badawi 1964, 254-5).

Sanhuri's reading, continued Badawi, is incorrect. It is wrong to consider the view of Ibn 'Abbas on Riba to mean only multiplied Riba (anatocism). Therefore, Art. 232 of the Egyptian Civil Code prohibiting anatocism suggests the unduly narrow view that anatocism and Riba are the one and same thing. Also wrong is Sanhuri's conclusion that Riba as a whole is prohibited only as a means, and not also as an ends, thus allowing Riba in case of need (Art. 233 of the Egyptian Civil Code). Finally, even though Badawi acknowledges the efforts of Sanhuri at 'moderating' the attitude of Arab legislations on interest in comparison with unbridled capitalist legislation, he still considers that this 'moderation' is in its essence opposed to the Shari'a.

'Our great legislator', concludes Badawi on Sanhuri, has been correct in his predictions that a change towards socialism would come to undermine the whole question of Riba, and Nasser's work towards obliterating Riba from the social fabric 'started indeed to suppress interests in debts by the Loan bank (*Bank at-Taslif*) in his declaration on the 1961 Anniversary of the Revolution' (id., 257). Perhaps then, continues Badawi, will it be easier to transfrom the whole system by replacing the transactions operating on the basis of interest by a 'merger (*jam'*) between commenda operations which truly share profit and loss' and achieve that the society manage the financial system as an expanding and fruitful totality in which loss is compensated by profit (Id.).

This, however, is still in the making, adds Badawi. Meanwhile, the system continues to function in contradiction with the Shari'a and the rules of the loan with interest in the Civil Code (mainly Art. 227) are opposed to the Shari'a regulations (Id., 270).

Thus, from the limited theory of Riba, Badawi has shifted over the years to what he called the expanded theory. In his later view, several modern transactions, foremost among which those which allow interest on loans, as in Art. 227 of the Egyptian Civil Code, are deemed to be opposed to the Shari'a.[2] How the principal architect of the Code read Riba offers an interesting contrast to the one expounded in 1964 by his erstwhile collaborator.

C- Sanhuri and the Defence of the Civil Code.

In his *Sources of Law in Islamic Jurisprudence* (*Masadir al-Haqq fil-Fiqh al-Islami*), which were developed in lectures given in Cairo between 1954 and 1959, Sanhuri offers a lengthy analysis of Riba.

Riba, in the general system of obligations and contracts, is classified along with other 'vices of consent', which, in the French legal terminology, nullify a contract. In this perspective, Riba is considered to be a major constraining factor bearing on the freedom of contract.

Because of the acceptance by the Egyptian Civil Code of interest arising from various contracts, and mainly loan, Sanhuri's understanding of Riba is qualified by the necessity to abide by the dispositions written in the Code.

The whole defence of Art. 227 is based on a subtle syllogism, which shares some of the analysis offered by Badawi in his 1939 article.

The starting point of the syllogism is that 'Riba is forbidden', and that there are three main reasons for the prohibition: '(1) To prevent the hoarding of people's foodstuffs; (2) To prevent speculating on currency, so that currency

[2] In his 1939 article, Badawi had legitimized a number of modern transactions, including stock exchange, insurance contracts, etc. (See supra.) In 1964, he seemed much less secure about the legality of these transactions. A fuller account of his views can be found in the Annex to this chapter.

does not become itself a commodity; (3) To avoid unfairness and exploitation when the deal is related to a single commodity' (Sanhuri 1954, 236).

The two first reasons derive from simple public policy considerations. The third reason sheds light on the question of Riba al-Fadl, which, according to the hadith, is defined as the prohibition of the sale with an increase (Riba), of two commodities of the same kind. For Sanhuri, this classification is an important element in the articulation of the syllogism.

This form of Riba, Riba al-Fadl, writes Sanhuri, is forbidden in classical Islamic law as a prohibition 'of means' (*Saddan lidh-Dhari'a*). It is not forbidden per se, because it is meant to stand in the way of the more fundamental Riba of the Jahiliyya, Riba an-Nasi'a. Riba an-Nasi'a, however, is absolutely prohibited. It is prohibited per se. There are consequently different degrees of prohibition, and some are less absolute than others. The forms of Riba that are prohibited for themselves can only be excused in case of absolute necessity. But those forms of Riba which are prohibited because they can constitute a first step towards the original Riba an-Nasi'a do not fall under the same prohibitive regime. They, unlike Riba an-Nasi'a, can be tolerated in case of need.

But for Sanhuri Riba an-Nasi'a merely means anatocism. It is the combined (*murakkab*) interest, which makes money deriving from interest as important as the original capital. This, he adds, has been forbidden by the Egyptian legislator in Art. 232 of the Civil Code.

However, in Sanhuri's elaborate syllogism, it is important to bear in mind that the original ban on Riba falls in the category of sales. It is in sales that the vice of Riba operates, as is testified in the juxtaposition of the good sale, allowed by the scripture, and the bad Riba, forbidden in the same verse 275 of the second Sura. 'Loan', writes Sanhuri, 'is not in Islamic jurisprudence one of the root (*Asl*) Ribawi contracts. It is the contract of sale which is the root, and a loan will be measured against a sale' (Sanhuri 1954, 239). But the opposite is not true. The sale contract cannot be measured against the category of loans.

Following the syllogism, the root and the derivative cannot be addressed in the same manner, and the prohibition attached to a root contract is more absolute than the prohibition attached to a derivative transaction. Consequently, what is not forbidden per se will yield, as in the example of Riba al-Fadl, to need. Need, and not necessity as in the root contract, will open the way to the alleviation of the prohibition. And in a capitalist society like Egypt, the need for loans is overwhelming, and common. It is of the essence of the economic system. As long as is does not become anatocism, as in Art. 232, it will be tolerated by the legislator in accordance with the Shari'a.

Thus is the Egyptian system vindicated (see more in Ibid., 237-244). By a series of syllogisms, Sanhuri succeeds in showing that Art. 227 is fair. He ultimately laments the mould forced on society by the capitalist system, and voices hope that it will be remedied by the rising socialist tide. But until then, society's loans against interest are completely compatible with the Shari'a.

V. 1985: Back to Square One.

Some forty years after the passing of the Civil Code in Egypt, the debate was opened again in Egypt. In 1985, the Rector of the Azhar himself brought suit before the Constitutional Court of Egypt on the ground that Art. 226 of the Civil Code, which allows 4 per cent interest on compensatory damage, is prohibited by the Shari'a. Since the Shari'a had become after the 1980 modification of the Constitution, 'the [as opposed to a] principal source of legislation' (Art. 2 of the Amended Egyptian Constitution), Art. 226 was deemed by the Azhar to have become unconstitutional.

The Constitutional Court did not address the case on its merits, and dismissed it because Art. 2 as amended could not 'be made applicable to former legal enactments', and because judging unconstitutional Art. 226 of the Civil Code would 'lead to contradiction and confusion in the judicial process, in a manner which would threaten stability' (Supreme Constitutional Court of Egypt 1985, 106).

But the Court avoided discussing the issue of Art. 226 outright. The century-old debate on Riba in Egypt was in all evidence not completely over.

* * * * *

References

Abu Zahra M. n.d., *Tahrim ar-Riba Tanzim Iqtisadi,* Ad-Dar as-Sa'udiyya, (London ?)

Badawi I.Z. 1939, 'Nazariyyat ar-Riba al-Muharram', *Majallat al-Qanun wal-Iqtisad*, Cairo, pp.387-447; 533-566.

Badawi I.Z. 1964, *Nazariyyat ar-Riba al-Muharram*, al-Majles al-A'la li-Ri'ayat al-Funun, Cairo.

Eccel C. 1984, *Egypt: Islam and Social Change*, Berlin, Klaus Schwarz.

Hill E. 1987, *Al-Sanhuri and Islamic Law*, Cairo Papers in Social Science, Vol.10, American University in Cairo.

Homoud S. 1985, 'Address', in *Proceedings* of the First International Meeting, Islamic Banking Conference, New York.

Kerr M. 1966, *Islamic Reform: the Political and Legal Theories of Muhammad Abduh and Rashid Rida*, Berkeley.

Landes D. 1958, *Bankers and Pashas*, London.

Manar 1904, 'Sunduq at-Tawfir fi Idarat al-Barid', Vol.7, pp.28-29.

Manar 1906, 'Fasl fi-Hikmat Tahrim ar-Riba', Vol.9, pp.332-350.

Manar 1917, 'Ribh Sunduq at-Tawfir', pp.526-528.

Mandaville J. 1979, 'Usurious Piety: the Cash Waqf Controversy in the Ottoman Empire', *International Journal of Middle East Studies*, Vol 10, pp.289-308.

Saleh N. 1986, *Unlawful Gain and Legitimate Profit in Islamic Law*, Cambridge University Press.

Sanhuri A. 1954-1959, *Masadir al-Haqq fil-Fiqh al-Islami*, 6 Parts in 2 Vol., Part 3.

Saud M. 1985, 'Lucheon Address', in *Proceedings* of the First International Meeting, Islamic Banking Conference, New York.

Supreme Constitutional Court of Egypt 1985, 'Decision on Shari'a and Riba', *Arab Law Quarterly*, Vol.1 Part. 1, pp.100-108.

* * * * *

Annex (See section IV) Badawi's 1964 views on 'some Contracts legal in appearance, but which are considered by some jurists to be Ribawi'. (Badawi 1964, 203-219).

[As will be seen from the following text, Badawi's opinion on these transactions is much less clear than when he dealt with similar transactions in his 1939 article.]

1. *'Bay' al-'Ayna'*

In this sale, 'the commodity is sold for a delayed price (*Thaman mu'ajjal*). Then the seller buys it back from the buyer for a price paid immediately, and the latter price is inferior to the former one' (Badawi 1964, 203). Despite the fact that this transaction represents the clearest case of legal subterfuge (*hila*) to avoid the Riba constraints, eminent jurists, such as Shafi'i have allowed it. There are cases, adds Badawi, in which this kind of sale has been tolerated by the Prophet, 'who knew that prohibiting the sales of dates against dates with an increase (*tafadul*) is premised on the prohibition of Riba an-Nasi'a itself and that this sale is not accepted as a prohibition of means (*saddan lidh-Dhari'a*). But this ...was meant for the purchase of a better kind of dates; the Prophet pointed at the sale of bad (merchandise) against money for the purchase of good merchandise so that the people can acquire what they needed in a way that avoids the means to the forbidden Riba itself, not that he permitted the forbidden by the way of a subterfuge' (Ibid., 203-4).

Badawi adds: against the reading of Shafi'i, most jurists, like Ibn Al-Qayyim and Awza'i, consider bay' al-'ayna to be anathema.

2. *'Bay' al-Wafa''*

This transaction is a sale of a commodity by the buyer on condition that the seller be allowed to get the commodity back upon paying its price. This, says Badawi, is a clear hila, and if some jurists accept it, it is not as they claim a way to avoid Riba, but as a mortgage (*rahn*) contract in which the buyer does not own the commodity and can use it only with the agreement of the true owner, the seller-mortgager.

3. *'Hitt wa Ta'ajjal'*

This transaction operates as a discount operation (*hatita*), which, says Badawi, is quite common in banking. It is admitted in a hadith of the Prophet, though some jurists like Shafi'i have been wary of extending it by analogy to other transations.

4. *'Al-Qard bi-Jarr Manfa'a'*

In Badawi's opinion, this loan for interest is nothing else but Riba, following Sarakhsi and Ghazali. And if some jurists like al-Kasani take a different view, it is because they have wrongly expanded the comparison. For not only is this loan comparable with Riba, 'it is pure Riba, and its essence. It is therefore categorically forbidden per se. This prohibition is a prohibition of ends, not a prohibition of means or a prohibition of excuses' (Ibid., 213).

5. 'Sale with Loan (*Bay' bis-Salaf*), or two transactions in one'

Badawi adopts the definition of the sale with loan, or the 'two transactions in one', from the definition of Sanhuri and Shafi'i. This transaction is in their view a sale premised on either a loan, or on a condition of an other sale, as in 'I sell you this slave for a thousand pounds if you sell me your house for so much'. These transactions are deemed illegal because of Riba, which operates as a destructive underlying cause by introducing uncertainty into the transaction (Ibid., 214-5).

*****

PART TWO

FINANCIAL PERSPECTIVES

THE PROGRESS OF ISLAMIC BANKING: THE CASE OF IRAN AND PAKISTAN

Abbas Mirakhor*
International Monetary Fund

Introduction

Among all the Muslim countries only the Islamic Republics of Iran and Pakistan have attempted to implement Islamic banking on a comprehensive scale. In both cases the decision to do so was marked by a great deal of conviction and courage. The history of economics knows few such actions with wide ranging consequences where the policymakers had so little hard analysis upon which they could base their decisions. While it is true that research into Islamic banking had proceeded since the 1940s, this was not sufficient, either in quality or quantity, to lay the foundation for policy decisions of such magnitude. Nor was Islamic *fiqh*, with its more than a millenium of history, of much help in discerning the economy-wide effects of the adoption of Islamic banking.[1] Fiqh's consideration of *riba* has always had a micro perspective. With very few exceptions (Sadr 1983 for example), the *fuqaha* (jurists) did not consider the macroeconomic implications of removing interest from the banking system and replacing it with modes of finance acceptable to Islam. There were also no historical records or an institutional memory of an Islamic society that had adopted a modern banking system without interest. Even today it is astonishing to realize how little theoretical research is available regarding the full range of issues concerning a financial system in which interest is to

* The author gratefully acknowledges helpful comments and suggestions of Ali Agah, Zubair Iqbal, Mohsin S. Khan, Shoja Nawaz, Ghasem Salehkhou, Iqbal Mehdi Zaidi, and Nawzish Ali Zaidi. The views expressed in this chapter, however, are the author's sole responsibility. They do not necessarily reflect those of the IMF.

[1]A good survey of fiqh's position on riba in English can be found in Saleh's book (1986).

play no role at all. Yet, despite the lack of sufficient theoretical analysis, not only with respect to the consequences of adoption of Islamic banking but also with regard to the types of problems that could be expected in the transition period, there is a great deal of evidence to suggest that a major segment of decision makers in both the Islamic Republics of Iran and Pakistan simply felt that to eliminate interest from the banking system was an Islamic duty. In both countries the policymakers and their advisors were under no illusion that interest and riba could be eliminated from the economy by a mere government edict. They felt that a start had to be made and that the government should take the first step in the direction of changing the banking system.

Any evaluation of the progress of Islamic banking needs to take into account conditions as they existed at the time the decision for adoption was made as well as the multiplicity of constraints currently operating in the two countries. It must also be borne in mind that the judgments of this article are based on its understanding of the economic implications of the rules and injunctions of Islam and it does not attempt to co-opt the jurisdiction of fiqh.

The plan of the chapter is as follows. In section I certain theoretical aspects of Islamic banking are discussed. The intention is to establish a reference point against which the progress of Islamic banking can be measured. Section II discusses the progress of Islamic banking in Iran and Pakistan, while section III contains some concluding remarks.

I. Some Theoretical Considerations on the Adoption of Islamic Banking for the Economy

There is now a general consensus among Muslim economists on the fact that the concept of riba is not restricted to 'usury'. Therefore, the prevailing view is that the Islamic prohibition against riba extends to interest and that the banking system in an Islamic society would violate this prohibition if it allows the use of an interest rate.

At least four characteristics define the prohibited interest rate: (1) it is fixed ex ante; (2) it is tied to the time period and the amount of the loan; (3) its payment is guaranteed; and (4) the state apparatus sanctions and enforces its collection. Islam's position on property rights can assist in providing an economic explanation as to why such a rate is ruled out. Islam recognizes two types of individual claims to property: (a) the property that is a result of the combination of individual's creative labour and natural resources, and (b) the property that is obtained through exchange, remittances of what Islam recognizes as the rights of those less able to utilize society's resources, outright beneficience grants and inheritance. Money represents the monetized claim of its owner to property rights created by assets that were obtained through (a) and/or (b). Lending money is, in effect, a transfer of these rights from the lender to the borrower and all that can be claimed in return for it is its equivalent and no more. Interest on money loaned represents an unjustifiable creation of instantaneous property rights. It is unjustifiable because interest is a property right claimed outside the legitimate framework of individual property rights recognized by Islam, and instantaneous because as soon as the contract for lending upon interest is concluded, a right to the borrower's property is created for the lender, regardless of the outcome of the enterprise for which the money is used (Mirakhor 1986). This property rights argument can also be used to explain Islam's prohibition of bribery, short-weighting, *gharar* (see definition *infra*), *ihtikar* (hoarding), among others, since they all represent unjustifiable and instantaneous property rights claims. Hence, money lent can only receive something in return if in fact it helps to produce additional property.[2]

One implication of the prohibition of interest is that it virtually eliminates all debt financing and debt instruments as they exist in conventional banking. If an Islamic financial system is not to operate on the basis of interest then how can financial transactions take place? Again, fiqh offers a micro-perspective explanation. It basically holds the view that individuals have a wide freedom of contract and as such the contracting parties are free to engage in any transaction unless prohibited by the Shari'a (Mirakhor 1986). This flexibility makes possible a virtually open-ended menu of various modes of financial transactions and instruments. There is nothing to stop the system from creating any contractual form so long as two conditions are met. First, that the contract cannot include any element of riba and second, that it cannot include any element of gharar. The difficulties arise in practice when riba and gharar have to be operationally defined. Although the definition of riba according to fiqh is far broader than interest, the consensus of scholars is that, according to all schools of fiqh, the prohibition against riba includes interest.

As for gharar, it can operationally be defined as a situation in which one of the contracting parties in a transaction is in possession of some information regarding the subject of the contract which is deliberately withheld from the other party. This definition brings gharar very close to the case of assymetric

2 This is also a possible explanation as to why *Qard al Hasana*, the non-interest bearing loan, has been so strongly emphasized in the Qur'an and manifold rewards from God have been promised. The *Shari'a* permits a borrower to repay more than he has borrowed provided that this is not stipulated in the loan contract and that the borrower does so willingly and not as a condition of the loan. (See also Saleh 1986, 41-44.)

information and moral hazard of the modern day contract theory. With few exceptions fiqh did not define, ex ante, the various riba-free methods of transaction available today. The practice was that the contracting parties would decide on a method of transaction; then the fuqaha would rule if that method was permissible. Muslim economists often state that to become Islamic a banking system will have to replace its interest-based transactions by profit sharing arrangements. This is, of course, the economists' inference. The position of fiqh is that no transaction between two contracting parties can have any elements of riba and/or gharar. There are a variety of possible non profit-sharing modes of transaction where these two conditions are absent.

Hence, if a financial system operates primarily with modes which satisfy the stipulated conditions but which are not profit-sharing it follows that from the fiqh's point of view the system is not rendered un-Islamic. Throughout the history of Islamic transactions a variety of methods of contracting were developed which were deemed permissible under the Shari'a Law of Contracts. A majority of these modes were well suited for an agrarian and commercial economy in which projects matured in reasonably short duration. In a modern economy with an industrial sector in which projects have longer gestation periods and where financing of such projects often involves more than two parties there was a need for more suitable riba-free methods.

The ingenuity of Muslim scholars helped devise a way to extend two existing modes of transaction, i.e., *mudaraba* and *musharaka*, to financing of industrial projects and to the banking system.[3]

Once the basic outline of a mudaraba/ musharaka-based banking were defined, the search for their economic implications began. Nearly all Muslim economists who have written on Islamic banking are in agreement that the cornerstone of such a system is profit sharing. It is possible to justify this assertion on the basis of Islam's position on economic justice and property rights and obligations (Mirakhor 1987) as well as on the prohibition of an ex ante fixed rate of return. Thus, for these economists an ideal Islamic financial system is one in which financial resources are primarily allocated on the basis of an expected rate of return and one in which the rewards to those who finance and to those who manage economic projects and enterprises are based on a profit sharing arrangement where only the share parameter is known in advance with certainty.

---

[3] A study of mudaraba and musharaka from an organization theory standpoint awaits the efforts of Islamic theorists and experts in this area. Such a study, particularly on the various forms of musharaka, can be a fruitful contribution to the theory of business organizations.

It is quite possible that in an Islamic society in which Islamic value systems have been internalized by the people and form the basis for preference formation and in which Islamic Law of Contracts is operative, the above ideal situation may, in fact, result. In the transition period, however, when the society is moving from a non-Islamic, or even an anti-Islamic position to an Islamic one, a profit sharing system can lead to perceived or actual difficulties that can only be eradicated by a strong social commitment to create a supportive legal and financial environment.

It can be argued, for example, that one reason for existence and entrenchment of the institution of interest in any economy is that it can effectively minimize monitoring costs and, given government sanction, obviate moral hazard. Additionally, once the lender is assured of repayment, the borrower has a freedom of action without the necessity of divulging all the information in his possession regarding the expected outcome of his venture or the manner in which he intends to carry out his plan of action. Profit sharing, by necessity reduces this freedom on the one hand and increases monitoring costs on the other.

Whereas both the Qur'anic injunctions and the provisions of the Shari'a Law of Contracts assure the absence of moral hazard, the perceptions exist that the present Muslim societies lack the conviction to promote and enforce either. This perception of existence of moral hazard seems to be the single most important cause of the difficulties of the transition period in the implementation of Islamic banking. However, this burden need not be as onerous as it appears. A wide variety of modes of transaction can exist to cover the spectrum between pure forms of profit sharing modes, such as mudaraba and musharaka, and weaker Islamic modes, such as mark-up transactions. All existing modes have been inherited from centuries past and there is no reason why Muslim bankers, economists, and financial experts cannot devise new types of organizational forms, modes of transaction and financial instruments to expand the existing menu and reduce the perception of risk surrrounding musharaka and mudaraba.

One example, which has not received much attention within the Islamic academic community, is the concept of cooperatives. It is a method of business organization whose roots can be found in the very core of Islam. In Iran it has been adopted both as an objective of the restructuring of the economy mandated by the constitution of the Islamic Republic and as a method of enhancing Islamic banking. There the commercial and specialized banks, in their mudaraba and musharaka activities with the private sector give priority to entrepreneurial cooperatives. This not only promotes cooperation in the society but also reduces moral hazard. From the conceptualization of Islamic banking as one in which the assets and liabilities of the system are acquired on profit-sharing basis important propositions are derived. It has been shown that in such a system: (a) 'the real values of assets and liabilities would be equal at all points in time'(Khan 1987b, 11); (b) the 'prospect of instantaneous equilibrium between the asset side of the banking system, deriven mainly by the real sector of the economy and the liability side' means 'that by necessity there must be a close relationship between investment and deposit yields...' (Khan 1987b, 11); (c) 'due to the fact that the return to liabilities will be a direct function of the return to asset portfolios and because assets are created in response to investment opportunities in the real sector, it will be the real sector that determines the rate of return to the financial sector rather than the reverse.' (Khan 1987b, 12); (d) 'adjustment to shocks that result in banking crises and disruptions of the payments mechanism of the country' is more rapid than in the conventional system (Khan 1987b, 31; see also Mirakhor and Zaidi 1988, for an open economy discussion of the adjustment process in an economy adopting Islamic banking); (e) there is no disruption in the intermediation process of the banking system (Iqbal and Mirakhor 1987); (f) savings and investment need not decrease and there are reasons to believe that should certain Islamic injunctions become operative and the Shari'a Law of Contracts adopted, both will increase (Haque and Mirakhor 1987); (g) monetary policy can be used to stabilize the economy both in closed (Khan and Mirakhor 1987) and open economy models (Mirakhor and Zaidi 1988); and finally, (h) in an open economy context, to the extent that borrowed (through profit-sharing modes) external resources are channelled into productive investments, such investments can be expected to generate a stream of returns at least sufficient to repay the associated loans (Mirakhor and Zaidi 1988).

II. Islamic Banking in Iran and Pakistan

Due to the fact that these are the only two countries in that part of the Muslim world that have replaced interest-based banking with Islamic banking it would be tempting and convenient to analyze their progress jointly. The two share many factors in common, but above all they share in the conviction that ultimate solutions to the economic problems of the human society are to be found in a functioning Islamic system. They are committed to the Islamization of the economy.

There are, however, differences in their approach in pursuing their objectives. Heretofore Pakistan's approach has been cautious and deliberate. It took Pakistan some 30 years after its creation to begin to take serious steps toward Islamization of its banking system. Despite this seemingly slow progress, no serious research can question the society's commitment to this objective. As early as a few months after its creation, the objective of Islamization of banking was unequivocally pronounced by the Father of the Nation, Qaid-e A'zam Mohammed Ali Jinnah, on the occasion of the opening of the State Bank of Pakistan on July 1, 1948. The Islamization of the economy as an aspiration to be pursued by the nation was affirmed and given concrete expression in the Objectives Resolution passed by the Constituent Assembly of Pakistan in 1949, thus making Islamization an integral part of the nation's blueprint for its future. The entrenched structural inflexibilities which resulted from a cognitive dissonance in the intervening years, typical of all Muslim societies, has made a goal congruence and thus a consensus on the speed of a national return to its pronounced objectives a slow process.

In Iran on the other hand, the Islamic Revolution, with its sheer momentum, has made the structure of the economy extremely pliable and permitted very rapid progress toward Islamization. Hence, despite the similarities between the two countries, the role and functioning of the government and the economy in general and Islamic banking in particular have been quite different. For these reasons the performance of Islamic banking in Iran and Pakistan will be treated separately in this chapter.

A. The Islamic Republic of Iran

The process of Islamization of the banking system in Iran has gone through three distinct phases since the success of the Revolution. In the first phase (1979-1982), the banking system was nationalized, restructured, and reorganized in order to remove the weakness of the inherited system (Iqbal and Mirakhor 1987). External and internal developments in this phase did not allow the policymakers to develop a coherent plan for the Islamization of the banking system, although various piece-meal attempts were made toward this objective.

The second phase began in 1982 and lasted until 1986. In this phase a legislative and administrative quantum leap was made in adopting and implementing a clearly conceptualized model of Islamic banking. The Law for Riba-free Banking, which was passed in August 1983, gave a deadline of one year to the banks to convert their deposits in line with the Shari'a and required that they Islamize all their operations within three years from the date of passage of the Law. During this phase the central bank was implicitly envisioned as a quasi-independent economic institution similar to that conceptualized in most western banking systems, with a considerable degree of autonomy from the government.

Administratively, the intermediation role of the banking system was given centrality though the central bank exercised extensive control on the operation of individual banks in its regulation and supervisory capacities.

The third and current phase, which began in 1986, promises a role for the banking system different from that in the earlier phases, although still within the framework of the Law for Riba-free Banking. The new change appears to conceptualize the banking system as an integral part of the Islamic government, so that it becomes a direct instrument of governmental policies. Even though this appears to represent a significant change in the role of banking as envisioned earlier, it is well within the framework of the expectations resulting from the turn of political events in Iran in recent years over the role of the government in the economy. The end result of that debate culminated in a recent position taken by Imam Khomeini which seems to have sharply defined the role of an Islamic government within the framework of *Velayat-e Faqih* (Petrossian 1988).[4]

This historic ruling cuts short all debates on the role of the government within the conceptualization of Velayat-e Faqih and makes clear that the government is to be the supreme instrument by which the objectives of Islam for the society are to be achieved. Without violating either the spirit or the letter of the Constitution, or negating the role assigned to the private sector or private property by the Constitution or by the *Sunna* (Life and Teachings) of the Prophet, the ruling leaves to the Majlis (representative assembly) to define the role of the government as well as that of the private sector in the economy (Petrossian 1988). Its immediate effect is to legitimize the trend in the increasingly interventionist posture of the government vis-a-vis the economy and should also hasten legislative action on the definition of private property. Finally, the ruling indirectly affirms the highly activist role of the banking

---

[4] The position referred to was enunciated by the Imam on January 6, 1988 in a letter to the President of the Islamic Republic of Iran. Knowledge of the arguments contained in the Justification of the Velayat-e Faqih is essential to an understanding of the contents of the Imam's letter. The basic arguments were presented in a book entitled, 'Islamic Government,' which has been translated by Hamid Algar (see Imam Khomeni, 1981). Velayat-e Faqih combines the electoral process, the concept of Islamic Shura (consultation) and the guidance of the fuqaha to arrive at the structure of the government responsible for the management of the society.

system in promoting social and economic development which began in phase three.

Much of the trend in the progress of Islamic banking in Iran has been influenced by factors with roots in the pre-revolutionary economic structure as well as post-revolutionary external and internal political developments. The post-revolution economy had inherited a host of difficult economic problems. Before the Revolution, the Iranian economy had become highly dependent on oil revenues as well as on importation of raw materials, intermediate goods and food stuff. The industrial sector was organized without due attention paid to efficiency or comparative advantage and with very weak forward and backward linkages to the rest of the economy. The agricultural sector, which was producing surplus commodities up until the late 1960s, was subjected to ill-suited policies that led to massive migration of farmers into the cities. Poor economic planning, influx of oil revenues, and rapidly increasing government expenditures stimulated the growth of a private sector enjoying import controls, exclusive licences, low interest loans, and low taxes on profits.

The result of these policies was that the Revolution inherited a private sector which had enjoyed monopoly and oligopoly position and had a perception of its role in the economy quite different from that expected under an Islamic system.

The success of the Revolution brought with it additional problems including massive capital flight (Iqbal and Mirakhor 1987), which almost led to the collapse of the banking and financial system. Problems began to multiply for the economy at a rapid pace as the Revolution took root. The economy, already vulnerable to external and internal shocks, was dealt severe blows including the freezing of its foreign assets, economic sanctions, interruptions in production, the influx of nearly two million Afghan refugees, a war, and drastic reductions in oil revenues.

Concurrently, the Constitution of the Islamic Republic specified objectives for the economy to be pursued, such as income redistribution, economic self-sufficiency, strengthening of the agriculture sector, creation of an active cooperative sector, and reduced reliance on oil revenues, all of which required fundamental restructuring of the society's economic behaviour and institutions. Reduction in oil revenues plus the political objective of not relying on external financial sources meant that the banking system would have to play a role far broader than that of pure intermediation.

The banking system was used as an instrument of restructuring the economy, away from services and consumption toward production, in four ways. First, credit to the service sector which constituted some 55 per cent of the GDP was drastically reduced to halt its further expansion in the short run and curtail its size in the medium term (Iqbal and Mirakhor 1987). This policy went into effect during the second phase and has continued ever since. Second, bank credit was directed towards encouraging the growth of the agriculture sector. Several modes of Islamic finance were designed to help farmers improve and expand production. Coupled with substantial government subsidies for seed, fertilizer, machinery, and crop insurance, the credit policy of the banking system has helped reviving the agricultural sector. This policy was initiated during the first phase and strengthened in the later phases. Third, Islamic banking was used to create incentives for the development of a cooperative sector spanning agriculture, industry and trade. Cooperatives were given priority in credit allocation and in direct investment as well as in musharaka financing by the banking sector. This policy received a great impetus in the third phase. Recently, the central bank has devised a plan under which 95-99 per cent of the needed finance, in the form of venture capital, would be provided for industrial cooperatives with innovative ideas. Priority is also given to cooperative ventures with projects which hold the promise of domesticating imported technology. Fourth, the banking system, in partnership with the government, undertakes to finance large industrial projects such as the Mubarakah Steel Project.[5]

As a vehicle for income redistribution, the banking system has been used to provide interest free (Qard al Hasana) loans, to build low-income housing, to provide financing for small scale agro-business and industrial ventures and cooperatives, without stringent collateral requirements. The banking system has also financed government expenditures and deficits, with a view on distributional impact. The pattern of consumption and production has been affected by the banking system not only through reduction of credit to the service sector but also through curtailment of credit to the production of luxury goods and commodities with a large import content, while at the same time credit to the production of necessities and intermediate goods has expanded. It is clear that with a reduction of oil revenues from 27 per cent of the GDP in 1977/78 to only 4 per cent in 1986/87, the banking system has been a major source of finance for achieving many of the social and economic goals of the Islamic Revolution. Moreover all signs indicate that this active role of the banking system will not lose its importance in the medium term.

[5] The Tehran Metro is the latest example of large scale social overhead capital investment projects in which the commercial banks undertook a joint financing responsibility alongside the government.

Table l. - Islamic Republic of Iran: Position of Banking System vis-a-vis Private Sector, March 1984- March 1986

In billions of Iranian Rials

	March 1984	March 1985	March 1986
Private sector deposits	5600.6	5918.3	7960.2
Sight	1955.8	2509	3168.6
Non-sight	3644.8	3409.3	4791.6
Old	3644.8	1087.9	258.3
Savings	2737.3	716.7	--
Time	907.5	371.2	--
New	--	2321.4	4533.3
Qard al-Hasana	--	780.0	940.6
Term investment			
Short-term	--	914.2	2477.0
Long-term	--	627.2	1115.7
Credit to private sector	4256.6	4500.7	5763.5
Loans and credits (old)	4256.6	3746.0	2938.9
Commercial Banks	2819.2	2288.4	1795.3
Specialized Banks	1437.4	1457.6	1143.6
New facilities	--	754.7	2824.6
Commercial Banks	--	583.5	2068.6
Specialized Banks	--	171.2	756.0

Source: Bank Markazi

Tables 1 and 2 shed light on the performance of Islamic banking in the last three years of its operation. Table 1 provides information on the liability side of banking and shows that the old interest-based deposits have been rapidly converted to the new Islamic modes. The size of the deposits in Islamic modes doubled between 1985 and 1986. Both long term and short term investment deposits showed a much more rapid growth (growth rates of 79 and 170 per cent respectively) than the Qard al Hasana deposits which increased 21 per cent over the same period. The growth of the deposit side was not only due to the acceptance of Islamic banking by the population, but also to the rapid expansion of banking in the rural areas. According to the Central Bank of the Islamic Republic, 975 new branches opened in the rural area in 1986/87.

These areas had little or no access to the banking system previously. Further expansion of the banking system into the rural areas is planned and the policymakers hope that much of the 60,000 existing villages can be provided with access to banking facilities in the medium term.

Table 1 also indicates that credit to the private sector using the new Islamic facilities increased from IRls 754.7 billion to IRls 2,824.6 billion between March 1985 to March 1986, nearly quadrupling its size in one year while the old interest-based facilities declined by 22 per cent over the same period.

Table 2 shows the asset side of the banking system. In the previous full year of the operation of Islamic banking (1984-85) concern was expressed that weaker Islamic modes of financing had been given greater emphasis than profit-sharing modes (Iqbal and Mirakhor 1987). The 1985/86 data shows some improvements in the asset acquisition behaviour of the banking system. The rate of growth of short term debt purchases, i.e. the purchase of debt documents of less than 12 months maturity issued against real goods, was reduced by 50 per cent. Legal partnerships, i.e., long term profit-sharing arrangements, increased by 1.6 per cent. Direct investment increased by 2 per cent. Short term transactions such as instalment sales increased by 1.7 per cent, while *salaf* transactions maintained its previous rate.

The exhibited slow trend (Table 2) toward greater utilization of profit-sharing arrangements can be expected to continue in the short run for three reasons:

First, the entrepreneurs have not been educated to the realities of government priorities and the full potentials of profit sharing modes of Islamic finance. In the old system an entrepreneur could obtain interest based financing with sufficient collateral provisioning. Many entrepreneurs do not seem to realize that they can submit cooperative project proposals for funding on a profit-sharing basis, often without stringent collateral requirements.

The second reason is an environment of uncertainty in the Iranian economy. This is mainly due to the war. But it was also caused by the policy of the government towards the private sector. The behaviour of the private sector before and immediately after the Revolution as well as expropriations and nationalizations undertaken by the government have created some tension between the government and the private sector. The present economic policymakers have on occasion questioned the motives of the private sector and it was perhaps this apprehension that prompted the government to set up its own distribution centres shortly after the war, despite the almost legendary distributional efficiency of the Iranian bazars. On the other hand, the private sector has, for some time now, been asking for clear-cut guidance and a legislative mandate specifying the role and scope of the private sector permissible under the Constitution.

Given the war and a hostile international economic environment, many of the government regulations and rulings affecting the private sector, e.g., price-quantity control regulations, import-export policies, and exchange rate regulations, were designed on a short term basis and appeared to the private sector incoherent and at times even contradictory. This has lead the private sector, in turn, to initiate very short term trade and commercial projects with quick payoffs. Although it has a constitutional mandate to do so, the legislature has been unable to forge a consensus on the rights and responsibilities of private property as well as the role of the private sector in the economy. The new ruling by Imam Khomeini (Petrossian 1988) should clear the way for the Majlis to remove this barrier and allow the private sector to make long term plans.

Table 2. Islamic Republic of Iran: Breakdown of New Banking Facilities, March 1985-March 1986

In billions of Iranian rials

	March 1985	In Per cent of Total	March 1986	In Per cent of Total
Lease Purchase	27.9	3.7	22.1	0.8
Installment sale	247.5	32.8	973.8	34.5
Civil Partnership	109.1	14.5	384.2	13.6
Mudaraba	134.6	17.8	508.3	18.0
Salaf transactions	26.8	3.6	99.8	3.5
Ju'ala	2.4	0.3	35	1.3
Legal partnership	37.0	4.9	182.3	6.5
Direct Investment	4.4	0.6	74.4	2.6
Other	1.6	0.2	46.2	1.6
Total transactions affecting profit of investment deposits	591.3	78.3	2326.7	82.4
Debt purchasing	85.0	11.3	176.5	6.2
Qard al-Hasana	78.4	10.4	321.4	11.4
Total transactions not affecting profit of investment deposits	163.4	21.7	497.9	17.6
Total transactions	754.7	100.0	2824.6	100.0

Source: Bank Markazi

The third reason for the slow growth of Islamic profit sharing financing is embedded in the structure of the banking system in Iran. Currently there are six commercial banks and three specialized banks. The three specialized banks existed prior to the Revolution. They are well equipped for the task of project analysis and monitoring which is a necessary requirement in Islamic banking. The Islamic Banking Law authorized the commercial banks to engage in profit-sharing financing as well. But it will take considerable time before the commercial banks are able to develop the necessary expertise to engage in such financing. In the meantime, only the commercial banks are permitted to attract deposits. This creates a financing problem for specialized banks. For instance, the Bank of Industry and Mines is one of the specialized banks with a history of financing long and medium-term industrial projects on a profit-sharing basis. Yet, this bank is unable to obtain sufficient resources to meet the demand of the entrepreneurs for profit sharing.

As can be seen from Table 1, in 1985 the specialized banks were allocated about 23 per cent of the total banking credit. This amount increased by about 4 per cent in 1986. Although there are no data available on the breakdown of credit allocation to each of the three specialized banks, casual observation suggests that because of the central role which the Agricultural Bank and the Housing Bank have been assigned in reviving the agricultural sector and in providing low income housing respectively, the Bank of Industry and Mines may have not received enough credit expansion to fund industrial projects. Moreover, because the banking system is financing government deficits, the fixed rate of return on government financing establishes a floor for the commercial banks' rate of return which makes them reluctant to provide their excess liquidity to the Bank of Industry and Mines on the basis of profit sharing with an unknown rate of return.[6]

---

[6] It is rather odd that the Bank of Industry and Mines is not permitted to attract investment deposits on profit-sharing basis, even though nearly all of this Bank's projects are financed on the basis of expected rates of return that could permit it to offer its depositors reasonable rewards. This Bank could play a crucial role in investment and capital formation in the transition period while the commercial banks are building up their inventory of expertise in portfolio management, and in the evaluation and monitoring of industrial investment projects.

B. The Islamic Republic of Pakistan

Although there is no recent data (the latest figures go back to 1985) on the assets and liabilities of the banking system in Pakistan, all available evidence suggests that the adoption and implementation of Islamic banking has not disturbed the process of intermediation, bank liquidity and safety, and the effectiveness of monetary policy. An expressed intention of the designers of the process of Islamization of banking was to leave the structure of banking in Pakistan unchanged and to merely take steps to ensure that all modes of financial transactions within the system were non-interest based (see CII Report 1983).

The implication is that, unlike the banking system in Iran the intermediation role of the banking system was kept intact in Pakistan. It was also foreseen that the Islamization process would be undertaken in phases, allowing a deliberate and cautious move on the part of the policymakers and the bankers toward full Islamization. The liability side of the banking system quickly converted to Islamic modes (Iqbal 1987), demonstrating depositor acceptance of Islamic modes of non-interest bearing deposits. The asset side, however, has shown a much slower pace of Islamization. A high percentage of the assets of the banking system are concentrated on short-term, trade-related modes rather than on the more authentic Islamic modes of musharaka and mudaraba (Iqbal and Mirakhor 1987). Although the weaker Islamic modes are permissible under the Shari'a, they do not carry with them the positive aspects of profit-sharing modes, e.g., incentives for longer-term investment projects that can enhance capital formation and economic development.

It has been suggested (Iqbal 1987) that the bias in the asset acquisition of the banking system toward short-term trade financing is the result of the risk-averse posture of the policymakers and bankers in the Islamization process. As the banking system continues to shun profit- sharing modes and finances short-term commercial and trade-related projects, longer-term investment projects look elsewhere for funding. Given the shallow nature of capital markets, this means either disintermediation or, worse, capital starvation for industrial projects. Professional bankers believe that so long as the business community does not adopt Islamic ethical norms, the monitoring costs of profit-sharing projects will remain expensive, as they are subject to high moral hazard (Iqbal and Mirakhor 1987).

A suggested remedy is the adoption of the Shari'a Law of Contracts by the legal system so that bank contracts with enterprises can become legal documents presentable in court. At present, the disputes arising between banks and their clients can be presented in 12 Shari'a Tribunals for settlement. The assessment is that neither the number nor the perceived functions of these courts will allow for speedy settlement, thus placing a premium on non-compliance and default (Iqbal and Mirakhor 1987).

There is a further danger of disintermediation as it relates to the rate of return structure within the banking system. It was pointed out earlier that in Islamic banking the rate of return in the real sector becomes the instrument of financial resource allocation in the economy. By implication, if an Islamic banking system is looked upon as a pure intermediary, then the assets and liabilities of the banking system are acquired in a way that reflects the existing structure of real rates of return in various sectors of the economy. In that case, the rate of return to deposits will reflect the profit-earning capacity of the banking system. If for any reason this does not occur, the absence of the latter will lead to disintermediation; and the absence of the former will generate the misallocation of resources. Perhaps a tentative hypothesis regarding the efficiency of the intermediation role of Islamic banking is that in the long run the rate of return to the banking system is the same as that to the depositors plus the cost of intermediation; and that once Islamic banking has been implemented these two rates should eventually approach one another asymptotically. It is a fair argument that neither the length of time nor the existing constraints will allow the convergence of these two rates in the short-run. Moreover, detailed data on the rates of return on all modes of assets and liabilities acquisition are unavailable.

Nonetheless, Tables 3 and 4 provide information on the rates of return on equity and on PLS saving deposits of five commercial banks and can be used as proxies for the rate of return to the banks and to depositors in order to allow an assessment, albeit incomplete, of the present and future prospects of the intermediation role of the banking system in Pakistan.

Table 3. Rates of Return on PLS Saving Deposits
Nationalized Commercial Banks in Pakistan 1981-1986

Bank	Dec. 1981	Dec. 1982	Dec. 1983	Dec. 1984	Dec. 1985	Dec. 1986
Allied Bank	8.50	8.00	7.00	8.55	7.00	7.10
Habib Bank	9.00	8.50	8.50	7.25	7.80	7.30
Muslim Commercial Bank	9.00	8.50	7.25	8.15	7.70	7.10
National Bank	8.50	8.00	7.25	9.00	7.80	7.30
United Bank	8.50	8.00	8.50	7.10	7.0	6.50
Average	8.70	8.20	7.70	8.01	7.46	7.06

Source: Zaidi 1987, 3.

Table 4. Rates of Return on Equity Nationalized Commercial Banks in Pakistan 1981-1986

Bank	1981	1982	1983	1984	1985	1986
Allied Bank	10.40	12.92	14.75	14.79	15.34	17.92
Habib Bank	43.79	44.80	39.60	37.79	30.01	26.71
Muslim Commercial Bank	26.46	32.29	28.13	24.95	19.82	18.27
National Bank	14.23	17.75	19.18	20.14	20.51	18.43
United Bank	15.90	17.82	19.14	28.95	15.54	14.13
Average	22.16	25.12	24.16	25.32	20.24	19.09

Source: Zaidi 1987, 6.

As can be observed from these tables, the trends in the average rates of return seem to correspond to one another but there are some features of these tables worth noting. First, the large variation which exists among the rates of profits of the banks (Table 4) is not reflected in the rates of return on PLS deposits (Table 3).

Under normal circumstances, if the banks would be allowed to pay rates of return to depositors commensurate with their own profits, deposits would shift from low-rate banks to high-rate banks. The only condition is that the rate differentials should be high enough to cover search and other costs of switching deposits from one bank to another. Regulation of the banking system in Pakistan has been designed to pre-empt large shifts of deposits within the banking system in order to maintain stability. Thus, the competitive edge among the banks in attracting deposits does not hinge on the economic performance of the banks in the short or medium term.

The second noticeable feature of the table is the fact that the trends in the profit rates of the individual bank are generally not reflected in the rates of return to their depositors. The profit rates of Allied Bank, for example, show an increasing trend while the rate of return to its depositors shows the reverse. Perhaps a positive feature of the rate of return regulation is that it has ameliorated the potential fluctuations in the rate of return to depositors. The profit rates of the Habib Bank, for example, show a decline of 17.08 per cent between 1981 and 1986 while the rate of return to its depositors reveals a decline of 1.7 per cent.

Nevertheless, if a salient feature of an Islamic banking system is that the rate of return to depositors is an efficient signalling device for the rate of return to the real sector as well as the productivity and efficiency of individual banks, this is so far not clearly reflected in the performance of the banking system. If the rate of return on equity (Table 4) of the banks is taken as a proxy of the rate of return to the economy as a whole, then the performance of the banking system so far indicates that if Islamic banking is allowed to operate properly and the depositors are permitted to share in the profits of the banks as partners, there is sufficient incentive for the expansion of the banking system as well as an enhancement of its intermediation role. The tightly regulated environment at the present, however, does not allow the market realities to be reflected in the rates of return.

One analyst has recently observed that 'the State Bank of Pakistan has specified ranges of profits ostensibly to guide banks and specialized institutions in their lending operations. Presumably, estimated rates of profitability arising out of different modes serves as a basis for determining these ranges. In effect, the role of the market in determining risk-reward relativities has been limited' (Iqbal 1987).

Consequently, both the rates of return to the banking system and to the depositors are fundamentally and heavily influenced by regulation, rather than by market information. Given this reality, it is a rational reaction on the part of the bankers to choose minimum-risk modes of financing that will not be effective in promoting efficient resource allocation and economic development and, in the long run, Islamic banking. It has been suggested (Zaidi 1987) that the present situation can be improved upon by the revision of profit-sharing formulas and the weighting system which regulate the rate of return to the banks and their depositors. Perhaps a further step could be to allow the formulas to become more sensitive to interbank competition and market realities by introducing into them a weighted index of banks' profit performance.

Although improvements in the existing formulas may make the functioning of the rates of return as a resource allocation mechanism more efficient, the most serious challenge to the intermediation role of Islamic banking in Pakistan is government borrowing. At present, the government borrows directly from the public at predetermined rates higher than the banks pay on their PLS deposits. Moreover, lending to the government is perceived to be less risky. For these reasons disintermediation is a likely outcome threatening the proper functioning of Islamic banking.

Concluding Remarks

The experiences of Iran and Pakistan have shown that the adoption of Islamic banking has not led to the collapse of the banking and financial system as some had feared. On the contrary, the quick acceptance of the system by the public, as reflected in the rapid growth of the private sector deposits in Islamic modes in both countries has demonstrated the potential effectiveness of Islamic banking in mobilizing financial resources in all Islamic countries. The asset side, however, has not shown a tendency toward rapid conversion to profit-sharing modes of Islamic finance in either country, due, in large part to the policy stances of the authorities.

Despite their similarities, the models of banking followed in the two countries have features which sharply differentiate the path of progress of the two systems. This difference can be mostly attributed to the role of government and central banking in the two countries. In Pakistan, Islamic banking was adopted and implemented in a manner that leaves the intermediation role of the banking system undisturbed. In Iran, in contrast, the banking system is looked upon as a powerful instrument of achieving the goals and objectives which the Islamic Revolution mandates for the economy. In Pakistan the progress of Islamic banking has been constrained by an interrelated network of elements, the roots of which, it is argued, lie in the lack of operating Islamic ethical norms in the business environment. This chapter argued that if Islamic banking is adopted solely to play an intermediation role, then the only effective instrument allowing it to perform this function efficiently is the structure of the rates of return signals emitted by the real sector of the economy. It follows that the financial sector must be allowed reasonably free and efficient access to the market so that it can receive proper expected rate of return signals.

Similarly, the banking system must be allowed a relatively unconstrained opportunity to translate these signals into rates of return to its depositors. If allowed to operate freely, but within an Islamic framework where the Shari'a Law of Contracts and Islamic economic behavioural injunctions are operative, Islamic banking could efficiently allocate the financial resources of the society to ensure economic progress.

The regulating posture of the policymakers toward Islamic banking in Pakistan has been marked by a great deal of caution. The banking community has also shown a reluctance to engage in medium or long-term industrial financing on a profit-sharing basis. Islamic banking in Pakistan appears to be at a crucial crossroads and its further progress requires greater commitment, by all involved, to changing the environment in which it must operate. If Islamic banking is to play its intermediation role efficiently, then the regulatory, legal, and economic conditions must be such that the financial system will have a fair chance to perform as expected. If the only modes of Islamic financing continue to remain short-term trade transactions, e.g., via mark-up, then the rates of return to the banks and the depositors may begin to show a downward trend because of the diminishing marginal productivity in short-term trade markets as they slowly become saturated with financing. Moreover, as has been pointed out, emphasis on short-term financing will have inimical effects on investment, capital formation, and economic development.

In Iran the adoption of Islamic banking has had both a different set of objectives and different course of progress than in Pakistan. Three distinct phases of this progress have been identified. Each phase meant a quantum jump in utilization of the banking system to achieve the mandated economic goals of the Revolution and each phase was prompted by impatience of the public and the authorities with the pace of Islamization. It is probable, for example, that during the second phase, government policymakers have been irked by the semi-autonomous and quasi-independent status of the banking system. And in the third phase, the line of demarcation establishing the previous status for the banking system has become blurred as the banking system was integrating rapidly with the rest of the Government. As such, the banking system is being perceived not only as the major source of financial resources to underwrite the goverment's fiscal deficits, but also as an effective tool in pursuance of Islamic economic objectives such as the modifications and shifts in the pattern of consumption, investment, and production behaviour in the economy as well as in restructuring and in redistribution of income.

This trend implies that market rates of return do not constitute strong imperatives in providing resource allocation signals for the banking system. If there is a rate of return which is used as a guideline in allocating financial resources, it must be the policymakers' perception of some long-run social marginal productivity of the projects. Perhaps for this reason the rates of return to the deposits are determined arbitrarily, but they are so ex post, and cannot reflect the actual rates of return to the real sector. However, since financial resources are allocated to projects whose long-run social benefits outweigh their shorter run and purely economic marginal productivity (e.g., expanded credit availability to the agricultural sector, government cooperatives, and social overhead capital), the rates of return to the depositors will have to be less than if resources were allocated to projects with higher and more immediate rates of return. Hence, the private sector deposits, in effect, subsidize projects that in the policymakers' view have important social benefits. Clearly, a more efficient portfolio management of the banking system can be helpful in reducing this burden on the present generation of the depositors if the policymakers could, through planning, identify and prioritize projects which in their view need to be financed. They would then allow the banking system to allocate its remaining resources according to the rate of return prevailing in the real sector.

A high degree of ideological consensus and faith in Islam has brought the society to bear enormous sacrifices to ensure the survival and growth of the Islamic system in Iran against extremely heavy odds. The particular model of Islamic banking employed in Iran has institutionalized the degree of commitment of the economy and the people to the goals of Islam. It will take some time before the objectives pursued, e.g., the creation of a cooperative sector in the economy, materialize and bear fruit. Since Islamic banking is an integral part of the process of goal pursuance, its progress cannot be fully judged at the present. What is certain is that the conventional criteria, even those that can be derived from theoretical analyses of Islamic banking now available, cannot be applied to the case of Iran. The model presently used in Tehran has its own logic and must develop its own criteria to judge the performance of the banking system. The economic implications of the Velayat-e Faqih has not yet fully crystalized. Thus far, neither government policy nor legislative actions to implement the programs of the Velayat-e Faqih have been of much help in clarifying the economic role of the government and that of the private sector. The recent ruling of Imam Khomeini should permit the emergence of a clear consensus on these issues.

One problem which both the Islamic Republics of Iran and Pakistan share, and which has significantly influenced the performance of Islamic banking, is the intractability of financing government deficits through the financial system via a predetermined rate of return. This process has generally had an adverse effect on the performance of Islamic banking in both countries because the fixed rate of return establishes a 'floor' and a point of reference against which all expected rates of return will be measured.

This problem is more acute in Pakistan than in Iran. In Iran the government borrows solely from the banking system at rates lower than those paid by banks to their depositors. In Pakistan, in contrast, the government borrows directly from the public at rates higher than paid-on PLS deposits of the banks. The risk-adjusted differential in the two rates is high enough to attract deposits away from the banking system and leads to a much greater threat of disintermediation. Since Islamization of banking in Pakistan was meant to strengthen its intermediation role, this government policy is undoubtedly harmful to the Islamization process. The intractability of the problem stems from the fact that it occurs at a point of conjunction for monetary and fiscal policies in an Islamic economy.

Unlike Islamic banking, there has been so far no consensus among Muslim economists as to the role of fiscal policy or as to a menu of fiscal policy measures appropriate for a modern Islamic economic system. In fact, there has been very little theoretical study of the fiscal policy of Islam. The meagre works available have concentrated mainly on Zakat as the principal fiscal measure. And even on this issue there is debate as to the exact nature of 'Zakatable' sources and the potential revenue capacity of an Islamic state (Ariff 1982). Muslim economists are divided as to whether Islam imposes a revenue or an expenditure constraint, or both, on an Islamic government.

Within the conceptualization of the Velayat-e Faqih model of an Islamic society, however, issues are far clearer; once the government decides what it must do to achieve the economic goals of Islam, it has the power and the responsibility to raise revenue through taxation if its own revenue resources are insufficient. In other models also, the role and objectives of the Islamic society are reasonably well defined (Ariff 1982), and closely correspond to those in the Velayat-e Faqih model. But in these other models, the government's role in pursuing the economic objectives of Islam for the society is, directly or indirectly, revenue constrained.

There are additional developments in Iran which should reduce the government's reliance on the banking system, such as new tax legislation and a rapid increase in non-oil exports. At present, the population makes considerable contribution to the war expenditure voluntarily and outside the government budget by providing cash, goods, and services directly to the armed forces, through the *Masajed* (Mosques), or by taking supplies directly to the front. But the war effort also requires a major financial commitment from the government's budget. Once the war is ended, the budget deficits may not be as great a burden on the banking system as they are presently. This conclusion is reinforced by the fact that, even with the war and declining oil revenues, the deficit has been reduced from 14 per cent of GDP in 1980/81 to 4 per cent in 1985/86. Thus, it is likely that the financing of the deficits will be much less of a problem for Islamic banking in Iran in the future than in Pakistan.

The general conclusion which can be derived from the study of Iran and Pakistan is that Islamic banking is a powerful instrument of mobilizing the financial resources of an Islamic society. However, because government policies in Iran and Pakistan strongly influence the asset acquisition behaviour of the banking system, it is far more difficult to judge, on the basis of the banking system's performance to date, the efficiency of Islamic banking in allocating mobilized resources.

* * * * *

References

Ahmad K. 1980, *Studies in Islamic economics*, The Islamic Foundation, London.

Ahmad Z. 1984, *Concepts and Models of Islamic Banking: An Assessment*, presented at the Seminar on Islamization of Banking, Karachi.

Ahmad Z. 1987, 'Interest-Free Banking in Pakistan', *Journal of Islamic Banking and Finance,* Vol.4 No. 1, p 8-30.

Ahmad Z. et al. 1983, *Money and Banking in Islam,* Institute for Policy Studies, Islamabad.

Ariff M. 1982, *Monetary and Fiscal Economies of Islam,* International Center for Research in Islamic Economics, Jeddah.

Bank Markazi Jomhouri Islami Iran 1983, *The Law for Usury/Interest-free-Banking,* Tehran.

Chapra M. U. 1985, *Towards a Just Monetary System,* The Islamic Foundation, London.

CII (Council on Islamic Ideology) 1983, 'Report on Elimination of Interest', in Ahmad Z. et al..

Haque N. U. & Mirakhor A. 1987, 'Saving Behavior in an Economy without Fixed Interest', in Khan M. S. and Mirakhor A., *Theoretical Studies on Islamic Banking and Finance,* The Institute for Research and Islamic Studies, Houston.

Haque N. U. & Mirakhor A. 1987, 'Optimal Profit-Sharing Contracts and Investment in an Interest-Free Islamic Economy', in Khan M.S. and Mirakhor A., *Theoretical Studies on Islamic Banking and Finance*, op. cit..

Iqbal Z. & Mirakhor A. 1987, *Islamic Banking,* International Monetary Fund, Washington, D.C..

Iqbal Z. 1987, 'Islamization of Banking in the Islamic Republic of Iran and in Pakistan', paper presented at the International Institute of Islamic Economics, Islamabad.

Khan M. S. 1987 a, 'Islamic Interest-Free Banking: A Theoretical Analysis' in Khan M. S. and Mirakhor A., *Theoretical Studies on Islamic Banking and Finance*, op. cit..

Khan M. S. 1987 b, 'Principles of Monetary Theory and Policy in an Islamic, Framework', paper presented at the International Institute of Islamic Economics, Islamabad.

Khan M. S. & Mirakhor A. 1987, 'The Financial System and Monetary Policy in an Islamic Economy', in Khan M. S. and Mirakhor A., *Theoretical Studies on Islamic Banking and Finance*, op. cit..

Khomeini, Imam R. 1981, *Islam and Revolution*, Algar H. tr., Mizan Press, Berkeley.

Mirakhor A. 1986, 'Some Theoretical Aspects of an Islamic Financial System', paper presented at the First International Seminar on Islamic Banking, Bank Markazi, Tehran.

Mirakhor A. 1987, 'The Economic System in an Islamic Society', *Middle East Insight*, Vol. V No 3, pp 32-46.

Mirakhor A. & Zaidi I. 1988, 'Stabilization and Growth in an Open Islamic Economy', unpublished, International Monetary Fund, Washington, D.C. An earlier version of this paper was presented in a seminar in the International Institute of Islamic Economics, 1987, Islamabad.

Petrossian V. 1988, 'Khomeini Opens the Way for Economic Reform', *MEED*, Vol. 32 No. 3, p 10.

Sadr M. B. 1983, *Al Bank Al-la Ribawi Fil-Islam* (The Non-Interest Bank in Islam), Dar At-Ta'aruf, Beirut. Originally published in 1969.

Saleh N. 1986, *Unlawful Gain and Legitimate Profit in Islamic Law*, Cambridge University Press, London.

Zaidi N. A. 1987, 'Profit Rates Policy for PLS Depositors', *Journal of Islamic Banking and Finance*, Vol.4, No 4.

*****

CURRENT THOUGHT ON ISLAMIC TAXATION A CRITICAL SYNTHESIS

Munir Morad
Centre of Near and Middle Eastern Studies, SOAS

Introduction

The object of this chapter is to assess the current debate over Islamic taxation. The relevant issues will be examined in the light of *fiqh*, jurisprudence, and the relatively new concept of Islamic economics. The chapter's main argument is derived from the following question: has Islam already provided a comprehensive model of taxation applicable in modern times, or should Islam's role be restricted to offering the moral base from which Muslim governments will draw their fiscal and tax policies ?

Throughout Islamic history, taxes have constituted a powerful means of governmental manipulation. They have therefore always commanded a special position in the body politic of the state. But tax funds did not invariably act to support the functions of the state. In times of mounting opposition, religious levies also found their way to fund insurrection (Ismail 1973, 131). The downfall of the Shah's regime in Iran was accelerated by the religious levies which were increasingly used for revolutionary measures.

As a rule, however, the willingness and scrupulousness of the populace to pay its taxes are a reflection of the loyalty of the taxpayer to the receiving authority. It demonstrates a recognition of the ruler's legitimacy. Indeed, the collapse of the taxation *modus operandi* is seen as one of the salient reasons for the ruin of the Abbasid state in the middle of the thirteenth century. The cost of financing the army rose beyond the economic means of the state, and the consequent tax extortion led to additional dues imposed on the public, which often surpassed regular taxes (Lokkegaard 1950, 92-93; see also Ibn Khaldun 1958, I, 49).

Before discussing Islamic taxation proper, this chapter addresses the evolution of the concept of Islamic economics. A section on fiqh then highlights jurisprudential development and some of its dialectical qualities which are relevant to the debate over a modern Islamic economy. The next section discusses *zakat*, the main form of religious taxation. The term will be used in its broadest sense, to include other levies postulated by Islam. The use of the word synonymously with taxation largely arises from the emphasis in contemporary Islamic economic literature on zakat as a comprehensive framework for taxation in fiscal studies. But many areas are yet to be defined in the emerging fiscal debate among Islamic economists, and they will be presented in section IV. The closing section of the chapter will sum up the arguments and propose a set of possible outcomes for the future development of Islamic taxation.

I. The Debate over Islamic Economics

Islamic economics does not qualify as an independent science. No 'Islamic economy' has yet fully developed, and the history of Islam provides few precedents on which Muslim scholars can test their hypotheses and base their theories. In the words of a pioneer of Islamic economics, 'the birth of Islamic economics could not be rightly proclaimed until an Islamic economy has found expression in the society,...or until a methodical examination of past economic experience has been carried out' (Sadr 1979, 334).

As far as modern economies are concerned, traditional Islam has in the words of Sadr left an area of vacuum, *mintaqat faragh*, for the legitimate authorities to contend with, through a process of *ijtihad* (original thinking) and *ikhtiyar* (discretion). Islamic economics, at the present stage, can therefore only be described as a *madhhab* (doctrine, belief), and not as *'ilm* (science) (Ibid., 478, 400-404, 416).[1] In describing, as some scholars do, the developing discipline as 'meta-economics', the emphasis on the human and moral qualities of an Islamic economy has been suggested (Faruqi 1973, 1-8). But the terminological difficulty reflects the uncertainty in the intellectual battle launched to base a modern economic theory on the teachings of Islam.

At the heart of Islam's economic philosophy is the concept of *istikhlaf* (relegation).[2] It encompasses the divine appointment of man by the Creator as His khalifa (trustee, successor) to take charge of earth and its resources: 'And He it is Who has made you successors in the land' (Qur'an, VI:166); 'And spend out of what He made you to be successors of ' (Qur'an, LVII: 7). Therefore, although Islam recognizes the right to ownership, wealth is expected to perform a social role regulated by Islamic injunctions (Hasab

[1] Although the word ikhtiyar has been used by Sadr, he has employed the word *Dhatiyya*, subjectivity, more often. The preference may not be entirely accidental, since Dhatiyya emphasizes the theoretical nature of Islamic economics.

[2] Istikhlaf should not be confused with *khilafa,* caliphate.

1981, 28-31). The Islamic economy is answerable to the stipulations of Allah as manifested in the Qur'an and in the other sources of the Shari'a.

For the economy to qualify as Islamic, it must fulfil three criteria: dual ownership (where the private and public sectors can operate); limited economic freedom (through a defined measure of state intervention); and social justice, which must guarantee a fair distribution of resources within the Muslim community (Sadr 1979, 215). Public good and social balance are the two main objects of the economy, but realism (*waqi'iyya*) is also stressed as a means of differentiating Islam's mode of distribution from the other idealistic models such as communism (Ibid., 305). Poverty and wealth can coexist in a Muslim society.

Islam's emphasis on the spiritual aspects of the problem of poverty, however, has not prevented Muslim economists from exploring the possibility of a fiscal system capable of accommodating social welfare. The system's main objective would consist in securing what has come to be called solidarity (*takaful*) (Gammal 1980, 321-333). But although solidarity through taxation has turned into a leitmotiv of modern Islamic economic writings, it is doubtful that the traditional forms of taxation, and especially zakat, are sufficient to meet the demands of a state charged with expanded public welfare responsibilities (Ariff 1982, 17). No Muslim country, including the relatively rich oil states of the Gulf, has succeeded in establishing a welfare system of the calibre of those operated in developed countries.

Criticism of Western schools of economic thought has provided the emerging discipline with its main intellectual challenge. Muslim economists are particularly critical of what they see as the deterministic aspects of the modern science of economics, and the final nature of its rulings. In this logic, Islamic economics 'rectifies this error. Taking human volition into account, it seeks to guide man in the light of Islamic injunctions and to orient man's economic attitudes towards the Islamic ends and ideals'. The role of the Muslim economist must accordingly be that of 'building bridges between the is and the ought' (Siddiqi 1981, 69-70).

It is then not surprising that Islamic economics have remained highly theoretical, as Muslim economists tend to operate from an academic platform. The contributions to the literature have grown rapidly, but the writings of the majority of Muslim economists often strike an idealistic chord and remain preoccupied with theoretical arguments. Full employment, no inflation, and an optimum rate of economic growth are promised (Chapra 1985, 34-44), however incompatible these goals may appear in the practice of complex industrialized economies.

The major source of difficulty confronting Muslim theoreticians today lies in the fact that the practical value of Islamic economics is restricted by the absence of adequate antecedents, and the limited scope of empirical research. This situation was summed up by the editor of a major collection of papers in the field: 'Since we are still in the process of crystallizing Islamic economic postulates, the scope for empirical research appears to be rather limited at the present stage of development of Islamic economics, which is highly theoretical' (Ariff, 23).

Efforts at establishing a concrete discipline of Islamic economics have also been delayed by theological arguments about the validity of the discipline when it operates outside the laid boundaries of fiqh. The theological strata of the Muslim world are very reluctant to accept such a sensitive area of human activity as the economy to grow into an independent branch of studies.[3] The *'ulama* (the jurists of the clergy), as well as the state apparati may never recognize Islamic economics unless and until the discipline's rulings are sanctioned by fiqh (Sadr, 308-316). The study of economics and taxation in Islam requires the relevant fiqh provisions to be examined first.

II. The Role of Fiqh

There are four major schools of fiqh in the Muslim Sunni world: Maliki, Hanbali, Shafi'i, and Hanafi. Though traditionally considered outside the orthodoxy, and in the wake of the rapprochement between Sunnis and Shi'is throughout the twentieth century, some Shi'i 'ulama have tended to classify the Shi'i Imami fiqh as a fifth, Ja'fari school (Mughniyya 1977). Since many of the pioneers of Islamic economics are Shi'i,[4] it is important to include their contributions in this survey.[5]

[3] Criticism is often exchanged between the *fuqaha* and the Muslim economists over the issue of the authority to influence economic policy. According to one economist, 'we have great respect for jurists who have made great contributions and we look to them for guidance, but to blindly follow the sayings and rulings of some of the fuqaha would lead us to great errors', (Ahmed, Iqbal and Khan 1983, 1955)

[4] The most notable example was Muhammad Baqer as-Sadr (died 1980), who wrote, in addition to *Iqtisaduna* , 'Our Economy'(1979), another important book on economics, *Al-Bank al-la Ribawi fil-Islam* , 'The non-usurious bank in Islam'(1981). Although his treatment of the issues discussed in both books were highly theoretical, his *ijtihad* (original thinking) in economic theory was received favourably by scholars from the Shi'i as well as from the Sunni communities. In *Al-Bank al-la*

Fiqh has undergone several distinct developments since the rise of Islam. Initially, the individuals charged with administrative or judicial authority, under the early Muslim state, exercised *ra'i* (opinion) in matters in which they found no antecedents to fall back on. Fiqh, which literally means comprehension, was first applied in this sense. However, by the end of the fourth century of the Hegire, fiqh had grown into a comprehensive system covering all aspects of religious, political and social life (Faruki 1975, 20-33), and become increasingly perceived as the science which coordinates and encompasses all the branches of Islamic studies (*Encyclopaedia of Islam* 1927, II, 102).

In terms of Islamic economics, this totalistic definition has tended to impede the development of any independent economic authority that would operate outside the traditional realm of fiqh. The fuqaha insist on a discussion of the economy which takes full account of the received system of scholarship, and strictly adheres to their prevailing methods. Islamic economics have thus recently been discussed by a number of jurists as 'fiqh *al-Iqtisad*', the fiqh of economics (Shirazi 1983). And though ijtihad may seem a potential platform from which Muslim economists could operate more freely, the concept is not yet universally acceptable to all schools of fiqh. The training and ordination of mujtahids who would specialize in economics have so far carried little favour with the 'ulama (Jamali 1984).

Disagreements among the various schools of fiqh have added a new dimension to the controversy. The Maliki school, for instance, which is dominant in the Maghreb, is more elaborate on the issue of taxation than the others (Malik 1982, 119-135). Its 'ulama generally take deeper interest in tax issues and have even occasionally clashed with the state over taxation (Rodinson 1966, 158). The Shi'is, on the other hand, dispute the legitimacy of *Kharaj*, land tax, and *'ushr*, custom duties, because they were introduced by the Caliph 'Umar Ibn al-Khattab, whose regulations have not wholeheartedly been received in the Shi'i community. However, it can be argued that this attitude was taken more in line with sectarian political disputes than because of theological objections:[6] the

---

Ribawi, Sadr explored the possibilities of a banking system built on the teachings of Islam, mainly in reference to the objection to *Riba*, interest.

[5] For the Sunnis, the Qur'an, Sunna, *Qiyas* (analogy), and *ijma'* (consensus), constitute the four sources of law. To these, Shi'is add *aql* (reason) as another source or principle on which ijtihad can be based. Some Shi'i 'ulama dispute qiyas as a valid instrument of fiqh (See Muzaffar 1979, 181-182).

[6] The Shi'is hold their own opinion on the issue of the payment of zakat by rebellious tribes during the so-called apostasy wars, when after the

revolutionary government in Shi'i Iran has scarcely touched the tax system inherited from the *ancien regime*, and Khomeini's writings provide little discussion of taxes outside the traditional religious levies (Khomeini 1981, I, 312-369; II, 90-92, 497-501; Khomeini 1982, 232-266). There remains that the disparity between theory and practice is not the reserve of the Shi'i school of fiqh. Sunni fiqh also disapproves of taxation not demanded by the Shari'a. And where these occur, they are treated as exceptions (Qaradawi 1969, II, 991-992).

All in all, over the issue of taxation, fiqh has generally concerned itself with what ought to be, rather than with actual application. It tries to provide a set of universal principles and morals which may not always find much expression in practice. The fuqaha have so far produced little in terms of a workable system of Islamic taxation. Where attempts were made, they have generally tended to repeat obsolete traditions.

III. The Problems of Definition

On the substantial level, taxation has proved to be one of the most contentious aspects of the *Mu'amalat* (Transactions) section of fiqh, and the jurists of the different schools do not agree on a common code of practical implementation. Where the wider application of the Shari'a in the area of taxation has been considered in some countries like Pakistan and Sudan, the state had to contend with the express lack of consensus among the jurists over questions such as tax threshhold, base, coverage and methods of spending of the zakat funds. Introducing Islamic taxation has also raised political questions: the replacement of modern taxes by Shari'a-endorsed levies applies not by virtue of citizenship or allegiance to the state, but by virtue of religious affiliation. In countries like Sudan -where there are important non-Muslim constituencies- this could challenge the concept of nationhood on which taxation is based.

The difficulty in defining taxation is compounded by the variety of religious levies some of which, like Kharaj and 'ushr, are not mentioned in the Qur'an.[7]

Prophet, some tribes of Arabia went back on their commitment to Islam. For Shi'i historians, the war broke out mainly because of the disputed accession of the first Caliph, Abu-Bakr as-Siddiq, who came to lead the community when power should have gone to 'Ali Ibn Abi-Taleb, the first Imam for the Shi'is (See Amin 1980, 97-99).

[7] This explains partly why some Shi'is have been able to question these taxes. In Shi'i fiqh, most items under Kharaj and 'ushr are taxable under Khums. For the classical Sunni treatise on Kharaj, see Abu Yusuf 1977.

And even though zakat is unanimously recognized as a religious tax, there is wide disagreement on its range of application. Shi'is, for their part, attach more importance to *Khums* (the 'fifth'), and tend to consider zakat as a charity tax (Mughniyya, 169-176). But while zakat was not designed at the beginning as an income tax (Lokkegaard, 78), it later evolved to incorporate a number of other levies, including taxes on wealth (Aghnides1916, 525). The issues of zakat base and coverage, nonetheless, still remain unsettled. Among Islamic economists, some believe that it ought to include levies on property including industrial and real estate. And the disagreement has also been centred on whether public assets are taxable (Ariff 1982, 17).

Islamic economists are clearly concerned about the restricted base of the zakat tax in the Shari'a, and are exploring for this reason the legal possibilities of expanding its present base. There are already some authors who, notwithstanding the narrowness of zakat imposition, discuss its fiscal potential in the management of the economy (Kahf 1982, 125-140). But in Saudi Arabia, zakat constitutes less than one percent of annual government expenditure on essential services (Salama 1982, 363), and it is difficult to see how it can realistically be adopted at this stage as a comprehensive fiscal instrument.

With respect to zakat taxes, disagreements persist over basic issues. The 'ulama insist that zakat must be levied at a flat rate, and they reject indexing or proportional taxation (Gammal, 154). The right of the State to levy additional taxes, however, is recognized by some jurists (Sadr 1979, 712-716). This may or may not help reconcile the two groups of Islamic economists who have remained sharply divided so far between those who dispute the imposition of a proportional zakat levy[8], and those who see flexibility as essential for the creation of a modern Islamic economy.[9]

---

[8] Like Salama, who strongly disapproves of progressive taxation: 'The zakah rate is defined and established on a flat rate basis and no authority on earth has any right to alter the zakah rate... Zakah therefore cannot be used as a source of revenue for financing state expenditure'. (Salama 1982, 342.)

[9] An example of this trend can be found in Mannan 1970, 291. The critics of the flat rate rightly argue that in Islamic history the taxes levied by the state were seldom an accurate reflection of the Shari'a. In fact the state often violated these regulations by levying lower taxes on favoured groups, while taxing others more than the prescribed limits (Labib 1978, 74).

IV. Undefined Areas

Taxation has changed from a relatively simple to a very complex process in economic life, and this truism applies both to the economies of the Muslim states and the economies of non-Muslim countries. With the advent of industrialization, the central role of land taxation has waned. There have also been changes in the functions and fiscal roles of taxation, and taxation has become an essential prerogative of the State, as well as a measure of its economic well-being.

The difficulties facing the implementation of an Islamic tax system in the modern age are equally theoretical and administrative problems. From the point of view of the Shari'a, taxation is seen as a means of raising revenue for the state, but also a way to restore social justice. Tax provisions modelled on these two essentials, however, are not necessarily compatible with each other, and the recent literature of Islamic economics has failed to concern itself with the details of the tax system advocated.

Tax payment in Islam is governed by the ability to pay, and is therefore unrelated to considerations of benefit.[10] On grounds of equity and expediency, the Shari'a postulates that people should contribute to the finances of *Bayt al-Mal* (State treasury) according to their means. A Muslim is deemed to have no ability to pay zakat unless his income or proceeds of wealth are above the *nisab* (legal threshhold) set by fiqh. But whereas income is indicative of the ability of a person to pay in this system, ownership of property is irrelevant and consequently untaxable. Furthermore, Islam recognises two distinct forms of wealth, *zahir* (apparent), and *batin* (concealed), and wealth which is concealed from the scrutiny of tax authorities with legal fictions may not incur taxation under some schools of fiqh.[11]

The discrepancy between theory and practice in Islamic taxation is nowhere more evident than in the mode of levy. The Shari'a postulates a direct system of taxation, levied on income and wealth, and disfavours an indirect system based on consumption. But the most consistent tax for contemporary taxes is constituted by custom duties: imported goods enter a country at a limited number of ports, where books can be kept and dues collected. Furthermore,

---

[10] Perhaps a close definition of taxation in Western fiscal literature is 'a compulsory contribution from the person to the government to defray the expenses incurred in the common interest of all, without reference to special benefits conferred' (Seligman 1925, 432)

[11] The practice of legal fictions is considered reprehensible though valid according to hanafi, shafi'i, and ja'fari jurisprudence. See e.g. *Encyclopaedia of Islam,* s.v. 'zakat'.

direct taxation is hardly practical if, as in the subsistence economies of many rural areas of the Muslim world, the bulk of the wealth serves to support a large family. And even if some form of capital taxation is possible under specific circumstances, it could hardly provide the regular and stable revenue that a government requires to finance its activities.

Taxation of commercial activities on the basis of zakat is also problematic. A zakat tax has a limited use in an economy where few established channels of retail distribution exist. Income tax and tax on profits have even a more restricted scope: low levels of income and profits mean that a large proportion of salaried workers and of businesses should be exempted because they remain below the nisab. And it is difficult to imagine a systematic submission of tax returns when illiteracy is high and the local bureaucracy inefficient.

Conclusion. The Case for Pragmatism and Research

Over the past two decades many Muslim countries have witnessed a growing interest in the possibility of a comprehensive Islamic economy. By acknowledging that the study of Islam need not be confined to the theological aspects of the Shari'a, Muslim writers have sanctioned a new set of values which have led to the tentative transformation of the 'Mu'amalat' section of fiqh into 'Islamic economics'. The change in name reflects the rising status of the subject.

At the same time however, it has become apparent that this process calls for a continuous critical assessment. In the discussion on Islamic economics, and on zakat in particular, the gap between theory and practice remains wide, and there is a pressing need for a flexible fiscal formula which could be of use for the different economies of the Muslim world. It might also be interesting to look into the possibility of a negative taxation, which would answer Islam's emphasis on social justice while encouraging wider participation and enthusiasm from the public.

As things stand, Islamic economists have much to do before a level of applicability can be reached that would enable enthusiasts to operate with confidence. Presently, the state of development of the Islamic world is so different from the context in which original levies were designed that the early formulas need thorough rethinking before being applicable. Many aspects of the theory and practice of Islamic taxation must be critically analyzed before they acquire a rigorous underpinning. Further progress is necessary to put Islamic economists and fiqh specialists on a more solid ground.

*****

References

Abu Yusif (Ya'qub Ibn Ibrahim) 1977, *Kitab al-Kharaj*, Cairo: al-Matba'a as-Salafiyya.

Ahmed Z., Iqbal M. & Khan, M.F. eds. 1983, *Fiscal Policy and Resource Allocation in Islam*, Islamabad.

Aghnides N. 1916, *Mohammedan Theories of Finance*, New York: Columbia University.

Amin A. 1980, *Al-Imam 'Ali Ibn Abi-Taleb*, Kuwait: Tawjih Islami.

Ariff M. 1982, *Monetary and Fiscal Economics in Islam*, Jeddah: King Abdulaziz University.

Chapra M.U. 1985, *Towards a Just Monetary System*, Leicester: the Islamic Foundation.

Encyclopaedia of Islam 1927, London: Luzac & Co.

Faruki K.A. 1975, *Islamic Jurisprudence*, Karachi: National Book Foundation.

Faruqi I. ed. 1973, *Contemporary Aspects of Economic and Social Thinking of Islam*, Indiana: Muslim Student Association of the U.S. & Canada.

Gammal M.A. 1980, *Mawsu'at al-Iqtisad al-Islami*, Cairo: Dar al-Kitab.

Hasab F.A. 1981, *Fil-Fikr al-Iqtisadi al-Islami,* Beirut: 'Alam al-Ma'rifa.

Ibn Khaldun 1958, *The Muqaddima*, Vol.1, Franz Rosenthal tr., London: Routledge and Kegan Paul.

Ismail M. 1973, *Al-Harakat as-Sirriyya fil-Islam*, Beirut: Dar al-Qalam.

Jamali M.F. 1984, 'Ra'i fi-Takwin al-Mujtahid', *Al-Fikr*, XXXIX:5, Tunis.

Kahf M., 'Fiscal and Monetary Politics in an Islamic Economy', in Ariff ed.

Khomeini R. 1981, *Tahrir al-Wasila,* Vol.I and II, Beirut: Ta'aruf.

Khomeini R. 1982, *Clarification of Questions,* Borujerdi tr., London.

Labib S. 1978, 'Egyptian Commercial Policy in the Middle Ages', in *Studies in Economic History of the Middle East*, Cook ed., Oxford: Oxford University.

Lokkegaard F. 1950, *Islamic Taxation in the Classic Period*, Copenhagen: Branner & Korch.

Mannan M.A. 1970, *Islamic Economics: Theory and Practice*, Lahore: Muhammad Ashraf.

Malik (Imam Malik Ibn Anas) 1982, *Al-Muwatta'*, Tarjumana and Johnson trs., Norwich: Diwan.

Mughniyya M.J. 1977, *Al-Fiqh 'alal-Madhahib al-Khamsa*, Beirut: 'Ilm lil-Malayin.

Muzaffar M.T. 1979?, *Usul al-Fiqh*, Najaf, Iraq.

Rodinson M. 1966, *Islam et Capitalisme*, Paris: Editions du Seuil.

Sadr M.B. 1979, *Iqtisaduna*, Beirut: Ta'aruf. Originally published in 1961.

Sadr M.B. 1981, *Al-Bank al-la Ribawi fil-Islam*, Beirut: Ta'aruf. Originally published in 1969.

Salama A.A. 1982, 'Fiscal Analysis of Zakah with Special Reference to Saudi Arabia's Experience in Zakah', in Ariff ed.

Seligman E.R. 1925, *Essays in taxation*, New York: Macmillan.

Shirazi M.H. 1983, *al-Fiqh al-Iqtisad*, Qom.

Siddiqi M.N. 1981, *Muslim Economic Thinking*, Leicester: the Islamic Foundation.

Qaradawi Y. 1969, *Fiqh az-Zakat*, Vol.2, Beirut: Irshad.

*****

THE PERFORMANCE OF ISLAMIC BANKS: TRENDS AND CASES

Volker Nienhaus
Economics Department, University of Bochum

Many articles, essays and books have been written on theoretical and ideological aspects of Islamic banking,[1] but only a few publications deal with the actual business of interest-free financial institutions.[2] What is missing is a comprehensive empirical study that analyses the performance of Islamic banks and evaluates their successes and failures against the results achieved by conventional banks under similar circumstances. The present chapter certainly cannot fill this gap. Its aim is more modest: It is an attempt to summarize facts and figures excerpted from numerous annual reports of Islamic banks and to give a preliminary assessment of notable trends and cases. They are related to developments in the conventional banking sector of selected countries. This shall draw the attention to areas where further research seems to be most promising and/or needed.

The chapter is not comprehensive. It is selective in (at least) two respects: (1) It does not cover all operating Islamic financial institutions (the number of which may have reached 50 by now). For some banks, annual reports were not available, and others started business less than two years ago. However, the oldest and the largest Islamic banks are included. (2) The selectivity is more serious with respect to the conventional banks. The choice of conventional banks for the purpose of comparisons was somewhat arbitrary (or 'pragmatic'). Because it was impossible to evaluate over a hundred annual reports of conventional banks, the comparisons were based on data for banks

[1] See for example IERB (1982), Ahmed, Iqbal, Khan (1983), Chapra (1985), W.M. Khan (1985), M. Khan (1986).

[2] Probably the most comprehensive empirical study so far is Ahmad (1987); with special reference to Iran and Pakistan see Iqbal, Mirakhor (1987); general surveys and case studies are presented by El Din (1986), Huq (1986), Mudawi (1986), Nienhaus (1986), Salama (1987), Wilson (1985).

included in the list of the 'Top 100 Arab Banks' which is compiled and published annually in the December issue of 'The Banker' . Most Islamic banks, however, are not among the largest financial institutions of their countries; they are of much smaller size, so that smaller conventional banks would probably be more adequate candidates for comparisons. Nonetheless, and despite the possibility of biased results, the comparison with large conventional banks seems to be defendable and useful for a preliminary evaluation of the performance of Islamic banks.

The chapter starts off with some terminological remarks and is then divided into two sections: The first section presents the data for a quantitative assessment of the achievements and shortcomings of Islamic financial institutions; it also gives an interpretation of disclosed figures. The second section deals with qualitative aspects of the activities of Islamic banks; the discrepancy between the ideology and practice of Islamic banking shall be discussed and the differences between a 'commercial' and a 'developmental' approach will be outlined. The conclusion of the chapter is that Islamic banking is no longer a negligible phenomenon; its future growth, however, requires some financial innovations, and the developmental impact of Islamic financial institutions will be relatively limited as long as the commercial approach remains privileged in the business activities of most Islamic banks.

I. Deposit, Income and Profits: Meaning and Calculation

It is important to note that often the same words are used by different banks and have different meanings. These differences must be taken into account when a comparison of the performance of conventional and Islamic banks is made.

A. Deposits

If money is paid into current, savings or fixed term accounts at a conventional bank, this money constitutes a deposit. Interest is paid on savings and time deposits, but usually not on current accounts. As in a conventional bank, credit balances on current accounts at an Islamic bank are deposits; they constitute an unconditional liability of the bank against the clients, namely to repay on demand. Current accounts at Islamic banks are unremunerated and usually offer no overdraft facilities.

If the clients of Islamic banks want a return on their money, they must pay into investment accounts (also called 'participation accounts' or 'PLS [profit and loss sharing] accounts'). However, credit balances on these accounts are not deposits in the conventional sense. The returns are not fixed in advance; the clients participate by a certain percentage in the financial results of the utilization (investment) of their funds by the bank. These results could be, at least in principle, negative (i.e. a loss). Then the clients have to bear a part of the loss; this reduces the nominal value of the credit balances of their investment accounts. In such a case, the clients could not claim a full repayment of the money paid in. The full repayment, however, is constituent for a deposit in the strict sense.

Although such differences are of legal and economic relevance, the term 'deposit' shall be used in this chapter for both savings and fixed term accounts in current and investment accounts in Islamic banks.

B. Income and Profits

Banks employ funds of shareholders and depositors to generate an income. Roughly speaking, the total income of a conventional bank originates from service charges and fees, from equity participation and from interest-based trade and corporate financing. The total income of an Islamic bank also originates from charges, fees and equity participation, but the trade and corporate financing is not based on interest. Islamic banks can apply mark-up techniques (like *murabaha* for trade or *ijara* for real assets) or PLS arrangements (like *musharaka* for corporate financing). These differences in techniques may be relevant for a qualitative evaluation of the business of conventional and Islamic banks, but they are not decisive for an assessment of the quantitative performance.

1. Total (Gross) Income

If the total income from banking services, equity participation and financing activities is related to the total funds that have been utilized for its generation, this would be a first indicator for the performance of a bank. The total funds utilized by a bank can be approximated by the total assets (less contra accounts) as shown in the balance sheets. An income/assets ratio that increases over time and/or is higher than that of other banks can point to an improving or better use of funds and a superior performance. Such a conclusion, however, is only provisional because the income /assets ratio does not reflect any cost elements:

- If, for example, a bank pays higher salaries than other banks (with a similar number of employees), then substantial parts of the total income are not to the benefit of the depositors or the shareholders but are absorbed by the bank's staff.

- But not only the salaries and other operating expenses must be paid from the total income (or gross revenues); provisions and depreciations for bad debts must also be covered. It may well be that a bank with a high gross income suffers from bad loans and has to make substantial provisions (so that the net income will be much smaller).

In these cases, that part of the revenues that could be passed on to the depositors and shareholders would be reduced and the 'income generating power' (for depositors and shareholders) would be diminished. Later sections of this chapter will quote some examples proving that this is not only a hypothetical but a very real problem for banks. Therefore, the (gross) income/assets ratio cannot be the only measure for the performance of a bank.

2. Net Income

If operating expenses, depreciations and provisions are subtracted from total income, the resulting net income is that part of the revenues which can be passed on to the depositors and shareholders.

In a conventional bank, the net income is the sum total of interest paid to depositors plus residual net profits due to the shareholders.

In an Islamic bank, there is no interest paid to depositors; they participate in the financial results of the placement of deposits, these results can be identical with the difference between total income and operating expenses and provisions respective depreciations, but there are also other methods for calculating the 'residual income' of the depositors. These methods for calculating the depositors' shares have an effect on the distribution of the financial results between the depositors and the shareholders, but they do not affect the total amount available for distribution.

Therefore, the net income may be defined as that part of the total income (respective of the gross revenues) that can be distributed to the shareholders and the depositors of a bank. It is the sum total of the (fixed interest or residual PLS) income of the depositors plus the residual profit of the shareholders. The profit of the shareholders can be passed on to them in different forms, e.g. by paying a cash dividend, by the issue of bonus shares or by an increase of the value of the existing shares after retaining the profit and increasing the reserves.

3. Gross Profits

It is often said that the depositors of Islamic banks participate in the profits (or losses) of the bank ('PLS accounts'). To avoid misunderstanding, a clear distinction between two types of profits should be made, namely the gross profits which comprise the depositors' and the shareholders' shares, and the net profits which consist of the shareholders' shares only. Much confusion arises from the fact that some Islamic banks use the word ' profit' or even ' net profit' for what is actually the gross profit as defined above (i.e. the depositors' shares are included).

In the simplest case, the gross profit is identical with the net income. However, most Islamic banks make some adjustments before they calculate the return on deposits: They exclude, for example, any income that was generated without a direct recourse to depositors funds (e.g. fee for banking services) from the pool to be distributed between depositors and shareholders. In conventional banks, the sum total of interest paid plus net profits would correspond to the gross profits of Islamic banks. Gross profits are of importance for internal calculations in Islamic banks, but most of the banks do not show gross profits in their annual reports. This is not a too serious deficit because for a comparison between Islamic and conventional banks the net income (i.e. the income generated for depositors and shareholders) is the more relevant figure.

4. Net Profits

The net profits of conventional banks are the difference between the net income and the interest paid to depositors. Similarly, the net profits of Islamic banks are the difference between the net income and the return on deposits (calculated on the basis of gross profits). The ratio of net profits on capital (plus reserves) reveals how lucrative a bank is for its shareholders. The performance of banks is often measured by relating the net profits to capital plus reserves or to total assets. However, these ratios do not reflect the income that has been generated for the depositors. If, in the case of two banks with the same capital, deposits and total assets show different profit/assets and profit/capital ratios, one cannot immediately conclude that the bank with the higher ratios had a better performance. It may be that the lower ratios of the second bank are due to higher returns paid to the depositors (which reduce the residual net profits). If this is the case, the net income/assets ratio of the second bank must be higher than that of the first bank.

The net income/assets ratio would be a very appropriate measure for the performance of a bank; the net profit/assets or net profit/capital ratio provide supplementary information on the distribution of the net income between depositors and shareholders. Particular conditions must be fulfilled if the net profit/assets or net profit/capital ratios should allow similar conclusions regarding the performance of banks: The rates of return (interest rates) for different types of deposits must be the same for all banks and the respective composition of deposits should be very similar. In practice, however, the rates of return and especially the composition of deposits differ substantially between Islamic and conventional banks. Therefore, an important proviso in the analysis is that net income/assets ratios for the conventional banks could not be used in the empirical comparison between conventional and Islamic banks in the next section of this article.[3]

II. Financial Results: Observations and Interpretations

When Islamic banking introduced itself to the Western business community, many people came to believe that substantial amounts of petro-capital could be channelled through these new financial institutions and that they would enter the Western markets as providers of risk capital.[4] But after a while it became apparent that interest-free banking hardly meant corporate financing on the basis of profit and loss partnerships (as it was propagated by the theory and ideology) but mainly trade financing on the basis of mark-up and - to a lesser extent - hire purchase and leasing. The initial enthusiasm cooled down, and the reports in the media became more critical.

A. General Trends

The skeptical attitude toward interest-free banking was supported by some spectacular losses and financial troubles of individual Islamic financial institutions. The following are the most prominent examples:

- Dar al-Maal al-Islami (DMI) - the mother company of an international network of Islamic banks, investment and insurance companies - had placed surplus funds on the international gold market and lost 28 mn US$ in 1983 and 19.5 mn US$ in 1984 (which was more than 10 per cent of the paid-in capital).

[3] These figures are not provided in The Banker's 'Top 100 Arab Banks'. There 'total revenues' (which correspond to total [gross] income) were recorded only until 1982 and for not much more than half of all banks.

[4] See for example the papers and speeches of a seminar in Baden-Baden (F.R. Germany) in 1981, collected in Ali (1982).

- Kuwait Finance House (KFH) had channelled most of its funds into the Kuwaiti real estate and construction sector and was so badly hit by the collapse of that market that it had to transfer the net income of 1984 to a special reserve; neither shareholders nor depositors received any return on their funds.

- Islamic Bank International of Denmark (IBID) experienced such a heavy loss in 1985 and 1986 (amounting to more than 30 per cent of the paid-in capital) that the shareholders had to inject fresh capital amounting to roughly 50 per cent of their initial subscription.

- Faisal Islamic Bank (Sudan) (FIBS) came under public fire because it was accused of hoarding foodstuff.

- The Islamized commercial banks in Pakistan were criticized because of increasing costs of funds and decreasing returns on deposits after the transformation to the interest-free system.

All these troubles are realities and cannot be denied; nevertheless one has to be cautious not to rush to faulty conclusions. Except for the unfavourable trend in Pakistan,[5] all the quoted troubles of individual banks had very specific and rather unique reasons; they are not permanent phenomena but rather temporary difficulties in some years. To see the troubles in the right perspective, one should also take a look at the performance of the troubled institutions in the years before and after the critical period and compare their problems with the performance of conventional banks operating under similar circumstances.

Doing this, one has to note that DMI was not the only financial institution that lost on the gold market, that in Kuwait many other banks ran into trouble for similar reasons like KFH (late consequences of the Souk al-Manakh crash in 1982), and that FIBS has recovered in the years after 1984. It is therefore dangerous to draw general conclusions from particular cases. For a general evaluation of the performance of Islamic banks one has to take a more comprehensive view with respect to both the number of banks and the number of years. An attempt in this direction has been made in the following sections.

[5] On the decreasing returns on PLS deposits in Pakistan see Zaidi (1987).

1. Size and Market Shares of Islamic Banks

Islamic banks differ widely in size: The largest bank (KFH) has total assets of nearly 3 bn US$ while the smallest bank (Faisal Islamic Bank of Kibris, FIBK, in Northern Cyprus) had less than 10 mn US$. Such absolute figures, however, are not sufficient for an assessment of the quantitative importance of a bank in its national context: Internationally small banks can have large market shares nationally.

(a) Ranking by Total Assets

The Banker started to publish a list of the 100 largest Arab banks (in terms of total assets) in the year 1980 with a ranking based on the balance sheets for 1979. It included one Islamic bank - KFH - on rank 94. KFH climbed to rank 34 for 1984 and dropped a little to rank 36 for 1986 with total assets of roughly 3 bn US$. Since 1982, a second Islamic bank - Faisal Islamic Bank of Egypt (FIBE) - is listed; it also improved its position substantially since its first appearance on rank 77, to rank 43 for 1986 with total assets of about 2 bn US$. The Banker lists no more Islamic banks, but the total assets of three or four more Islamic banks are big enough to qualify for ranks between 70 and 90 in 1985/1986: Dubai Islamic Bank (DIB), International Islamic Bank for Investment and Development (IIBID), (1986 figures n.a.), Jordan Islamic Bank for Finance and Development (JIBFD) and Masraf Faysal Al-Islami of Bahrain (MFIB). Table 1 shows where these banks should have been ranked approximately, and table 2 gives the absolute figures for the total assets (in US$).

Table 1: Position of Islamic Banks among Top 100 Arab Banks (See Annex 1 for Notes to Tables, and for sources; Annex 2 for Banks' acronyms)

Year	KFH	FIBE	IBID	DIB	JIBFD	MFIB
1980	94					
1981	68					
1982	51	77				
1983	42	66				
1984	34	47				
1985	39	45	74	97		78
1986	36	43	n.a.	87	87	76

Table 2: Total Assets of Islamic Banks (in mn US$)

	1985	1986		1985	1986
ABIIB	268.36	252.41	FIBS	192.07	207.3
ABIL	48.49	63.53	IBBL	61.01	82.56
ABTFH	40.13	63.90	IBID	19.46	22.64
BIB	166.71	169.41	IIBID	723.85	822.03
DIB	415.97	470.34	JIBFD	344.73	469.80
FFI	44.45	79.68	KFH	2781.86	2947.93
FIBE	2078.70	2056.00	MFIB	667.16	707.54
FIBS	192.07	207.03	QIB	166.26	166.26

The ranking among the top 100 Arab banks shows at least for some Islamic banks that they have grown to financial institutions of a respectable size within a relatively short period of time. Their size becomes even more considerable when their total assets are not only compared with the top banks all over the Arab world but with the top banks of those countries where the Islamic banks are located. KFH, FIBE and MFBI have become among the seven largest banks of their countries (including offshore banks in Bahrain and adding funds under management to total assets of the balance sheet of MFIB), and JIBFD has become the fourth largest bank in Jordan.[6]

The comparison of total assets alone does not tell very much about the 'real' importance and performance of these banks, but it shows that Islamic financial institutions are no longer negligible quantities and should be considered by financial analysts, businessmen and policymakers - at least in some parts of the Muslim world.

(b) Deposits and Market Shares

Situation. Except for Iran and Pakistan, where the whole banking system was 'Islamized' in the first half of the 1980s, Islamic banks in all other countries operate in 'mixed systems' which have been and still are dominated by conventional (interest-based) banking. For an assessment of the quantitative importance of Islamic banks, their market shares have been calculated. The market shares are defined as the shares of the deposits of Islamic banks in the

[6] The ranking is based on figures of the 'Top 100 Arab Banks'. This list may be incomplete for conventional banks as it is for Islamic banks; thus, the actual rank may differ from the figures given here.

total (private) demand, savings and time deposits of the respective country.[7] The figures for the Islamic banks were taken from their annual reports; the figures for total deposits were calculated from IMF statistics where government deposits are separated from demand, savings and time deposits. The exclusion of government deposits seems justified because for most Islamic banks deposits from the public sector are only of subordinate relevance: The resource base (capital and deposits) of most Islamic banks is in the private sector.

Over the last five years, Islamic banking gained considerable quantitative importance in a number of countries: As shown in table 3, the market shares of the Islamic banks are close to 20 per cent in Egypt, Kuwait and Sudan and roughly 10 per cent in Jordan and Qatar; Islamic banks are less important in the U.A.E. (where the oldest Islamic commercial bank is located) and in Bangladesh (where the first Islamic bank started only in 1983). Islamic banking is still marginal in Turkey with a market share of less than 1 per cent, but the two interest-free financial institutions in Turkey are among the most dynamic Islamic banks anywhere, and it may well be that their national market shares will grow considerably and rapidly.[8]

[7] This method was proposed by Moore (1987). It is certainly not perfect, but it gives an idea of magnitudes and changes over time.
[8] For other countries where Islamic banks are operating, sufficient data were not available, but it is reasonable to assume that the market shares of Islamic banks in countries like Guinea or Tunisia are modest.

Table 3: Market Shares of Islamic Banks (in per cent)

	1980	1981	1982	1983	1984	1985	1986
Bahrain (BIB, ABIIB)	1.03	1.42	2.86	3.45	7.44	16.19	15.92
Bangladesh (IBBL)				0.47	1.52	3.22	3.90
Egypt (FIBE, IIBID) A	1.61	4.51	6.14	8.63	9.37	12.76	[9.8]
Egypt (FIBE, IIBID) B	2.39	6.27	8.27	11.17	12.34	16.80	[12.3]
Jordan (JIBFD)	1.90	3.35	3.90	5.40	6.82	7.72	8.60
Kuwait (KFH)	5.70	8.21	23.32	17.33	17.13	17.64	18.03
Qatar (QIB)					6.71	7.98	10.37
Sudan (FIBS)	6.86	10.87	15.00	13.34	12.68	7.74	7.08
Sudan (4-6 banks)	7.0	11.2	15.3	15.9	17.8	16.9	
Turkey (FFI, ABTFH)						0.41	0.74
U.A.E. (DIB)	[1.32]	1.28	1.35	2.03	2.35	3.06	3.27

Egypt:A including, B excluding public entities' deposits.
Sudan (4-6 banks): taken from Moore (1987).

The market shares of Islamic banks in table 3 do not include the so-called 'Islamic products' offered by Western financial institutions especially to clients in the Arab Gulf region. In the case of Egypt, the quantitative relevance of Islamic banking is certainly much higher than indicated by the market shares of only two Islamic banks because these figures neither include the deposits in the interest-free departments of conventional banks nor the money that is invested in interest-free financial institutions of the rapidly growing 'informal' financial sector.

Trends. It is often argued that Islamic banking has reached its culmination point: The high growth rates of the initial years have vanished; the Islamic banks have found a market gap, but it is only of limited size. After filling the gap there is no room for further expansion. In short, the thesis is that the older Islamic banks in particular, reached their 'limits of growth', they lost the dynamics of the early years and entered into a period of 'consolidation' and relative stagnation.

For a test of this presumption, data have been compiled in table 4 for six 'old' Islamic banks which have been operating for over seven years.

Table 4: Growth of Deposits in 'Old' Islamic Banks (in per cent)

	since	80-81	81-82	82-83	83-84	84-85	85-86
DIB	1976	[19.3]	23.5	64.0	52.1	38.1	11.7
KFH	1978	97.9	60.9	47.5	1.9	1.9	4.7
FIBS	1978	106.7	97.9	26.9	7.5	6.1	9.0
FIBE	1979	234.8	68.9	53.5	25.8	4.2	-6.6
JIBFD	1979	117.6	41.4	63.4	41.3	24.3	24.1
BIB	1979	91.3	121.3	30.7	10.4	80.6	1.6

The following can be observed:

- With only one exception (FIBE 1985/86), the growth rates of deposits remained positive for all Islamic banks since 1980/81.

- However, the growth rates declined over the last years; the maximum was reached in 1982/83 or before (with the exception of Bahrain Islamic Bank [BIB]).

This trend seems to confirm the thesis of decreasing dynamics of (old) Islamic banks. But one should not rush to conclusions: Firstly, it should be noted that high initial and subsequently decreasing growth rates occur (as a consequence of the arithmetic of growth rates) even if the increase in deposits would be identical in absolute amounts every year. Secondly - and more important - one should not only look at the decreasing growth rates of the Islamic banks but should also take into consideration the growth rate of the deposits of the other banks (i.e. the growth of total non-governmental deposits). Such a comparison discloses that the 'relative' growth of Islamic banks was better in most cases than the growth of the other banks. This better relative growth resulted in increasing shares of Islamic banks in total deposits, i.e. in an increase of the market shares of the old Islamic banks. The following observations are of particular interest (see table 5 below):

- The market share of the oldest Islamic bank - DIB, operating since 1976 - was stagnating for years around 1 to 1.5 per cent; then it increased for two years to 2 per cent, and in the last years to 3 per cent and more. This pattern is in clear contrast to what is expected according to the hypothesis of deteriorating dynamics.

- Despite a sharp drop in the deposit growth rates from 50 per cent and more before 1982/83 to less than 5 per cent subsequently, KFH was able to keep its market share of 17-18 per cent - even after the year 1984 in which no return was allocated to the investment accounts.[9]

- The market shares of JIBFD and BIB continuously increased from 1.9 respective 1.0 to 8.6 respective 6.7 per cent. This is also contrary to what should occur when dynamics dwindle.

- The figures for FIBE show some fluctuations, but a clear trend did not emerge.

- The only bank that actually lost market shares (from a maximum of 15 per cent in 1982 to 7 per cent in 1986) is FIBS. This negative trend seems to be in conformity with the hypothesis of limits of growth for, and decreasing dynamic potentials of, Islamic banks. However, the market shares which FIBS lost were probably not won by conventional banks but by other Islamic banks in Sudan which started operations in 1982 and later; as already shown in table 3, the Islamic banking sector as a whole did not contract over the last years.

Table 5: Market Shares of 'Old' Islamic Banks (in per cent)

	since	1980	1981	1982	1983	1984	1985	1986
DIB	1976	[1.3]	1.28	1.35	2.03	2.35	3.06	3.27
KFH	1978	5.70	8.21	12.32	17.33	17.13	17.64	18.03
FIBS	1978	6.86	10.87	15.00	13.34	12.68	7.74	7.08
FIBE	1979	1.61	4.43	5.62	6.89	7.06	9.83	7.43
JIBFD	1979	1.90	3.35	3.90	5.40	6.82	7.72	8.60
BIB	1979	1.03	1.42	2.86	3.45	3.91	6.42	6.68

Summarizing these observations on the 'relative' deposit growth of old Islamic banks, one can say that even if some individual banks may have reached their maximum market shares (around or somewhat below 10 per cent), this hardly proves that the Islamic banking sector as a whole has reached its limits. There

[9] The government may have infused funds into KFH during the most critical period, but the same was done for other banks; so the figures are biased for all banks.

are enough examples that old banks continue to grow and to gain market shares, and it can be observed in some countries that new interest-free financial institutions give a fresh impetus to the Islamic banking sector. The rate of expansion may be more moderate today than in the early 1980s, but this does not mean that Islamic banks entered into a period of stagnation.

2. Overall Performance

The increasing market shares would hardly emerge if Islamic banks utilized substantially and permanently the funds of shareholders, and especially of depositors, in a less effective way than conventional banks. Therefore, growing market shares are a first indication for a reasonable performance and success of Islamic banks with regard to income generation. However, this indication alone is not sufficient. The market shares (i.e. the shares in total deposits) may increase (at least for a while) even if the financial results of Islamic banks were worse than the average of conventional banks: This could happen if substantial numbers of clients are so 'riba-averse' that they would have no deposits in conventional banks and would never shift their deposits to interest banks even if they could earn higher returns there. Further, the creation of Islamic banks may lead to a mobilization of savings which previously were kept completely outside the financial system. Therefore, the balance sheets and profit and loss accounts respective income statements of Islamic banks need a closer examination.

Table 6: Capital/Assets Ratios of Islamic Banks (in per cent)

	1979	1980	1981	1982	1983	1984	1985	1986
ABTFH							21.8	10.7
ABIL						21.6	29.9	23.7
ABIIB						40.3	19.0	23.7
BIB		51.0	33.5	21.3	17.3	16.1	10.1	10.0
BIM						24.0	15.7	n.a.
DIB	n.a.	n.a.	13.7	11.3	7.4	5.1	4.5	5.1
FFI							19.5	9.0
FIBE	30.5	10.0	3.9	3.4	2.8	2.4	2.2	4.7
FIBS	12.9	7.5	8.2	9.9	30.1	29.7	27.4	25.7
IBBL					32.0	9.2	4.9	4.2
IBID					33.7	16.1	25.8	37.2
IIBID			33.7	6.6	2.3	1.9	1.2	n.a.
JIBFD		13.0	9.6	9.3	5.9	4.5	3.9	6.1
KFH	4.3	3.1	5.2	6.3	4.4	4.1	4.5	4.4
MFIB					12.6	7.0	11.9	16.6
QIB						15.6	10.1	7.4

Table 7: Net Income/Assets Ratios of Islamic Banks (in per cent)

	1979	1980	1981	1982	1983	1984	1985	1986
ABTFH							14.9	19.9
ABIL						4.9	2.8	4.2
ABIIB						6.2	6.7	6.9
BIB		9.2	6.6	11.5	8.3	8.9	5.8	6.6
BIM						n.a.	n.a.	n.a.
DIB	n.a.	n.a.	6.1	8.0	6.8	8.3	4.9	5.4
FFI							9.9	11.3
FIBE	4.8	6.1	6.6	7.5	7.1	7.5	7.2	n.a.
FIBS	7.5	7.5	10.2	10.3	7.2	4.3	6.4	5.0
IBBL					1.6	5.4	5.3	5.4
IBID					5.0	6.1	14.0	9.4
IIBID			5.4	6.9	9.5	7.4	5.3	n.a.
JIBFD		3.4	2.8	3.9	2.6	2.3	1.9	1.8
KFH	6.2	8.3	9.7	9.2	5.3	4.9	3.3	3.6
MFIB					n.a.	n.a.	n.a.	n.a.
QIB						5.0	6.1	5.8

Table 8: Gross Profit/Assets Ratios of Islamic Banks (in per cent)

	1979	1980	1981	1982	1983	1984	1985	1986
ABTFH							13.0	17.5
ABIL						4.7	2.6	4.1
ABIIB						5.0	6.2	6.0
BIB		4.8	3.9	6.2	6.1	7.1	4.3	4.5
BIM						n.a.	n.a.	n.a.
DIB	n.a.	n.a.	3.9	4.9	4.6	4.3	2.5	2.2
FFI							7.0	8.9
FIBE	2.7	5.0	5.8	7.0	6.5	6.6	5.9	n.a.
FIBS	3.4	3.8	7.4	7.6	4.2	3.0	3.0	0.9
IBBL					0.3	3.1	3.6	3.2
IBID					0.0	2.2	-0.8	0.3
IIBID			4.1	4.5	5.1	5.2	3.9	n.a.
JIBFD		0.0	0.0	0.0	1.5	1.9	2.2	2.2
KFH	4.6	5.7	7.1	8.1	4.6	0.0	2.2	2.4
MFIB					n.a.	n.a.	n.a	n.a.
QIB						1.9	3.8	4.2

Table 9: Net Profit/Capital Ratios of Islamic Banks (in per cent)

	1979	1980	1981	1982	1983	1984	1985	1986
ABTFH							26.9	89.6
ABIL						2.1	1.4	3.5
ABIIB						8.1	6.5	4.4
BIB		7.3	6.3	18.5	13.7	16.3	9.8	10.8
BIM						-1.6	5.4	n.a.
DIB	n.a.	n.a.	9.0	10.8	12.7	11.0	4.4	4.9
FFI							24.7	48.3
FIBE	8.9	20.2	17.5	16.8	20.6	17.2	18.2	10.3
FIBS	22.0	32.7	51.7	71.0	7.1	7.2	5.9	0.7
IBBL					-3.8	10.2	9.6	0.1
IBID					2.1	2.1	-12.9	-12.1
IIBID			10.1	30.2	31.4	26.5	0.0	n.a.
JIBFD		0.7	10.6	20.5	14.1	19.3	13.6	7.9
KFH	31.1	47.4	33.4	36.4	11.5	0.0	4.6	7.2
MFIB					4.1	10.9	7.7	8.6
QIB		4.6	14.3	13.0				

Tables 6 to 9 show that the Islamic banks are a very heterogeneous group; they are different in nearly all dimensions which are relevant for an assessment of performance.

- The capitalization of the banks in relation to their total assets ranges from 4-5 per cent (1986: DIB, FIBE, IBBL, KFH; 1985: IIBID 1.2 per cent) to roughly 25 per cent and more (1986: ABIL, FIBS, IBID). The capital/assets ratio decreased for most of the 'older' banks (which is not unusual); it increased substantially for FIBS in 1983 due to an increase of the paid-in capital. The capital/assets ratio remained very high for IBID; this is mainly due to a substantial decrease of deposits in 1985 as a reaction to heavy losses.

- The (total) income/assets ratio ranged from a modest 2 per cent (JIBFD) to an extraordinary 20 per cent (ABTFH) in 1986. For most 'older' banks, the income/assets ratio reached a maximum in 1982 (BIB, FIBE, FIBS, JIBFD) or in 1981 (KFH) and declined subsequently. The economic slowdown in the Arab world seemingly affected most of the older Islamic banks (and also the conventional banks) in that region and reduced the income generating potentials of the funds at the disposal of these banks.

- The gross profit/assets ratio showed a similar pattern to the income/assets ratio, but with more pronounced annual fluctuations in some cases (esp. KFH); a continuous decrease of the income/assets ratio combined with a continuous increase of the gross profit/assets ratio can be observed in one case (JIBFD).

- The net profit/capital ratio is a measure for the profitability of a bank for its owners. This ratio generally dropped after 1982, in some cases drastically (FIBS, IBID, IIBID, KFH). Relatively stable or increasing ratios can be found only for three of the younger banks (ABTFH, FFI, QIB). Negative net profits (losses) were reported by two banks in their first year (BIM, IBBL); such initial losses can be considered as 'normal'. Two banks had zero net profits in one year (KFH in 1984, IIBID in 1985), and one bank suffered heavy losses in two subsequent years (IBID in 1985 and 1986).

Obviously, there are substantial differences in the performance and success within the Islamic banking community. This, however, is not so surprising if one remembers that the Islamic banks are spread over a large number of countries with very different business environments. The interpretation of the performance indicators should be made against this background, i.e. taking into account such indicators not only for one but for a number of Islamic and conventional banks operating in the same country.

B. Developments in Selected Countries

There are not many countries where more than one Islamic bank is operating and where a comparison between Islamic banks is possible. But the figures in The Banker's ' Top 100 Arab Banks' allow a partial and selective comparison of the performance of Islamic banks with that of some conventional banks for a few countries.

1. Bahrain

Three Islamic banks operate in Bahrain, but all have different types of licences: BIB is a local bank with a full commercial banking license, ABIIB can also operate in Bahrain but only as an investment bank, while the local activities of MFIB with an offshore banking licence are very restricted. With respect to the Bahraini market, only BIB and ABIIB should be aggregated (as in table 3) for the calculation of the market shares of Islamic banks in Bahrain.

Table 10: Islamic and Conventional Banks in Bahrain

Total Assets (in mn BD)

Lic.	Bank	1980	1981	1982	1983	1984	1985	1986
CBL	AACB				364	420	444	383
CBL	BBK	1135	1560	2271	2291	2205	2056	1737
CBL	BIB	30	46	76	95	104	167	169
CBL	NBB	790	1037	1118	1492	1669	1418	1513
IBL	ABIIB					125	268	252
OBL	ABC	1952	4788	7892	8762	11055	13066	14582
OBL	ARLA	1497	2089	2181	1723	1853	1700	1654
OBL	BMEB				392	446	558	504
OBL	GIB	2091	4507	6178	7434	7379	7741	8065
OBL	GRB	825	1228	1243	1269	1186	1070	863
OBL	KAB			385	449	574	649	487
OBL	MFIB				133	256	667	708

Net Profit/Assets Ratio [Pre-tax profits on assets] (in per cent)

Lic.	Bank	1980	1981	1982	1983	1984	1985	1986
CBL	AACB			8.92	1.89	1.59	1.42	0.30
CBL	BBK	1.41	1.32	4.16	1.92	1.34	1.00	0.44
CBL	BIB	3.73	2.09	3.93	2.37	2.61	0.99	1.09
CBL	NBB	1.89	2.04	2.73	2.50	1.79	1.37	0.79
IBL	ABIIB					3.27	1.23	0.90
OBL	ABC	4.62	5.79	1.81	1.28	1.19	1.00	0.88
OBL	ARLA	0.84	0.89	0.88	0.89	1.12	0.75	0.63
OBL	BMEB				2.95	0.14	0.06	0.49
OBL	GIB	0.57	0.98	0.96	0.85	0.88	0.90	0.89
OBL	GRB	0.52	0.51	0.38	0.32	0.41	0.47	0.42
OBL	KAB				1.08	1.04	0.82	0.18
OBL	MFIB				0.66	1.03	0.30	0.43

Net Profit/Capital Ratio [Pre-tax profits on capital] (in per cent)

Lic.	Bank	1980	1981	1982	1983	1984	1985	1986
CBL	AACB			78.02	13.66	12.65	11.50	2.29
CBL	BBK	19.61	21.79	48.38	18.85	12.30	8.29	3.35
CBL	BIB	7.38	6.34	19.61	14.71	17.72	10.78	12.06
CBL	NBB	26.67	24.56	25.61	23.01	18.84	13.51	7.11
IBL	ABIIB					8.10	6.47	4.43
OBL	ABC	21.48	31.18	12.67	10.73	11.02	10.51	14.01
OBL	ARLA	9.46	12.12	11.37	8.45	8.50	5.31	4.03
OBL	BMEB				6.58	0.44	0.19	1.64
OBL	GIB	10.14	20.90	16.11	13.38	12.60	10.48	9.67
OBL	GRB	11.11	34.53	20.58	13.57	14.72	13.56	9.53
OBL	KAB				4.72	4.38	4.07	0.84
OBL	MFIB				4.09	10.89	7.73	8.60

Capital/Assets Ratio (in per cent)

Lic.	Bank	1980	1981	1982	1983	1984	1985	1986
CBL	AACB			14.66	13.14	12.03	12.57	13.89
CBL	BBK	6.78	6.72	9.95	10.42	11.34	12.29	14.40
CBL	BIB	50.95	33.47	21.25	17.27	16.06	10.09	10.04
CBL	NBB	50.95	33.47	21.25	17.27	16.06	10.09	10.04
IBL	ABIIB					40.33	19.01	20.32
OBL	ABC	21.52	18.56	12.05	11.76	10.08	9.09	8.65
OBL	ARLA	7.63	7.18	8.43	13.12	13.22	15.06	16.02
OBL	BMEB				29.85	35.20	28.32	31.94
OBL	GIB	4.32	4.94	6.70	6.03	7.89	9.24	9.27
OBL	GRB	4.61	1.42	2.26	2.52	3.12	3.83	5.21
OBL	KAB		15.00	31.16	27.17	21.25	18.95	25.26
OBL	MFIB				16.13	9.45	3.92	4.98

Licence: CBL= Commercial banking license
IBL= Investment banking license
OBL= Offshore banking license

Comparing the two Bahraini Islamic banks with each other, one can see (table 10) that BIB, as the older and in terms of capital and deposits smaller bank, is performing better than the newcomer ABIIB in its first three years in terms of net profit on capital, while ABIIB had higher income/ and gross profit/assets ratios. That BIB is more profitable for its shareholders can be explained to a large part by the fact that it is much higher leveraged than ABIIB whose capital/assets ratio is about twice that of BIB. But if the trend of the last three years continues, this trend could be reversed in the next years so that ABIIB may perform better than BIB.

For a comparison with conventional banks, only net profit/capital ratios (and capital/assets ratios) can be taken from The Banker's listings. Three non-Islamic commercial banks (which are much bigger than the Islamic banks) are included. The net profit/capital ratio of BIB was the highest of all five banks in the last two years while ABIIB was better than two conventional banks in 1986 but worse than all the others before. BIB's capital/assets ratio was the lowest in the last two years and the highest in the years before (except in 1984 when ABIIB started operations).

Taking these observations together, one can suspect that the leverage effect is more important for the profitability of a bank for its shareholders than the adherence to Islamic or conventional banking principles.

2. Egypt

Figures for two Islamic banks operating in Egypt were available (see table 11). FIBE is one of the oldest Islamic banks and the second largest in terms of assets. IIBID started in 1981 and is of medium size. Reliable figures on the Islamic activities of other financial institutions (interest-free departments in conventional banks, 'informal' Islamic financial institutions) were not available.

Table 11: Islamic and Conventional Banks in Egypt

Total Assets (in mn E£)

	1980	1981	1982	1983	1984	1985	1986
NBE	4354	5724	7624	7510	9124	11223	7372
BM	3143	4017	4017	6109	7536	9827	6511
BC	2401	3947	3947	4567	5259	5993	3891
AAIB	2218	2994	3687	4436	4445	3585	3421
BA	1823	2824	2840	3216	4003	4003	3032
AIB	1353	1918	2273	2274	2433	3087	2247
FIBE	197	589	997	1504	1862	2079	2056
MIB	429	608	773	931	1496	2300	1207
SCB	491	806	951	1029	1054	1814	1091
EAB	351	447	546	649	759	1119	608
IIBID	15	89	412	680	724	n.a.	

Net Profit/Assets Ratio [Pre-tax profits on assets] (in per cent)

	1980	1981	1982	1983	1984	1985	1986
NBE	1.50	3.17	2.82	2.57	2.11	1.56	0.95
BM	1.19	n.a.	3.50	3.09	2.94	2.62	2.47
BC	2.22	3.73	3.74	2.21	1.26	1.04	0.88
AAIB	1.27	1.10	1.13	1.05	0.39	-0.38	n.a.
BA	1.75		2.26	1.85	1.75	1.31	0.00
AIB	0.36	1.90	1.14	1.16	0.95	0.77	0.83
FIBE The Banker		[8.4]	[7.8]	[7.8]	[7.3]		
FIBE corrected	2.01	0.68	0.57	0.58	0.42	0.41	0.46
MIB	2.64	2.54	3.95	2.73	2.24	1.74	1.45
SCB	2.29	2.16	1.69	1.36	0.87	0.78	n.a.
EAB	4.21	2.94	4.56	4.55	4.26	3.65	2.36
IIBID		3.41	1.98	0.73	0.51	0.00	n.a.

Net Profit/Capital Ratio [Pre-tax profits on capital] (in per cent)

	1980	1981	1982	1983	1984	1985	1986
NBE	67.69	120.82	107.22	33.43	27.73	20.79	13.73
BM	47.72	n.a.	159.00	137.37	141.78	142.96	n.a.
BC	19.18	32.37	32.48	20.88	11.94	10.23	8.76
AAIB	16.45	16.61	19.48	18.80	10.82	-6.94	n.a.
BA	55.48	n.a.	68.62	57.37	54.58	44.59	14.23
AIB	2.47	16.30	11.05	11.12	9.94	7.66	7.64
FIBE The Banker		[169.2]	[232.4]	[253.5]	[278.1]		
FIBE corrected	8.85	20.16	17.51	16.77	20.56	17.24	18.25
MIB	89.80	57.32	61.64	31.18	28.33	29.62	26.04
SCB	44.06	50.00	39.18	27.59	16.71	16.84	n.a.
EAB	86.87	58.33	92.22	80.85	68.85	62.34	43.68
IIBID	3.41	1.98	0.73	0.51	0.00	n.a.	

Capital/Assets Ratio (in per cent)

	1980	1981	1982	1983	1984	1985	1986
NBE	2.26	2.70	2.69	7.51	7.70	7.33	6.58
BM	2.44	n.a.	2.11	2.20	1.97	1.73	n.a.
BC	11.48	11.18	11.18	10.95	10.24	10.18	9.84
AAIB	7.31	6.13	5.64	5.46	5.73	5.13	11.02
BA	3.14	3.32	3.27	3.20	3.20	2.71	2.16
AIB	14.16	10.95	9.67	9.73	9.37	10.92	10.86
FIBE	10.00	3.74	4.01	2.86	2.47	2.21	4.72
MIB	2.97	5.45	7.58	9.76	6.78	5.28	5.91
SCB	4.66	4.09	4.42	4.96	5.47	4.09	3.84
EAB	4.27	4.79	5.24	5.95	6.40	5.49	5.32
IIBID		33.36	6.56	2.31	1.92	1.17	n.a.

Both FIBE and IIBID are among the banks with rather low capital/assets ratios in the last years. This, however, is not a major point of concern for an Islamic bank because its investment accounts constitute no fixed liabilities but could be adjusted in cases of non-performing financings.

The net profit/capital ratios of FIBE were not exceptional, neither on the positive, nor on the negative sides.[10] IIBID's profits, however, dropped to zero in 1985 (no figures for 1986) after good results in the three preceding years. One can say that the Islamic financial institutions produced an income for their shareholders which was neither very high nor very low but rather average.

This income, however, was gained only by utilizing over-average amounts of deposits. The net profit/assets ratios of FIBE are the lowest among the Egyptian banks from 1981 to 1983; in 1984 one conventional bank had a lower ratio, and in 1985 the ratios of one conventional bank and the other Islamic bank were worse.

The relatively poor and slightly deteriorating net profit/assets ratio of FIBE might be in reaction to the distribution of the net income respective gross profits which is biased in favour of the depositors. If one Egyptian Pound invested by a conventional bank and by an Islamic bank yields the same return, but if the depositors receive a larger part of these returns from the Islamic bank than from the conventional bank, then the profits for the shareholders and the profit/assets ratio would be lower for the Islamic bank. But such a distributional bias in favour of the depositors must become visible in the returns on deposits as declared by the Islamic bank: They should be well above the rate of interest paid for savings and time deposits by conventional banks. However, FIBE's rate of return on deposits decreased from a maximum of 12.5 per cent in 1981 to 9 per cent in 1984. The rates were not available for 1985 and 1986, but a look at the figures for income and deposits after 1984 makes it hard to believe that the returns on deposits have increased.[11] IIBID paid between 14.1 and 12.3 per cent in 1982 and 10.0 to 6.0 per cent in 1984 (no rates for other years available). But while the returns on deposits decreased in these Islamic banks, the (fixed maximum) interest rate for savings deposits in commercial banks was increased from 8.5 to 10 per cent in July 1982 and for time deposits from 8.5-11.5 to 8.5-13 per cent. This means that in the last years the Islamic banks probably have paid to their depositors not more but less than conventional banks. Therefore, the low net profit/assets ratios do not reflect a distributional bias in favour of the depositors. They seem to be the result of (increasing) difficulties of the 'official' Islamic banks to find profitable outlets for the funds of their depositors.[12]

---

[10] The extremely high ratios calculated by The Banker for 1981 to 1984 are wrong because net and gross profits have been confused.

[11] Moore (1987, 7) estimates that the returns were not more than 7 or 8 per cent in 1985 and 1986.

[12] It was reported that the informal interest-free financial institutions paid much higher profits (up to 25 per cent and more).

3. Jordan

The JIBFH has grown up to the fourth largest bank of the country. The performance of JIBFD is very similar to that of a conventional bank whose total assets are roughly the 30-fold of JIBFD's, and of a second one of roughly the double size (see tables 3 and 12). The most remarkable feature is that JIBFD continuously increased its market share during the 1980s.

Table 12: Islamic and Conventional Banks in Jordan

Total Assets (in mn JD)

	1984	1985	1986
AB	10588	11738	12654
PB	528	658	776
JIBFD	252	345	470

Net Profit Capital Ratio (in per cent)

	1984	1985	1986
AB	27.68	16.94	14.01
PB	18.47	15.37	12.78
JIBFD	22.33	16.62	12.88

Net Profit/Assets Ratio (in per cent)

	1984	1985	1986
AB	1.22	0.79	0.72
PB	0.79	0.64	0.60
JIBFD	0.87	0.52	0.48

Capital/Assets Ratio (in per cent)

	1984	1985	1986
AB	4.47	4.88	5.35
PB	4.21	4.13	4.87
JIBFD	4.53	3.86	6.06

4. Kuwait

Most Kuwaiti banks had one or more bad years with no profits after the Souk al-Manakh crises in 1982 and in the depressed economic situation after the drop of oil prices in the middle of the 1980s. For 1985, three of the six largest conventional banks revealed zero profits in their balance sheets (see table 13). The Islamic bank - KFH - had this problem one year before (in 1984).

Table 13: Islamic and Conventional Banks in Kuwait

Total Assets (in mn KD)

	1980	1981	1982	1983	1984	1985	1986
NBK	5065	6940	8039	9046	8631	8962	10369
GB	4306	5340	6266	7088	6181	6301	6196
CBK	3707	5132	6127	6552	5954	5661	5429
ABK	3767	4492	4981	5728	5153	5232	5108
BB	1508	1958	1932	2344	3100	3457	3579
BKME	2029	2647	3534	3530	2975	3028	3014
KFH	621	1247	1971	2731	2778	2782	2949

Net Profit/Assets Ratio [Pre-tax profits on assets] (in per cent)

	1980	1981	1982	1983	1984	1985	1986
NBK	1.06	0.96	0.93	0.93	0.78	0.84	0.87
GB	0.56	0.59	0.72	0.64	0.54	0.00	0.22
CBK	0.86	0.95	0.95	0.87	0.58	0.00	0.25
ABK	0.46	0.59	0.81	0.77	0.61	0.25	0.30
BB	0.55	n.a.	0.81	0.80	0.65	0.00	0.49
BKME	0.72	0.69	0.74	0.73	0.69	0.16	0.34
KFH The Banker	[8.0]	[9.6]	[9.8]	[5.4]	[0.0]	[2.1]	n.a.
KFH corrected	1.46	1.72	2.28	0.50	0.00	0.21	0.32

Net Profit/Capital Ratio [Pre-tax profits on capital] (in per cent)

	1980	1981	1982	1983	1984	1985	1986
NBK	16.56	18.08	17.16	15.33	11.83	11.83	12.12
GB	9.66	10.69	11.82	9.43	7.31	0.00	2.52
CBK	13.05	15.93	16.55	14.70	8.82	0.00	3.14
ABK	8.00	10.98	13.75	11.75	8.92	3.37	3.53
BB	9.49	n.a.	11.89	9.80	5.13	0.00	3.24
BKME	11.97	10.71	11.69	11.54	9.04	1.85	3.68
KFH The Banker	[228.2]	[214.5]	[167.0]	[103.4]	[0.0]	[64.9]	n.a.
KFH corrected	47.43	33.42	36.43	11.46	0.00	4.62	7.24

Capital/Assets Ratio (in per cent)

	1980	1981	1982	1983	1984	1985	1986
NBK	5.90	4.92	5.90	6.16	7.05	7.16	7.16
GB	5.97	5.19	6.90	6.75	8.18	8.57	8.89
CBK	6.10	5.86	5.70	6.14	6.95	7.70	8.13
ABK	5.77	5.10	6.68	6.38	7.33	7.74	9.24
BB	6.58	5.08	8.60	7.86	16.10	15.22	15.01
BKME	5.54	7.11	5.88	6.78	8.53	9.14	9.42
KFH	3.09	5.13	6.33	4.38	4.14	2.36	2.44

From 1980 to 1982, KFH yielded the highest net profits on assets of all Kuwaiti banks listed in the 'Top 100'.[13] After the critical years 1983 and 1984, the bank started recovering, but the net profit/assets ratio is still much lower than it was before the crisis.

The net profits/capital ratio obviously recovered faster so that KFH showed the second highest (and increasing) ratios in 1985 and 1986.

KFH's capital/assets ratio is the lowest of the Kuwaiti banks; it decreased continuously since 1981 (with a slight increase in 1986). It is well known that the Kuwaiti authorities supported banks to avoid collapses. KFH was one of them, but it seems that it is strong enough to recover and to regain profitability in a relatively short period of time.

5. Turkey

Figures for Turkish banks are, of course, not included in the ' Top 100 Arab Banks' . Therefore it is not possible here to assess the performance of the two interest-free financial institutions in Turkey - ABTFH, FFI - against the performance of conventional banks. Instead, the Turkish institutions shall be compared with the other Islamic banks.

In terms of total assets, the Turkish banks - which both started operations in 1985 - are among the smallest of the Islamic banking community. Their

---

[13] However, the ratio was not so extraordinary as calculated by The Banker for 1980 to 1985: As in the case of FIBE, gross and net profits were confused.

capital/assets ratios were around 10 per cent in 1986 which is near the average of the group of Islamic banks.

In terms of (relative) income and profits, the Turkish banks clearly outperformed all other Islamic banks: They held - with one exception - the top positions in income on assets, gross profits on assets, and net profits on capital in 1985 and 1986. It is remarkable that the ratios for 1986 were even higher than the already high ratios for 1985. However, it must be noted that the increase of the net profit/capital ratio may - at least partially - be caused by the high inflation in Turkey (around 35 per cent in 1986): Inflation leads to a nominal increase of profits while the nominal value of the capital does not change accordingly. Therefore, the net profit/capital ratio will be inflated.

Although FFI came to better results than all other Islamic banks outside Turkey, ABTFH's performance was even more excellent. The differences between FFI and ABTFH are significant: the income/assets, net profit/assets and net profit/capital ratios of ABTFH were roughly the double of FFI's. A closer look at the annual reports for 1986 shows that:

- The number of accounts and the amounts of deposits at FFI were about 50 per cent higher than at ABTFH, but this is hardly a sufficient explanation for the large difference in profitability. For both banks, less than 10 per cent of all deposits were on current accounts.

- Both banks give a breakdown of their placements of funds by sectors or economic activities. There are some differences in the placements, but they are much too small to explain the pronounced differences in income and profits.[14]

- The main difference between FFI and ABTFH can be found in the composition of deposits: A little more than 2/3 of ABTFH's deposits are on Turkish Lira accounts and only 1/3 on foreign currency accounts, while more than 2/3 of FFI's deposits are on foreign currency accounts and only less than 1/3 on Turkish Lira accounts. If there are more profitable opportunities for the (interest-free) employment of Turkish Lira than for the national or international placement of foreign currencies (mainly DM and US$), then this discrepancy could explain (most of) the differences in income and profits.

---

[14] It may be, however, that the type of business which is financed in the same sector differs.

It will be interesting to observe the future of these two banks; the interim report of ABTFH for the first half of 1987 showed further improvements of the performance ratios. Maybe Turkish banks can be taken as examples for the successful implementation of profit-oriented strategies and for the efficient management of interest-free financial institutions in a newly industrializing country.

III. Theory and Practice - Discrepancies and Prospects

The theory of Islamic banking emerged in the 1950s and 1960s when macroeconomic models of interest-free economies were developed and some hints were given how interest-free banking could work at the microeconomic level.[15] In these models most if not all interest-based financing was replaced by financing on the basis of partnerships (*mudaraba*, musharaka) where the bank and the entrepreneur share the expected profit but also the risk of (unexpected) losses. Advocates of Islamic banking pointed out that this would be the main difference between interest-based and Islamic banking, and they based their ideological claim of an allocative and distributive superiority on it.

A. The Dominance of Short-Term Trade Financing

It is doubtful whether the first 'practitioners' of Islamic banking were aware of these theories. What they were (or very soon became) aware of, however, was the fact that participation financing can be very risky, especially in a world where Islamic banks compete with conventional banks and where the interest rate for loans sets a limit to the participation ratios of Islamic banks (when entrepreneurs compare the offers of Islamic banks with conventional alternatives).[16] Therefore, the Islamic banks looked for alternative ways for the employment of funds. Their starting point was that *riba* (interest) is prohibited in financial transaction while profits from trade are permissible. Consequently, the Islamic banks went beyond the scope of the customary activities of commercial banks and became traders themselves: instead of providing money, the Islamic banks provide the goods their clients need. On request of a client, the bank buys goods (merchandise, machinery, etc.) and sells or rents them to him. The selling price or rent covers the cost price plus a predetermined mark-up or profit-margin for the bank (murabaha or mark-up financing). Most funds of most Islamic banks are employed in various kinds of

[15] See for example Siddiqi (1973/83), Mannan (1970).
[16] This is explained in more details in Nienhaus (1983).

trade, rent and leasing (ijara) activities with fixed returns for the bank. Only a small fraction of the total financing is based on participation principles.

The expectations and hopes that Islamic banks would be active mainly in the field of corporate financing on participation basis - thus providing badly needed risk capital especially to small and medium sized enterprises - were disappointed.[17]

The share of medium to long term corporate financing in total financing of Islamic banks is generally very low, and if an Islamic bank goes beyond the short term financing of working capital, the financing is provided not on the basis of participation but of hire-purchase or leasing contracts.

If Islamic banks take recourse to participation techniques (mudaraba, musharaka), this is done rarely in medium and long term corporate but mainly in short term trade financing.

The annual reports of most Islamic banks do not disclose very much about the types of financing (trade or corporate, short or long term) and give no breakdown of financing according to the techniques and types of contracts (participation or fixed returns for the bank). Nevertheless, some statements and figures can be found which support the thesis that short term trade financing is clearly dominating in most Islamic banks.

---

[17] This disappointment is the background for the proposal that the authorities should force Islamic banks to increase the share of participation financing gradually; see Cizakca (1987, 89). This proposal implies not only a discrimination of Islamic banks against conventional commercial banks, it also exposes the depositors of Islamic banks to a higher risk than they (respective of the bank management on their behalf) may be willing to take. More important, the proposal seems to be based on a confusion between the mode and purpose of financing. The aim of the proposal is to reduce short term trade and to increase medium and long term corporate financing, i.e. to shift from one purpose of financing to another. But for this, it is neither necessary nor sufficient to prescribe a shift in the modes of financing: On the other hand, corporate financing could well be done under non-participation arrangements like leasing contracts (so that PLS techniques are not necessary). A prescription to use more participation modes of financing may have the effect that the banks replace some murabaha contracts by musharaka arrangements in trade financing (so that more use of PLS techniques is not a sufficient condition for more corporate financing).

FIBE's annual report for 1405 H./ 1985 A.D. allows the calculation that the bank's long term financing was less than 3 per cent of total financing.

FFI states for 1986 that 'Profit & Loss Sharing deals occupied a rather small volume of its total financing, due to various market problems encountered during this period.'

ABTFH has published a breakdown of its placements by the end of 1986; 93.8 per cent of the investments were trade financing, 6.2 per cent were invested in profit and loss sharing projects.

QIB explains in its annual report for 1406 H. that it is its policy 'to invest in short and medium term investments' which is felt necessary 'to match the short and medium term nature' of its deposits. 90 per cent of QIB's investments are due within one month.

KFH declares in the annual report for 1986: 'The principal activities ... include the provision of banking services, the purchase and sale of property and other trading activities' . Joint venture business with third parties is also mentioned, but its quantity is insignificant.

BIB uses musharaka contracts for investments in buildings and land, but they are not more than 6-8 per cent of total financing and investments.

ABIIB's source of income are 'investment returns' originating from profits from murabaha transactions only (except a small income from deposits with other Islamic banks).

IBBL had a relatively high share of musharaka type investments in the last years, but it decreased continuously and stood at 10.5 per cent in 1986 while the share of murabaha investments increased rapidly.

The obvious neglect of medium and long term PLS corporate financing - and the resulting discrepancy between ideology and practice of Islamic banking - is not caused by ignorance or ill-will of the bank managers.

Some Islamic banks emphasize that they do not classify themselves as development banks or investment banks but explicitly as commercial banks, not dealing with long term projects but with short term trade finance. They point out that in most Islamic countries the state runs specialized banks to meet the demand of the corporate sector for medium and long term financing.

In addition, they can draw the attention to the fact that most of the deposits of Islamic banks are of short term nature. It would be very risky to finance medium and long term projects out of short term funds.

Further, the low percentage of participation financing may not only be due to an insufficient supply by the banks but also to a weak demand by well-doing entrepreneurs: Entrepreneurs with good profit expectations may prefer financing their projects on the basis of fixed interest so that they do not have to share the expected profits with someone else.

Finally, for most entrepreneurs it is not very attractive that the traditional form of Islamic partnership financing (musharaka) gives the bank a right to interfere into the management of the partner's business. This problem, however, could be solved by the development and legalization of new types of PLS contracts (like PTCs in Pakistan or new types of shares of joint stock companies with no voting rights as introduced in Bahrain in 1986).

Summing up one can say that there is a discrepancy between the philosophy or ideology which emphasizes the social and developmental impact of Islamic banking and the partnership approach in financing, and the short-term trade oriented and mark-up based business of most of present day Islamic banks.

B. Problems of Financial Intermediation and Transformation

There are no fundamental differences between Islamic and conventional banks with respect to financing techniques, types of projects or the financed entrepreneurs. It cannot be denied that there are legal differences between the contracts applied by Islamic and conventional banks, but the economic differences - which are so pronounced in the ideology - look only marginal at the microeconomic level. But there are some more important differences at the macroeconomic level which do not constitute an advantage but rather a serious handicap for Islamic banking: The financial instruments for the liquidity management of Islamic banks are still underdeveloped; as a consequence, the macroeconomic transformation function is only partially fulfilled by Islamic banks. Banks as financial intermediaries between savers and investors must be able to transform amounts, risks and maturities.

Customers of Islamic banks usually can deposit money in investment accounts only for well-defined periods (like 3, 6, 12 months), and they have no contractual right to withdraw their funds before the end of that period (although the bank management may allow exceptions in extraordinary cases).

Islamic banks are not yet in a position to accept deposits in random amounts and with random maturities on a daily basis.

In conventional banks, the depositors are protected against the risk of nominal losses by the repayment guarantee of the bank, and they receive, in addition, a non-negative return. Deposits on investment accounts at Islamic banks, however, are exposed to the risk of nominal losses. The only protection against this risk is the prudence of the bank management in its financing and placement decisions, but the depositors have no institutionalized influence on the management.[18]

A certain portion of the legally short term funds is normally not withdrawn at maturity. These funds can be used for medium or long term financing so that the average maturity on the assets side of the balance sheet is longer than on the liabilities side. A precondition for this maturity transformation is that the bank is able to procure liquidity from external sources in cases of unexpected withdrawals. Without an interest-free 'money' and capital market, Islamic banks have no adequate instruments to meet this precondition for effective maturity transformation.

From a macroeconomic point of view, these are serious deficiencies of an Islamic banking system which is equipped with no other than the presently applied financial instruments. To overcome these defects, the creation of a new type of 'financial' certificates has been proposed which is in accordance with the Shari'a and for which a secondary market can be organized[19]: The Shari'a recognizes certificates when they represent the ownership of (parts of) real assets. There are no objections against the transfer of such certificates, and their price may be determined by supply and demand. To make it more concrete: suppose a bank buys some income generating real assets (like warehouses or petrol stations) which are leased out to commercial users. The bank then re-sells the objects by issuing certificates which legally are titles to a certain part of the leased out objects. The leasing contracts may be concluded for five to ten years, thus securing a continuous flow of rental income. It is possible to calculate a present value of the expected future income, and this - in relation to other opportunities for the profitable employment of funds - will determine a market price for the certificates.

To set up a secondary market, the issuing bank could start a daily 'over-the-counter' trading with prices continuously updated according to the actual

---

[18] It has been proposed that the banks should offer different types of investment accounts which are characterized by different risks (and profit expectation) resulting from placement of deposits.

[19] See Trolle-Schultz (1986).

demand and supply. Such a system would facilitate the short term and even very short term placement of surplus funds (by buying certificates today and selling them tomorrow). Once a sufficiently broad secondary market is established, the certificates could also be used by Islamic banks for their liquidity management: they could keep in their portfolios an amount of the certificates which could be sold on the market when there is an unexpected need of liquidity.

The creation of negotiable certificates of deposits (CDs) - which are directly linked and legally attached as a title to individualized real objects being leased out by the issuer of the CDs - should be seen as a very significant first step for the development of a more effective Islamic financial market.[20]

C. Commercial vs. Developmental Orientation in Islamic Banking

Most of the presently operating Islamic banks are interest-free commercial banks. They offer banking facilities to roughly the same segment of the economy as the conventional banks. A grave weakness of the banking system in most Islamic countries is that it is mainly engaged in the financing of domestic and international trade and of some manufacturing projects in major cities, while the rural areas are widely neglected. At best, branches of conventional banks collect deposits which are passed on to the head-offices and are invested in the commercial centres of the country. But there is not much financing available for farmers, craftsmen, small industrialists or traders outside the big cities.

---

[20] Financial innovations are needed not only in the deposit business but also in the financing business. If financing on a participation basis is encouraged, new techniques should be developed which reduce the very high income risk for the bank under PLS arrangements. It has been proposed elsewhere to reconsider what should (or must) be the basis for participation financing, what should (or could) be the 'results' which are allocated to the bank and the entrepeneur; the concrete proposal was to replace the profit (as it calculated in the balance sheet or income statement) by the value added. The value added may become negative, but only under exceptional conditions; normally, the value added can be predicted much better than the (gross) profit, and it is much more difficult for malevolent entrepreneurs to manipulate the value added than the profit figures. The proposal of a 'Value Added Participation' was elaborated first in Nienhaus (1986a).

The neglect of the rural areas by financial institutions can become an impediment for national development. Except for a few oil-rich Arab states, most Islamic countries have a large agricultural sector which absorbs the greatest part of the labour force and contributes substantially to the national income. This important sector must be integrated into the financial system of the country.

Developing Islamic countries are in need of investment funds; these can originate either from domestic savings or from capital imports. If the external debt of a country does not increase further, the agricultural sector must produce surpluses which set free productive factors that can be channelled into the manufacturing industry to facilitate its further growth and expansion. The integration of the agricultural sector into the national capital formation requires the integration of the rural population into the national financial system.

A precondition is that there should be financial institutions which are not only within physical reach for the population in small towns and villages, but which are considered as trustworthy by the people. Often the branches of conventional banks are not accepted by the rural population because the banking operations are based on interest and the financing activities are concentrated on the large business centres of the country and neglect the credit needs of the rural area.

It is a basic assumption that the rural population has the will as well as the capacity to save. 'Saving' means that parts of the actual income are not immediately consumed or used for the satisfaction of today's needs but are 'put aside' for use in the future (e.g. in old age, in case of illness, or for special occasions like a wedding). A developmental problem lies in the form of savings: People in rural areas keep their savings only to a small extent as financial assets (including deposits in the banking system). Rather, they 'save' - next to hoarding money - in the form of buying real assets (like jewelry, carpets, land, houses and durable consumer goods). This practice has negative consequences both on the individual microeconomic and on the social macroeconomic levels.

For the individual, the 'real asset saving' causes often very high transaction costs: When in cases of need savings assets have to be liquidated, this usually is possible only with substantial reductions of the (now) selling prices as compared to the (former) buying prices.

For the economy as a whole, the 'real asset saving' locks input factors in the production of savings assets; these factors could be shifted into lines of production with higher developmental impacts once the people would 'put aside' parts of their current income not by buying real assets but by acquiring financial assets respective depositing their money in bank accounts.

If one succeeds in affecting a change in the behavioural pattern of the population in shifting from saving in real assets to saving in financial assets (in a broad sense, including savings accounts with banks and financial papers), then the statistical macroeconomic savings ratio could be increased without restrictions in the level of 'effective' private consumption. Productive factors would be set free for investment purposes. It is of highest importance as a precondition for achieving such a behavioural change that the rural population has access to and confidence in financial institutions. What is important in this regard is, inter alia:

- that financial institutions are not only active in the large business centres of the country but work in the rural areas and not only with the big landlords but especially with the small people,

- that banks offer their customers different types of deposits to meet the different savings motives,

- that funds thus mobilized do not flow to distant commercial centres but rather are - at least in respectable parts - invested in the local community to give observable development impulses.

To establish a bank in a village or small town is very unusual, and those who have this intention probably will face some difficulties to raise the capital and to find suitable staff for their project. The uncertainties about the commercial feasibility of such a project are substantial, and the profit expectations for the capital owners are not very promising for the first years. But at least there is a hope that in the long run the dividends may become competitive if the bank succeeds in initiating economic development in the local community and is able to create its own group of self-employed people and new entrepreneurs whose activities and ventures are financed by the bank. To attain this goal, the bank could, for example, pay special attention to the financing of productivity improving devices for small craftsmen, farmers, traders, etc. who have factually no chance to get a loan from a conventional bank due to their lack of collaterals. The bank should not care so much about the (existing) collaterals but give more importance to the personal qualities of the client. The financing decisions should not depend on the 'physical capital' (collaterals) but mainly on the 'human capital' of the client. The expectation is that there will be no substantial defaults since the clients are aware of the fact that they have no alternative for future financing. The objective of the Islamic bank should be to change the behaviour of people (to 'educate the masses'), to integrate the rural population into the financial system thus widening the basis for the national capital formation, but also to decentralize the system and to create self-supporting regional 'sub-systems' in order to improve the individual as well as the collective economic situation of the majority of people living in rural areas.

The request to try to employ substantial parts of the funds in the same community where they have been mobilized does not mean, however, that the banks in rural areas should work in isolation and have no relations with the 'big business' in the commercial centres. On the contrary, it is of high importance for the smooth functioning of local Islamic banks in smaller communities that they can take recourse to an inter-bank market in order to place (short term) surplus funds for which they have no immediate employment themselves, or to get funds immediately when there is an unexpected need of liquidity. A cooperation of rural Islamic banks with interest-free commercial banks in the commercial centres seems to be necessary. This implies that there should be different types of Islamic banks in order to develop a banking system that performs all the macroeconomic functions that are accomplished by the conventional interest-based banking system and make a positive contribution to the national development.

Without an efficient financial market the ability of Islamic banks in rural areas to cope with liquidity surplus and shortage situations, their earning power, and their growth potential are seriously impeded.

IV. Conclusions

About 50 operating interest-free financial institutions prove that Islamic banking is viable at a microeconomic level. However, Islamic banks in general do not show a superior performance when compared with conventional banks; in many cases performance was even a little worse than the average, but it is apparent that Islamic banking can be operational and profitable. It will survive, and there are chances that the Islamic sectors in many countries will grow in the future (although some individual banks show signs of stagnation).

At the macroeconomic level some important questions are not yet settled. Neither Pakistan nor Iran have been able to set up a 'real' interest-free interbank or secondary market for Islamic financial papers. Adequate financial mechanisms still have to be developed. What also has to be developed is that type of Islamic bank which operates outside the commercial centres, integrates the rural populations into the financial system and promotes local development by providing finance for small business and self-employment. Few among the operating Islamic banks have a strong developmental orientation in their business activities.

- The FIBK was established in 1982, and the conceptual framework was designed by Dr. Ahmed El-Naggar who was the initiator of a first experiment with interest-free savings banks in Egypt in the 1960s.[21]

- The Sudanese Islamic Bank (SIB) was established in 1983. The merits of this bank lay in the introduction of innovative financing methods for the agricultural sector, especially for small farmers who had so far been neglected by the conventional banks.

- Other experiments that deserve more attention include (kinds of) credit cooperatives of Muslim communities in India and in South Africa.

Islamic banking is imperfect. Ideological claims of superiority are unfounded. But what we see so far is just the beginning of a development. The future will bring forth financial innovations; they will facilitate a 'smoother' functioning of interest-free banking. However, Islamic banks will always be in an instrumental disadvantage compared to conventional banks: whenever the Islamic banks develop new financial instruments, conventional banks are not restricted to imitate them if they find the new instruments promising. The reverse, however, does not hold: Islamic banks cannot copy all instruments

---

[21] For an outline and a preliminary assessment of the activities of this bank see Nienhaus (1987).

that are available to conventional banks. Thus the tool box of conventional banks will (actually or potentially) always be greater than that of Islamic banks. On the long run, the greatest challenges and potentials for Islamic banks may not lay in the markets which are served already by the conventional banks. Islamic banks could compensate their instrumental limitations if they are willing and able to integrate the rural areas into the national financial system. They could mobilize new depositors and create or educate their own entrepreneurs. This business may well become profitable, and for local Islamic banks it seems to be much less risky to apply participation techniques in their financing business than for big interest-free commercial banks. With financial innovations, with the emergence of an interest-free capital market, and with a more developmental orientation, there are good chances that Islamic banks can contribute substantially to the progress of their countries in the years to come. But this will not come by itself; it needs much commitment and efforts - and maybe also some critical comments from outside the Muslim world.

* * * * *

References

Ahmad, A 1987, *Development and Problems of Islamic Banks*, Islamic Research and Training Institute, Jeddah.

Ahmed, Z; Iqbal, M; Khan, M F ed 1983, *Money and Banking in Islam,* Institute of Policy Studies, Islamabad.

Ali, M ed 1982, *Islamic Banks and Strategies of Economic Cooperation,* New Century Publishers, London.

Chapra, M U 1985 *Towards a Just Monetary System,* The Islamic Foundation, Leicester.

Cizakca, M 1987, 'Rise of Islamic Banks and the Potential for Venture Capital in the Middle East' in Manisali, E ed, *The Middle East and Eastern Mediterranean - Recent Economic and Political Developments,* Istanbul 1987, pp 74-90.

El Din, A K 1986, 'Ten Years of Islamic Banking', *Journal of Islamic Banking & Finance* Vol. 3, No. 3, pp 49-66 (reprinted from Arabia).

Huq, M A 1986, 'Islamic Banking in Malaysia', *Thoughts on Economics* Vol. 7, No. 2, pp 1-21.

IERB - Islamic Economics Research Bureau ed 1982, *Thoughts on Islamic Banking,* Dhaka.

Iqbal, Z; Mirakhor, A 1987, *Islamic Banking,* IMF, Washington.

Khan, M 1986, 'Islamic Interest-Free Banking', IMF Staff Papers Vol. 33, pp 1-27.

Khan, W M 1985, *Towards an Interest-Free Islamic Economic System,* The Islamic Foundation, Leicester.

Mannan, M A 1970, *Islamic Economics - Theory and Practice,* Sh. Muhammad Ashraf, Lahore.

Moore, C H 1987, 'Islamic Banks: Financial and Political Intermediation in Arab Countries' , paper presented at a French/German symposium on Islamic economics, organized by the German Orient Institute, Bonn, 29-30 October 1987.

Mudawi, A B 1986, 'Medium- and Long-Term Finance by Islamic Financial Institutions', *Journal of Islamic Banking & Finance* Vol. 3, No. 2, pp 16-35.

Nienhaus, V 1983, 'Profitability of Islamic PLS Banks Competing with Interest Banks: Problems and Prospects', *Journal of Research in Islamic Economics* Vol. 1, No. 1, pp 37-47.

Nienhaus, V 1986, 'Islamic Economics, Finance and Banking - Theory and Practice', *Journal of Islamic Banking & Finance* Vol. 3, No. 2, pp 36-54.

Nienhaus, V 1986a, 'Value Added Participation (VAP) - A New Financing Instrument for Islamic Banks,' Workshop Paper No. 3, UNIDO Workshop on Industrial Financing Activities of Islamic Banks, Vienna, 16-20 June 1986.

Nienhaus, V 1987, 'The Potential Contribution of Islamic Banks to the Economic Development of Muslim Countries', paper presented at the international symposium on 'A New Strategy for Development from Below', organized by Faisal Islamic Bank of Kibris and International Association of Islamic Banks, in Northern Cyprus, 23-27 September 1987.

Salama, A A 1987, 'Utilization of Financial Instruments - A Case Study of Faisal Islamic Bank (Sudan)', *Journal of Islamic Banking & Finance* Vol. 4, No. 2, pp 24-40.

Siddiqi, M N 1973/83, *Banking without Interest,* Islamic Publications, Lahore 1973; new translation from Urdu: The Islamic Foundation, Leicester 1983.

Trolle-Schultz, Erik 1986, 'Savings and Investments through Islamic Banking and Finance' , paper presented at a seminar on Islamic Economics, organized by the Pakistan-German Society for Friendship and Cooperation, Bonn, 22 September 1986.

Wilson, R 1985, *Islamic Business - Theory and Practice,* 2nd ed, Economist Publications, London.

Zaidi, N A 1987, 'Profit Rates Policy for PLS Depositors' *Journal of Islamic Banking & Finance* Vol. 4, No. 4, pp 35-46.

* * * * *

Annex 1: Notes to Tables 1-13

(1) The figures for Islamic banks are taken from primary sources (mainly annual reports). Exceptions are the figures for FIBE 1986 and the capital/assets ratios in tables 10-13 which were taken from the December issues of The Banker (1981-1987). The total assets exclude contra accounts; in the case of MFIB, 'funds under management' are included in total assets.

(2) Islamic banks use different terminologies in their annual reports. The definitions of gross or net income and gross or net profits as they are understood in the tables are given in the first chapter above. The respective figures were taken/calculated from the balance sheets and income statements of the Islamic banks. Differences between, for example, 'net profits' as shown in the balance sheet and in the tables here are due to different definitions.

(3) The figures for conventional banks are taken from the 'Top 100 Arab Banks' in the December issues of The Banker (1981-1987). Each issue (e.g. the December 1987 issue) gives figures for the last year, i.e. the year under report (e.g. 1986) and the year before (e.g. 1985). The figures for the year under report of the previous issue (e.g. for 1985 in the 1986 issue) are not in all cases identical with the figures for the same year as given in the subsequent issue as figures for the year before the reporting year (e.g. 1985 in the 1987 issue). In these cases, the more recent figures have been taken (e.g. the figures for 1985 from the 1987 issue), assuming that the differences reflect corrections, or are final, in contrast to previously provisional figures.

(4) Figures in national currency were converted into US$ by using the rates published in the IMF's International Financial Statistics.

(5) Some Islamic banks use the Hijra calender (BIB, FIBE, FIBS, since 1984/1404, QIB). The Hijra years have been 'translated' into Gregorian years as follows: 1399=1979, 1400=1980, ...1405=1985, 1406=1986. The business year of some banks (e.g. BIM) runs from July 1 to June 30; the data for the full business year are given in that calendar year in which the business year ends.

(6) Most Islamic banks started operations during the period which is covered in the tables. A blank indicated that the respective bank was not yet operating in that year. For years in which it was operating but no figures were available from primary sources (like annual reports), this is expressed by 'n.a.'.

(7) Market shares (table 3) are defined as the percentage of Islamic banks deposits (taken from the annual reports) in total deposits of the country (= demand, time and savings deposits as published in IMF's International Financial Statistics, lined 24 and 25).

Annex 2: Banks Acronyms

Abbreviations

AACB	Al-Ahli Commercial Bank [Bahrain]
AAIB	Arab African International Bank [Egypt]
AB	Arab Bank [Jordan]
ABC	Arab Banking Corporation [Bahrain]
ABIIB	Albaraka Islamic Investment Bank [Bahrain]
ABIL	Al Baraka International Limited [U.K.]
ABK	Alahli Bank of Kuwait [Kuwait]
ABTFH	Al Baraka Turkish Finance House [Turkey]
AIB	Arab International Bank [Egypt]
ARLA	Arlabank International [Bahrain]
BA	Bank of Alexandria [Egypt]
BB	Burgan Bank [Kuwait]
BBK	Bank of Bahrain and Kuwait [Bahrain]
BC	Banque du Caire [Egypt]
BIB	Bahrain Islamic Bank [Bahrain]
BIM	Bank Islam Malaysia Berhad [Malaysia]
BKME	Bank of Kuwait and the Middle East [Kuwait}
BM	Banque Misr [Egypt]
BMEB	Bahrain Middle East Bank [Bahrain]

CBK	Commercial Bank of Kuwait [Kuwait]
DIB	Dubai Islamic Bank [U.A.E.]
EAB	Egyptian American Bank [Egypt]
FFI	Faisal Finance Institution [Turkey]
FIBE	Faisal Islamic Bank of Egypt [Egypt]
FIBK	Faisal Islamic Bank of Kibris [Cyprus]
FIBS	Faisal Islamic Bank (Sudan) [Sudan]
GB	Gulf Bank [Kuwait]
GIB	Gulf International Bank [Bahrain]
GRB	Gulf Riyad Bank [Bahrain]
IBBL	Islamic Bank Bangadesh Limited [Bangladesh]
IBID	Islamic Bank International of Demark [Denmark]
IIBID	Islamic International Bank for Investment and Development [Egypt]
JIBFD	Jordan Islamic Bank for Finance and Development [Jordan]
KAB	Kuwait Asia Bank [Kuwait]
KFH	Kuwait Finance House [Kuwait]
MFIB	Massraf Faysal Al-Islami of Bahrain [Bahrain]
MIB	Misr International Bank [Egypt]
NBB	National Bank of Bahrain [Bahrain]
NBE	National Bank of Egypt [Egypt]
NBK	National Bank of Kuwait [Kuwait]
PB	Petra Bank [Jordan]
QIB	Qatar Islamic Bank [Qatar]
SCB	Suez Canal Bank [Egypt]

* * * * *

ISLAMIC FINANCE IN PRINCIPLE AND PRACTICE
(With Special Reference to Turkey)

David Baldwin and **Rodney Wilson**
Economics Department, University of Durham

Introduction

There has been increasing interest in the subject of Islamic finance in recent years, with a growing academic literature, and numerous postgraduate theses. In this chapter some basic principles of Islamic finance are outlined, and the prohibition of *riba* discussed. The application of Islamic financial principles is assessed, and the emergence of the modern Islamic banking movement examined, focusing on the specific challenges faced by the Islamic banking systems of Saudi Arabia, Iran and Turkey. The influence of Islamic ideals on Saudi finance is discussed, both internally and internationally, as significant amounts of petrodollars were invested in the West in the 1970s and early 1980s. The Iranian experience is examined, as the Tehran authorities introduced comprehensive legislation Islamising their banking system. Finally, the impact of Islamic banks on Turkey is considered, the latter being perhaps the most secular state in the Middle East.

I. Islamic Financial Principles

The fundamentals of Islamic financial theory were expounded by the Prophet Muhammad over fourteen hundred years ago. Though the parameters may be fixed, innovative thinking is required to apply Islamic principles to modern, ever evolving, financial practice. The Islamic revival has been the stimulus for such thinking, which has emphasised that moral issues are always involved in financial dealings. Such transactions, by their nature, occur in a social context, and cannot be regarded as impersonal and value free, as most Western financial literature implicitly assumes.

The theory of Islamic finance is normative rather than positive. Finance is viewed as merely one facet of social relationships and an integral part of a wider economic system. It is not solely regarded as a field for the specialist. The need for specialist knowledge is of course recognised, but the specialist should not be isolated and concern himself with only narrowly defined interests. Rather the specialist should be conversant with the wider moral framework, and aware of spiritual as well as material needs.

There is a basic difference in perspective between the Western and the Islamic economist. Western neo-classical economics is ultimately concerned with the allocation of scarce resources amongst competing needs. In the Qur'an however, the bounty of God is stressed, with resources in abundance. In such a world one's needs can be satisfied without sacrificing another's. Competition is seen as neither necessary nor desirable by Muslim thinkers, whereas for many Western economists it is viewed as the natural order. Instead of being concerned with the regulation of narrow individual aspirations, the Islamic economist stresses wider social responsibility. Respect for private property rights is nevertheless emphasised in Muslim society, and in this regard at least, Islam has more in common with Western thinking than it does with socialism.

II. The Prohibition of Riba

Perhaps the most widely known tenet of Islamic finance in the West is the prohibition of 'riba'. What constitutes riba has long been the subject of debate amongst Islamic scholars. Some believe that riba refers to usury, whereas others believe that all interest is riba. Certainly one Muslim objection to interest payments is on grounds of equity. It is the poor and needy who are often forced to borrow, whereas the rich have surplus funds to save. Interest thus penalises the poor and benefits the rich. For the devout Muslim this is anathema, as it results in hardship and increasing social polarisation. Such practices could not be tolerated in a community of believers.

A further objection to interest is that it corrupts the recipient. It is viewed as unearned income, a reward without productive effort. Interest can be a deterrent to honest toil, as it may be tempting to rely on unearned income rather than working for a wage or salary. Western neo-classical economics sees interest as a reward for waiting or deferring consumption until a future time period. The Protestant ethic which underlies Western capitalism regarded saving as virtuous. Time is treated as a type of commodity by Western economists, which has a price. This is believed to be a trade-off between earnings and leisure, and wages are a reward for foregoing leisure.

Islamic scholars reject such notions. The just wage reflects the workers' contribution to society, not the time spent working. Time itself is valueless. Hence there can be no justification in a reward for time.

To the devout Muslim, abstinence needs no material reward. The earth's bounty is to be used, but God demands certain sacrifices such as fasting during the month of Ramadan. The rewards for such abstinence are spiritual, and the introduction of monetary incentives would only undermine the spiritual value of such practices. Furthermore, an incentive for saving may result in underconsumption, and a lack of effective demand in the economy. Hoarding is viewed as socially undesirable in Muslim societies, as it can result in unemployment and idle capacity. In this sense Muslim ideals are consistent with Keynesian views on economic management. Currency must circulate, and the accumulation of the means of exchange for its own sake is seen as undesirable.

III. Application of Islamic Ideals

Although there is little disagreement over the principles of Islamic finance, the interpretation of the prohibition of riba in practice has been subject to much greater controversy. Should the prohibition apply to all interest, or does it merely mean that interest rates should remain at moderate levels? Are interest charges for business loans permissible, as the borrowers are seeking to use their credit to generate profits? Are fixed interest loans preferable to those subject to interest rate variations, as at least the borrower knows the exact charges in advance, and there is no element of uncertainty? Finally, under inflationary conditions, should interest rewards be allowed to compensate savers for the depreciations of the value of their savings? A prohibition of nominal interest to compensate for inflation would penalise lenders, and subsidise borrowers. It could be argued that the prohibition of riba applies to real interest, not nominal interest, as with inflation, a ban on the latter may result in negative real interest.

Most Islamic states in practice have tried to restrain nominal interest rates. As inflation results in social strains in any Muslim community, and also poses moral dilemmas, the control of price increases has been an important economic priority for Muslim governments. In the Middle East, it is only in Turkey and Israel that inflation spiralled virtually out of control during the last decade. The consequences for nominal interest rates appalled the majority of devout Muslims. Interest rates in Israel are index-linked to the inflation rate, and in 1984 they rose to over 400 per cent. As there are some lags in adjustment, it is possible to have high real rates, especially as inflation starts to fall. Few Muslims in Israel, even those with citizenship, have held shekel denominated deposits under such conditions, as to do so would be sacrilegious.

Some states such as Saudi Arabia have a prohibition on all interest payments and receipts under their Islamic laws. Service charges are permitted, however, on bank loans, and in practice as they are calculated on a percentage basis, they resemble interest in many respects. The service charges are kept fixed however, and hence borrowers are not subject to the uncertainty as to the future costs of debt servicing which arises when interest rates vary. In Saudi Arabia most bank deposits are in current accounts which earn no income, but even deposits in savings accounts only earn a modest fixed return, not an interest receipt. There was no question of raising these returns when interest rates on dollar deposits in Bahrain and elsewhere rose to very high levels in the early 1980s, even though the Saudi Arabian monetary system was disrupted as a result of the exodus of capital. It was widely felt that it was better to suffer such disruptions, than to compromise on Islamic principles.

IV. Modern Islamic Banking

In Islamic states where commercial banks are free to charge and receive interest, many Muslim businessmen felt obliged to participate in riba transactions, even though they felt a moral guilt in doing so. To overcome this dilemma of conscience, specifically Islamic banks were founded, which could compete with conventional commercial banks, but which adhered to Islamic principles. The movement was started in Pakistan in the 1950s, but soon spread to the Arab World, with the opening of the Mitr Ghamr Savings Bank in Egypt in 1963, which later was superceded by the Nasser Social Bank. The impact of these institutions was modest, as the major state-owned banks continued to account for most of the banking business in Egypt. Nevertheless the Nasser Social Bank attracted deposits from an influential group of pious farmer landlords, and backed some significant agro-industrial ventures.

It was, however, the devout Muslim merchants of the Gulf who were largely responsible for the rapid expansion of Islamic banking during the last decade. These conservative merchants were reluctant to use the services of conventional commercial banks. Yet with the rapid business expansion of the Gulf following the oil price rises of 1973-74, some type of financial intermediation was clearly needed. Institutions such as the Dubai Islamic Bank (founded 1975), the Kuwait Finance House (1977), and the Bahrain Islamic Bank (1979) were established to serve such clients, while at the same time avoiding riba transactions. There was some government encouragement, with the states taking a minority shareholding in each of the institutions, but most of the finance came from the merchants themselves, especially in the case of the Dubai Islamic Bank which is 80 per cent privately owned.

The Islamic banks in the Gulf account for around five per cent of total bank deposits. Although their role in Gulf finance is modest, the bank's market penetration is considered a success, given that they represent a new type of institution adopting innovative financial techniques. Although there have been setbacks, notably as a result of dealings in precious metals, the track record of the Islamic banks has been favourable so far, and the returns to investors have been competitive with those offered by more conventional banks. As most deposits are of modest amounts, the total number of depositors is higher than their share of total deposits indicates. Many customers maintain accounts with both the new Islamic banks and conventional commercial banks. In this sense the Islamic banks complement rather than replace conventional banks. Nevertheless the ultimate objective for the Islamic banks is to provide a comprehensive range of banking services as a complete alternative to riba finance.

In Saudi Arabia there has been considerable support for Islamic banking, even though the kingdom had no specifically Islamic banks until recently. As all banks in Saudi Arabia are supposed to operate according to Islamic principles, the Saudi Arabian Monetary Agency saw no need to licence a specially designated Islamic bank. Indeed it was thought that granting such a licence would place the commercial banks in an invidious position. Hence the only Islamic financial institution in the Kingdom was the Jeddah-based Islamic Development Bank, but it is a development assistance agency, and not a bank which deals with the general public. Its principal aim is to provide riba-free finance for Islamic countries, especially those with low per capita income levels.

V. Moneylenders as Islamic Banks

Most Saudi citizens do not maintain accounts with the commercial banks in the kingdom. Instead they resort to moneylenders and moneychangers for their financial requirements. Some of these 'informal' bankers offer a wide range of financial services, including currency exchange, the handling of overseas remittances, deposit accounts and loans. Interest is not earned on loans, which are often in kind rather than cash. For example, if a client needs some item of equipment, the moneylender will usually purchase it on behalf of the client, and then either collect instalments from the client, or else enter a leasing arrangement. In either case the payments over a period will exceed the initial cost of the item, the difference representing the moneylenders' profit.

One Saudi Arabian moneylending and moneychanging family, the Rajhis, have grown to become the third largest commercial financial institution in the Kingdom, after the National Commercial and the Riyad Banks. Their assets exceed $180 million, and all of the business has been built up on the basis of riba-free transactions. In 1983 there were pressures for the Rajhis to register as a commercial bank, as unlike the other banks, they did not hold reserves with Saudi Arabian Monetary Agency, and were completely unregulated. Rather than register as a conventional commercial bank, the Rajhis decided to seek Islamic banking status, as they claimed their business methods conformed to Qur'anic principles in any case.

There was some hesitation on the part of the Saudi Arabian Monetary Authority, given the implications for the other banks, and the problems in acting as a lender of last resort for this type of financial institution. In the end, however, the Saudi Arabian Monetary Authority decided to licence the Rajhis officially in 1985 as deposit takers and exchange dealers, largely in order to help safeguard the stability of the domestic financial system. Although they are not obliged to act as lender of last resort with respect to institutions such as the Rajhis, it is widely believed they would if the need arose. It is only the unregistered moneychangers who refuse to submit properly audited annual accounts that lie outside the Monetary Agency's protective net. With the registration of the moneylenders as Islamic banks, the Monetary Agency has conceded that Islamic financial principles can be interpreted in different ways. Plurality exists as both the conventional commercial banks and the moneylenders claim to conform with Islamic principles, even though their methods of operation differ considerably.

VI. Islamic Banks in International Markets

Prince Mohammed Ibn Faisal of Saudi Arabia is one of the leading activists in the Islamic banking movement. Although he has not established a domestic banking operation within Saudi Arabia, he was the prime instigator of the Faisal Islamic Banks of Egypt and the Sudan, both of which were founded in 1977. Both banks received some local deposits, but much of their funds for lending came from Saudi Arabia. Hence in this sense the institutions represented a vehicle for the intra-regional recycling of petroleum revenue to less affluent Muslim states. Prince Mohammed Ibn Faisal, however, decided that it would be desirable to have an Islamic banking presence in Western financial markets. It was felt necessary to provide some mechanism whereby investors from Saudi Arabia and the Gulf could participate in Western markets on the basis of riba-free transactions. Consequently Dar al-Mal al-

Islami, the House of Islamic Funds, was founded in Geneva in 1981, with a paid up capital of $310 million.

Despite some initial teething problems, and losses during the 1983/84 financial year, Dar al-Mal al-Islami seems to have established a sound base, and is widening its lending and investment activities. There seems to be little problem in attracting deposits, although the 1983/84 losses deterred some investors, but the major difficulty has been to identify riba-free projects to profitably back in Western markets. There is no objection to dealing with institutions which participate in riba transactions, however, as long as the Islamic institution is not directly involved, although in the longer term it is hoped that such dealings can be avoided. In practice Dar al-Mal al-Islami functions as a kind of investment company, deploying most of its funds in equity markets and in property, although it also holds short term assets in the form of cash and commodities. It is the appropriate choice of liquid financial instruments which has caused greatest difficulty, as Islamic institutions cannot hold government bills or bonds which yield interest.

There is little doubt that the coming decade will see an increasing number of Islamic financial institutions represented in Western financial markets. The Rajhis maintain an office in London, not only for exchange dealings, but also to provide investment services for its clients from Saudi Arabia. Another Jeddah based group, the Baraka, are also represented in London. This group is primarily an investment company, but as its paid-up capital is $1.5 billion, and with its substantial deposit base, there is no doubt the Baraka will become a significant force in Islamic finance. Like Dar al-Mal al-Islami, the Baraka group maintains an offshore banking unit in Bahrain, and it has also opened branches in the Sudan, while further branches are planned in Turkey, Egypt, Tunisia and Malaysia. It seems likely that there will be increasing competition between the Baraka group, the Rajhis and Dar al-Mal al-Islami in the years ahead, although at present there seems to be no shortage of deposits for all these institutions.

VII. Constraints in Secular Societies

Problems inevitably arise when Islamic financial institutions operate in a non-Islamic environment. As the Islamic banks do not hold Western government securities as part of their liquid assets, they cannot be registered in Western Europe or the United States as fully fledged commercial banks. Commodity holdings are not recognised as liquid assets, and the maintenance of a large proportion of non-earning cash reserves would substantially reduce the banks returns on their assets.

The Bank of England has been reluctant even to register the Islamic banks as licenced deposit takers, and those operating in the United Kingdom are regarded as investment companies rather than so-called 'secondary' banks. Islamic banks do not want to be regarded as secondary in any case, but the lack of banking status has drawbacks. Islamic institutions cannot solicit for deposits from Muslim investors who reside in the United Kingdom. Nor can the Islamic financial institutions carry out normal banking operations in London, as they have to resort to conventional riba banks for the clearance of cheques and bankers drafts. The Islamic financial institutions cannot provide letters of guarantee or accept bills of exchange, hence they are precluded from participation in trade finance. The inability to offer such services is a major source of frustration.

VIII. Islamisation of Banking

In post-revolutionary Iran a major policy objective has been the Islamisation of the nation's institutions. According to this policy, it is felt that all institutions in an Islamic society should operate in accordance with Islamic principles, including banks and financial institutions. Merely permitting Islamic banks to operate alongside Westernised commercial banks is unsatisfactory. In a society of believers there is no place for riba financial institutions, indeed the workings of commercial banks are an affront to the faithful. Hence the Iranian government was not merely concerned to play a passive role by licencing Islamic banks and permitting commercial banks to continue operating as in the Arab states of the Gulf. Instead the Tehran government has introduced sweeping reforms, in order to ensure that the entire financial system conforms to Qur'anic ideas, and to the spirit of Shi'ism.

Iranian commentators have repeatedly attacked the Arab Islamic banking movement as a camouflage for capitalism. Merely using the word Islamic does not change the nature of the banks themselves. The phrase Islamic banking itself is a contradiction in terms according to these critics. The name bank comes from the Italian *banco*, meaning table, as in the past moneychangers from Lombardy used to place money on a table. Such practices are inappropriate in Islamic financial transactions which are based on trust. The word of a devout Muslim is believed, and he has no need to produce proof of his worth. This explains why even some Arab Islamic institutions are called houses rather than banks, the Kuwait Finance House and Dar al-Mal al-Islami being notable examples.

Merely providing interest free transactions, although a welcome development, is insufficient according to Tehran critics. Islamic financial institutions cannot be limited liability companies as obligations between Muslims who enter transactions must be absolute. There can be no escape from personal liability, and institutions can have no personality of their own in any case.

IX. Implementation of Islamic Financial Laws

Iran's new Islamic financial laws were passed by the Majlis, the country's parliament, in February 1984. They provided for the Islamisation of all Iran's financial institutions by March 22, 1985. Interest has been phased out of the system, and the banks now offer either interest-free current and savings deposits, or long-term investment deposits. With current account deposits customers can use chequing facilities, but only those with savings deposits are given preferential treatment with respect to loan applications. Incentives are also offered on savings deposits, including free tickets for the national lottery, the profits from which help the war wounded and their families. Those with long-term investment deposits cannot withdraw their funds without several months notice, but they are entitled to share in the bank's profits, in accordance with the Islamic *mudaraba* (equity sharing between bank and client) system.

Borrowers are encouraged to enter partnership arrangements with the banks, under which they share any profits which arise as a result of the investments which the bank has financed. The partnership arrangement may be only in respect of one project which the bank backs, or it may be with the business as a whole. In the case of a limited partnership the profits shared are only those which arise from the specific project for which funds have been obtained. Under a full partnership arrangement all profits are shared. Machinery purchases are often financed by the bank purchasing the item required on behalf of the client, who repays by instalment. An alternative arrangement is leasing conditioned to purchase, whereby the ownership is only transferred when the final instalment is paid. Under the Islamic banking laws banks may also finance trade through forward purchases on a client's behalf. There is a distinction drawn between such purchases and futures trading, which is regarded as speculative, and therefore prohibited. Under a forward purchase the bank pays for the commodity being traded on behalf of the import agent or wholesaler, who will repay the bank when he resells the merchandise to the retailer or final customer. The Arab Islamic banks have similar resale contracts, the time period for this type of credit typically being 90 or 180 days.

X. Employee Attitudes

In practice in Iran there has been some opposition to the new laws from bankers, and many bank employees are less than enthusiastic about the new systems. To facilitate implementation the banks have been reorganised into three groups, Malat, Melli and Tejarat. A Council of Money and Credit Regulation has been established to supervise the banking system, the Council consisting of representatives from the banks themselves, independent financial experts, and religious advisors, two of whom are Mullahs. The Central Bank retains its executive role, but the Council is responsible for bank policy, and the implementation of the new code.

The Arab Islamic financial institutions have had fewer personnel problems. All of the staff recruited by the Islamic banks are practising Muslims, apart from some employees in Europe. Many are experienced bankers who took salary cuts to join the new institutions, because they wished to work in an Islamic environment and refrain from participation in riba transactions. Their attitude is extremely positive, and they are genuinely seeking to make Islamic principles work. The bank employees view their jobs as part of their religious devotion. There is little doubt that in many respects a voluntary system of Islamic banking is preferable to compulsion. It should be interesting to compare the development of the systems on both sides of the Gulf in the coming years.

XI. Secularism and Islam in Turkey

To understand the position of the Islamic banks in Turkey, it is necessary to examine the position of Islam in the society, and to review the financial and commercial banking scene.

Although 99 per cent of Turkey's population is Muslim, the government seems to 'separate' religion from politics and other areas of public life. The Constitution of 1982 makes no mention of Islam: '*The Republic of Turkey is a democratic, secular and social state governed by the rule of law ... loyal to the nationalism of Ataturk, and based on the fundamental tenets set forth in the Preamble*' (Article 2).

The main reason for the secularism of Turkey arose from the concern for 'progress' and national strength. The founder of the Turkish Republic,

Mustafa Kemal Ataturk, believed that this could only be achieved by following an essentially Western model. In an effort to achieve this aim, Islam was disestablished, European laws and customs were introduced, and the Arabic script was replaced by the latin alphabet. Religious institutions such as the Sultanate and Caliphate, which had been an integral part of the Ottoman Empire, together with the religious orders, religious education and the religious legal system, were all abolished. The reformers took nationalism as a substitute for Islam and attempted to adopt territorial and linguistic rather than religious nationalism. The message of Ataturk was thus transformed into an official ideology.

However, for the Muslim, in theory, loyalty is to the religious community of the faithful, within which all men are brothers, regardless of language, customs, race or political affiliation and so nationalism would appear to involve a theoretical conflict with Islam. For many people the official ideology, Kemalism, comprising such principles as republicanism, nationalism, secularism and reformism, could not be a substitute for religion.

In recent years the visibility of Islam among the educated appears to have intensified. Several factors lie behind these changes. The first is that since 1960 the Westernised elite of Turkish society has felt able to co-exist with Islam, and a religious political party has been allowed to operate. (In a general election held on 29 November 1987 it gained 7.4 per cent of the votes). The present prime minister and many of his associates have also given vocal support to the re-emergence of Islam in Turkey. A second element which has enabled greater openness in Islam was the reintroduction of vocational education for the clergy after 1965, and this was later followed by an expansion of school religious education. A third factor has been the developments in the Middle East. This was not confined solely to the developments in Iran, but extended to the Arab oil-exporting countries which have been financing religious activity within Turkey.

Despite recent developments, a real divide still persists between Westernised Turks who have chosen Europe and traditional Turks who still consider themselves as part of the Islamic world. The question of the role of Islam in Turkey still arouses intense political debate and is potentially a very divisive issue.

XII. Inflation in Turkey

In 1980 the Turkish authorities designed a structural reform policy for the economy. The main aim of the policy was to promote exports and to liberalise imports and capital flows.

Although these reforms have generally been successful, balanced growth of the Turkish economy has been hampered in recent years by high inflation, which is the main economic problem facing Turkey today.

The rate of inflation rose in 1987 due mainly to increases in wages, food prices and continued depreciation of the lira in foreign exchange markets. The policy of managed floating of the currency to maintain export competitiveness limits the effect of stabilising influences on domestic prices through the exchange rate mechanism. According to the wholesale price index of the State Institute of Statistics (SIS) the inflation rate rose to about 50 per cent in 1987 compared to 30 per cent in 1986. In the same period the SIS consumer price index rose to 55 per cent from 35 per cent. Other indices published by the Treasury and the Istanbul Chamber of Commerce showed even faster wholesale and consumer price rises.

These inflation rates are modest compared to the rates in the 1970s, when prices rose by triple digit amounts, and the monthly rate exceeded 20 per cent. Nevertheless for the committed Muslim the trend is worrying, given the implications for interest rates. It would appear that only a marked tightening in fiscal and monetary policy could lead to a sustained decrease in the rate of inflation. In addition to these economic reforms, the financial sector has also undergone a period of change which has led to innovation and greater efficiency, and to a certain amount of competition among the financial institutions operating in Turkey.

XIII. Turkish Commercial Banking

Since 1980 the banking system in Turkey has been going through a period of major change. Prior to 1980 the banking sector had been able to obtain cheap funds from the public due to legal ceilings on interest rates. The rates paid to depositors were below the rate of inflation. The banks were able to lend these funds, at high rates, to finance domestic commerce and industry. The low cost of funds led to a rapid expansion of the branch network and by the 1980s most banks were under-capitalised and inward looking, and suffered from over-manning and a bureaucratic style of conservative management.

In July 1980 interest rates were partially deregulated but little competition resulted from this as the banks agreed not to compete among themselves for deposits by offering higher real rates. Lending rates have been negotiable for four years.

It was only on 1 July 1987 that the government finally freed interest rates on term deposits. This time, however, competition has broken out and interest rates on one-year deposits have risen from around 43 per cent to between 55 and 60 per cent. The effect of this has been to increase the cost of funds and thus decrease the profitability of the banks. The government hopes that in the long run competition among the banks will drive down rates.

There are nearly 50 banks in Turkey, including 23 foreign banks. Twelve of these banks are publicly owned. The two largest banks, Turkiye Is Bankasi and Ziraat Bankasi, a state bank, control about 60 per cent of all banking transactions. The major private banks such as Yapi ve Kredi Bankasi, Pamukbank and Akbank are all linked to industrial groups.

The Central Bank, founded in 1930, plays an important part in regulating the system. Banking supervision is now much tighter than in the past, and independently audited balance sheets must now be submitted annually to the Central Bank. In recent years the Central Bank has introduced a unified required reserve ratio, opened an inter-bank market for short-term maturities and overnight funds, and set-up a secondary market for government securities in order to conduct open-market operations to regulate bank liquidity.

It has mostly been the foreign banks in Turkey that have adapted to the new economic climate prevailing domestically by providing efficient services to customers using the latest technology. However, the differences that have existed between the Turkish private and state banks and the foreign banks are gradually disappearing as a result of the intense competition, particularly in the area of trade finance. The Turkish banks have been forced to increase their capital and to invest in modern technology to provide a service similar to that offered by the foreign banks. The start of the computerisation of the branch network will inevitably lead to staff reductions. Turkiye Is Bankasi, for example, cut its staff in 1986 by 520 to 21,864, due to computerisation of part of its network.

The government is also encouraging the development of new financial instruments. A new stock exchange has been set up in Istanbul and although market turnover is relatively small, this may increase rapidly with the privatisation of the State Economic Enterprises.

The government and the institutions would also like the population to have more confidence in the capital markets. At present a large amount of gold is held in private hands as a hedge against inflation and economic instability. Most economists believe that this capital is needed in the economy.

The establishment of joint ventures between Turkish and foreign banks over recent years, and the expansion of branches abroad by Turkish banks must be viewed as an opening up of the Turkish banking and financial sectors to the outside world . It is expected that this process of transformation will continue in the foreseeable future.

XIV. Islamic Banking In Turkey

Since its introduction 25 years ago, the concept of Islamic banking has been viewed with a certain amount of suspicion and scepticism in Turkish banking circles. As a result it was only in 1983 that any legislation was enacted to allow the establishment of Islamic banks in Turkey. The government of Prime Minister Turgut Ozal pledged specific legislation to allow their entry into Turkey's financial system in an effort to expand and improve economic ties with the Arab world. Turkey already had financial ties with the Islamic world through its membership in the Islamic Development Bank, which it joined in 1974. Since 1980 Turkey's economic and administrative ties with this organisation have been strengthened and Turkey is now one of the major shareholders and recipients of credit.

Islamic banks were given permission to operate in Turkey in 1983 as the result of Government Decree number 83/7506 of 16 December, issued by the Ozal administration shortly after taking office. These Islamic banks or 'Finance Institutions' (or 'Houses') as they are called in Turkey, were given permission to operate in accordance with regulations drawn up by the Central Bank. The rules themselves do not mention the words 'Islamic' or 'Shari'a' banking principles and some conventional bankers have criticised the establishment of Islamic banks on the grounds that they are contrary to the republican and secular constitution.

The 1983 decree states that the minimum capital required for establishing a finance institution in TL 5 billion (US$ 4.7) and that each institution must have at least 100 founding members (Article 3). The foreign shareholders are required to bring in capital in foreign exchange, although they may transfer profits abroad. Although largely established with foreign capital, these finance institutions consider themselves to be Turkish banks.

The institutions were given all the rights of other banks and thus they are allowed to finance industry, agriculture, foreign trade, issue letters of credit, establish joint ventures and partnerships and collect deposits. The right of leasing was also given to these finance institutions.

Savers can either open Turkish lira or foreign currency accounts, on which no profit is received, or they may deposit their money in a 'partnership account'. The money in the 'partnership accounts' is placed into the 'participation fund' which can make a profit or a loss depending on how the fund is managed. Depositors can place their savings, in Turkish or foreign currency, for periods of three or six months and one year or more. The institution takes 20 per cent of the profit, as expenses, and the client receives 80 per cent. In common with all other Islamic banks, the finance institutions in Turkey use the funds for mudaraba, *murabaha* (cost-plus trade financing), *musharaka* (profit sharing partnership between bank and client) and *ijara* (rental financing or leasing) transactions.

These institutions are exempt from lending limits imposed on other banks since 1983 because it is believed that their method of conducting business makes them less likely to go bankrupt. Also, unlike other banks, these finance institutions are allowed to carry out commodity trading. So far there are two Islamic finance houses in Turkey, Al Baraka Turk Ozel Finans Kurumu A.S. and Faisal Finans Kurumu A.S. The former began operations on 1 January 1985. Fifty per cent of the shares of this institution are owned by Sheikh Saleh Kemal's 'Al Baraka Investment and Development Company' and 13 per cent by the Islamic Development Bank. Turkish shareholders account for 20 per cent of the capital while the Islamic banks of Dubai (United Arab Emirates), Qatar, Bahrain and Jordan own the remaining 17 per cent. The most prominent Turkish shareholder is Kerkut Ozal, brother of the prime minister, and a former leader of the now banned National Salvation Party.

The latter institution, Faisal Finans Kurumu, began operating on 2 April, 1985. Its largest shareholder is Prince Muhammad Ibn Faisal al Saud's 'Dar al-Mal al-Islami' group.

The finance institutions have done much better than expected and the growth in both the number of accounts and in the value of deposits has been phenomenal. For example, at the end of 1985, the Baraka institution had 3,312 accounts and funds worth TL 12.57 billion and reported a profit of TL 1.3 billion. The Faisal Finans institution, after only 9 months of operations, had collected TL 16.32 billion in 5,210 accounts and reported a profit of TL 1.23 billion. Growth has continued at a rapid rate for both institutions. Funds accumulated in the form of Profit and Loss Sharing (PLS) accounts had reached TL 180 billion at the end of 1987, representing 1.5 per cent of the total TL 12.9 trillion deposited in Turkish banks.

The institutions have distributed profit to all PLS account holders above the prevailing interest rates paid by commercial banks operating in Turkey.

To compensate for their lack of branches both institutions have deposit-collecting agreements with commercial banks enabling them to attract funds from throughout Turkey. The finance institutions have now been granted permission by the Central Bank to open another five branches in major cities in addition to their Istanbul headquarters. In late December 1987 Faisal Finans opened branches in Ankara and Izmir and the Baraka opened a branch in Ankara. The Faisal Finans institution has also opened representative offices in Frankfurt and Jeddah. The purpose of these offices is to publicise the activities of the institution among the Turkish workers living in these countries and to suggest that they transfer their foreign currency savings through Faisal Finans. This would appear to be an ingenious way of raising the profile of institution and could prove to be a very useful and profitable source of foreign currency funds.

The economy has benefited from the flow of funds channelled into it by these finance institutions and both plan to devote greater attention in the future to the financing of Turkish enterprise.

The rapid growth of these finance institutions would appear to indicate that 'Islamic banking' in the 'secular' state can be both successful and profitable. It is likely that the next few years will see an increase in the number of finance institutions operating along Islamic lines in Turkey.

*****

Further Reading

Abdeen Adnan M., and Shook Dale N., *The Saudi Financial System in the Context of Western and Islamic Finance*, John Wiley, Chichester, 1984.

Ariff Mohammad (ed.), *Monetary and Fiscal Policies of Islam*, International Centre for Research in Islamic Economics, King Abdul Aziz University, Jeddah, 1982.

Bashir B.A., 'Successful Development of Islamic Banks', *Journal of Research in Islamic Economics*, Vol. 1, No. 2, 1984 pp. 63-81.

Iqbal Subair and Mirakhor Abbas, *Islamic Banking, The Experience of Iran and Pakistan,* International Monetary Fund, Occasional Paper No. 49, Washington, 1987.

Mayer Ann Elizabeth, 'Islamic Banking and Credit Policies in the Sadat Era : The Social Origins of Islamic Banking in Egypt', *Arab Law Quarterly*, Vol. 1, Part 1, 1985, pp. 32-50.

Rahman Afzalur, *Economic Doctrines of Islam, Banking and Insurance*, Vol. 4, Muslim Schools Trust, London, 1979.

Rodinson Maxime, *Islam and Capitalism*, Penguin Books, Harmondsworth, 1979.

Rodinson Mohammad N., *Banking Without Interest*, The Islamic Foundation, Leicester, 1983.

Wilson Rodney, *Banking and Finance in the Arab Middle East,* Macmillan, London, 1983.

Wilson Rodney, *Islamic Business : Theory and Practice*, Economist Intelligence Unit, Special Report, London, 1986.

Wilson Rodney, 'The Role of Islamic Banks in Financial Markets', *Arab Gulf Journal*, Vol. 4, No. 2, October 1984, pp. 53-61.

Wilson Rodney, 'Islamic Banking in Jordan', *Arab Law Quarterly*, Vol. 2, Part 3, 1987, pp. 207-229.

*****

Islamic Financial Institutions

	Country	Date of Foundation	Paid-up Capital ($ mn.)
Al Baraka Investment and Development Company	Saudi Arabia	1982	1,500.0
Al Rajhi Company for Currency Exchange & Commerce	Saudi Arabia	1985	180.0

Bahrain Islamic Bank	Bahrain	1979	15.3
Bahrain Islamic Investment Company	Bahrain	1981	13.3
Bank Islam Malaysia	Malaysia	1983	42.0
Beit Ettamouil Saudi Tounsi	Tunisia	1984	50.0
Dar al-Mal al-Islami	Switzerland	1981	315.0
Dubai Islamic Bank	UAE	1975	13.6
Faisal Islamic Bank of Egypt	Egypt	1977	40.0
Faisal Islamic Bank of Sudan	Sudan	1977	1.7
Faisal Islamic Bank of Turkey	Turkey	1985	400.0
International Islamic Bank	Bangladesh	1983	.....
Islamic Bank International	Denmark	1983	5.0
Islamic Banking System International Holding	Luxemburg	1978	34.8
Islamic Development Bank	Saudi Arabia	1975	2,000.0
Islamic International Bank for Investment & Development	Egypt	1981	6.0
Islamic Investment House	Jordan	1981	11.1
Jordan Islamic Bank for Finance and Investment	Jordan	1978	11.1
Kuwait Finance House	Kuwait	1977	51.4
Kuwait Finance House	(Turkey)	1983	20.0[a]
Nasser Social Bank	Egypt	1972	20.6
Qatar Islamic Bank	Qatar	1983	13.7

Saudi-Philippine Islamic Development Bank	Saudi Arabia	1982	5.0[a]
Tadamon Islamic Bank	Sudan	1983	50.0[a]
West Sudan Islamic Bank	Sudan	1984	....

Note: (a) Authorised rather than paid up capital.

*****

INDEX